dancing in the streets
tales from world cup city

DON WATSON

VICTOR GOLLANCZ
london

First published in Great Britain 1994
as a paperback original
by Victor Gollancz
A Division of the Cassell group
Villiers House, 41/47 Strand, London WC2N 5JE

A catalogue record for this book is
available from the British Library.

ISBN 0 575 05882 X

Photoset in Great Britain by
Rowland Phototypesetting Ltd, Bury St Edmunds, Suffolk
Printed and bound in Great Britain by
Guernsey Press Co. Ltd, Guernsey, Channel Islands

For Frau, as always

Thanks to: Ken Prestininzi, Zoe &
Yvette, Tony Hussey, Ian Preece,
Chrissie Glazebrook, The Twins &
Wee Ming-Belle.

Contents

1

Welcome to World Cup City –
Where Are You From?

World Cup City doesn't come with a street map, more like a psychological profile. It's a bit like Brigadoon – a mythological place full of revelry and excess that visits earth only occasionally. Like Brigadoon, which was a uniquely Hollywood version of a Scottish Highland village full of kilts and ceilidhs, if you stay aboard past a certain point, it takes you along with it. Unlike Brigadoon, World Cup City will finally drop you at Heathrow airport wearing an Irish baseball cap and a (fairly) close approximation of a Brazilian shirt, wondering what time it is, what day it is, where you live and how on earth you're going to get there.

It is not a hostile place. In fact, talking to strangers is more or less compulsory, that is as long as you are not guilty of the cardinal sin committed by the unfortunate Bill Buford (aka Bog Brush), author of *Among the Thugs*, who attempted to engage in eye contact during the game. Should you infringe in this way you will probably elicit the same response as Bog: 'What are you looking at, you queer cunt?' However, if you observe the one social rule – all conversation during the hallowed ninety minutes is to be had out of the corner of the mouth while keeping the eyes trained on the pitch – you will find that the curiosity of strangers is voracious. They will want to know about you and where you come from, what your native country is like, and what parts of World Cup City you have seen so far. If they are

American and have suddenly seen World Cup City assembled around them, they will want you to explain it to them.

But be warned, all this sociability aside it can be a dangerous place. Don't worry too much – the worst that's likely to happen to you is that you'll find yourself struggling home with a suitcase overstuffed with tacky merchandise. A T-shirt with Beavis and Butthead eulogizing Romario and Bebeto ('Romario is cool', 'Yeah, Bebeto kicks ass'), several others with the celestial numbers of 7 and 11 emblazoned on various parts, one proclaiming the New York Knicks as 1994 NBL Basketball Champions (a piece of pre-emptive marketing that proved to be misplaced optimism) plus a baseball shirt for every city you've landed in. Or of course there's the financial ruin that can result from the need for tickets. But for the long-term residents the dangers can be more severe. Think of Andrés Escobar who was gunned down in one of the obscure back alleys. Can it really be that serious? The answer evidently is yes, and amidst the detritus of the parade we have to acknowledge that World Cup City has its politics like everywhere else.

You will be left with a collection of images imperfectly captured on colour-print film, and with a series more perfectly imprinted on memory.

This will be the last of mine:

In the midst of a samba party in Old Pasadena one shirtless figure shuffles closer. Above his head he holds a cardboard placard. As he turns around I read: 'Tickets wanted'. We celebrants look at one another and shrug and then we read the second line: 'for France, 1998'.

In a sense World Cup City is the same city that we all live in, because all cities contain more allegiances than one, sometimes more than we are aware of. I began to notice this as the campaign to qualify for the competition reached its zenith, as London became a satellite of World Cup City. While it's the Yellow Brick Road that leads to Oz, for me at least it was the Edgware Road that led to World Cup City.

Not that apologies are necessary; the Edgware Road is as good a place to start as any. For one thing it's close to where I live, just around the corner, in fact. Dylan Thomas used to live in the Edgware Road.

Dylan's team didn't make it the night of the seventeenth of November, but he was there in New York in spirit, even more than usual. There was many a pilgrimage made to the Chelsea Hotel, where he died, and the White Horse Tavern, where he purchased the murder weapon, and many a glass raised in his honour, even if by another branch of the Celtic family.

The last thing he wrote about in *Adventures in the Skin Trade*, his uncompleted final book, was a drinking session on the Edgware Road, so it's appropriate that this should be the setting of the first bar from which World Cup City was glimpsed – the Portman Arms, a place that Dylan himself might have recognized, with its dark wood, mirrors and Victorian prints of flowing dresses and precocious children, even though the satellite TV that was the star of the show might have surprised him.

That night of the seventeenth, you could have looked out from the top of a tower block around here and seen all the thought bubbles rising up into the night sky. Dreams of World Cup City.

Of course there were some who still believed that England could qualify, but you could see all those bubbles bursting simultaneously at seventeen seconds past seven as Stuart Pearce allowed the ball to run to San Marino's David Gualtieri for one of the fastest and most embarrassing goals in World Cup history. Across at Goldbourne Road, in the Bab Marrakesh, the Moroccan supporters were sipping their mint tea and anticipating the USA, having completed a successful qualification in February. Down the road at the Porto Café, the Portuguese fans turned their attention towards Italy, wondering if the team could pull off a miraculous victory which might just give the explosive Paulo Futre the chance to prove himself as a worthy successor to the mantle of Eusebio. While down in Soho at Bar Italia the opposition were hoping for the draw they needed. The talk was of another number 10, Roberto Baggio, and whether he would come through this time at last.

Futre's tiny feet had already left their studmarks in the dreams of my native Scotland. For which I suppose I should be grateful. This time round there would be no defeats by Peru or Costa Rica, no humiliating 1–1 draws with Iran – even if this meant that there would not be any glorious 0–0 slaughterings of Brazil or 4–2 defeats of Holland.

But the bubble that rose above the Portman Arms wore the green, white and gold of the Republic of Ireland, the same flag that I grew up with being waved at Celtic Park; which at least gave me some stake in the proceedings, especially when the opponents were the North of Ireland who carried the hopes and wishes of all in the hated Rangers contingent. This was the Old Firm game on a national scale.

Sentanta, the Irish cable channel, is the umbilical cord that connects exiles everywhere with mother Ireland. Usually, the big games aside, there's little more than cursory attention paid in the Portman to its diet of Gaelic football. But a World Cup qualifier, the crucial last game, and against the North, is a once in a lifetime combination of factors.

There must have been neutrals who were not too distraught when Spain defeated Ireland at Lansdowne Road in their last home match, knowing that it would come down to a showdown like this.

For a couple of hours before the kick-off the pub was packed, and even the quantity of Guinness passing across the bar could do nothing to quell the tension. The first half only applied a further torque to the twist that was caught in everyone's gut.

The half-time trip to the Gents provides no more than cursory relief.

Sean was standing by the door, feeling like if he stayed here for a while then the second half wouldn't start just quite yet and he might get a little more time to summon up the mental energy necessary to go through with the second half. 'Jeez,' he said to me, 'I don't think I can stand any more of this.'

We both took a deep breath and stepped back into the breach.

Being in a crowd that supports the away team, watching the home team score on television, is a bit like feeling yourself being transposed into negative. Never have I experienced the contrast so sharply as when Jimmy Quinn scored for the North. The supporters at Windsor Park who had been singing the Unionist anthem 'The Sash' with particular vigour went mad. But in the Portman it was like an official announcement had been made that God was a Protestant after all.

Then the equalizer, struck with an equivalent grasp of spectacular dramatics by Alan McLoughlin. Was it really only three minutes later? Three minutes in which the Republic were on their way out. Even to me that moment expanded way beyond rational explanation. But the precious goal came and outside the Portman Arms and away in the distance beyond the end of the Edgware Road, World Cup City began to glimmer.

There was still the chance that Denmark could equalize in Spain, where they were playing against ten men, and it would all have been a mirage after all. A further eternity passed, but the ten men, feeling the will of an international confederation of Irishmen behind them, held on, and for the first time I saw a glimpse of the joyous madness of victory that you find in World Cup City.

Many a loyal Ulsterman shed a tear that night to see the enemy on the way to America.

This wasn't the only drama that night. Italy had scraped through with a single goal against the Portuguese. We now knew that we would not see Futre in the Finals, or Giggs as Romania in fairness took the Welsh side to pieces, or Cantona as Bulgaria's final-minute equalizer brought another campaign of inexplicable mediocrity by the talented French side to an end. Who were Bulgaria's players anyway? At that time we little suspected that they would last long enough for us to find out. But we would see Baggio. Perhaps this time.

And then the draw was made. Ireland would be playing against Italy, Norway and Mexico. The first game was to be against Italy, in New York.

In Gerry Conlon's book *Presumed Innocent*, on which the film *In the Name of the Father* was (very) loosely based, he describes the moment when he knew he was to be set free. The thoughts that go through his mind are New York, Ireland, the World Cup.

These are the thrills that freedom represents after years of incarceration, and all of them were to be combined in a single event.

Ireland versus Italy in New York. It was to be one of those events that is bigger than football. The Boys in Green meet the Azzurri. The two great immigrant communities play host to the travelling armies from the homeland. The World Cup in America; the more I thought about it, the more it seemed like a fascinating contradiction in terms, an event of consummate weirdness. I had to be there.

I studied a plan of the fixtures and came up with an itinerary. I would cut a cross section across America, travelling from east to west. I'd start in New York with the irresistible romance of Ireland/Italy, and then head for places and find out what was going to happen when I got there. Chicago, the city of the Blues, of House and of the novels of Nelson Algren and Saul Bellow. San Francisco, setting of *Vertigo*, one of my favourite movies of all time, and then the sprawling megalopolis of Weird – Los Angeles and the World Cup Final. An American odyssey with football matches, a trip to the heart of World Cup City.

All that remained was to book my passage, and locate a few of my fellow travellers. A few days later I asked the barman in the Portman if any of the regular crowd were planning a trip.

'Oh yes,' he said, 'they're all going.'

Really?

'Or that's what they'll be saying at closing time at least. Why's that, anyway?'

I'm going out myself, and I was looking to link up with some others.

He tells me he's lived in the States himself for ten years or so.

'You won't have any trouble,' he assures me. 'Just go to any pub in Brooklyn or Queens – you won't be on your own. There's plenty of them out there, Murphys, O'Sheas, Connollys. Just follow the colours, you won't be on your own.'

As it turned out, he was right.

Through the Irish FA I was put on to the secretary of the London branch of the Republic of Ireland Supporters Club, Tony Booth, who told me that the road to World Cup City was to lead through Harlesden, where their next meeting was to be held.

All cities have more than one time zone. Lack of public transport or a combination of economic factors can leave one district lagging a matter of years behind others. Harlesden is one of the parts of London that has failed to keep up with the pace of change. The Tube used to run peak hours only, leaving you stranded for hours, just half a mile from civilization. As a result it has maintained a mood of its own.

Fifty per cent of the population is black, the rest is Irish. It's like two parallel cultures existing in the same place, scarcely touching. Walking into Harlesden makes you think – for a nation so small, Ireland has spread its influence across the globe, and, unlike, say, the Scots, it has remained visible in the host culture.

It was a summer evening of gentle but persistent drizzle when I went off in search of the London Irish.

Two bouncers in bow ties stood outside the Top 32 Club, one of the great temples to the worship of the great bacchanalian god of the craic that are scattered across London – Highbury Corner, Kilburn High Road and here.

One of the bouncers asks if he can help me.

'It's OK,' his colleague who sees my Celtic badge tells him. 'On you go, son.'

Inside the windowless dance hall the low lights pick out a panoply of orange, green and white. Tony at the front is addressing the faithful.

'I won't tell you who to talk to,' he says to me later as I button-hole him in the bar. 'Or who not to – although there's one or two I could warn you about.'

Cheers, Tony.

There's a buzz of anticipation in the air. The travel agents are here and supporters are poring over printed sheets giving the details of air passes, rail passes, package deals.

Are you going across? I ask a friendly-looking lad at my shoulder, whose name turns out to be Adrian. His eyes shine and a pleased as punch grin splits his face. Am I kidding? Of course he's going.

It's going to be an expensive business, presuming they get into the later rounds.

He laughs. 'Presuming?' he asks. There's no presuming about it. He's got it planned out as far as the semi-finals at least.

A slight trace of a Highland brogue about my accent means some Scots and most English take me for Irish. But the Irish always take me for Scottish and Adrian is no different.

There's a trace of suspicion.

'Celtic or Rangers?' he asks, meaning are you for us or agin' us. I point to the badge. So that's all right, then.

This is the only time all evening when anyone questions my loyalties, or just exactly what I'm doing there. There is none of the suspicion or the paranoia that you read about from English fans. There's people here with Irish accents, English accents, Scottish accents. So I want to join the party? Fine. No problem. Welcome aboard.

We get into a conversation about London. I tell him I'm resigned to being a reluctant Londoner now, a Scottish Londoner, but a Londoner nevertheless. Adrian still wants to go home, back to the boys in Cork. One of these days.

We're joined at this point by Sylvie, short for Sylvester, who looks like a gangly Christian Slater, dark hair swept back from high cheekbones. Adrian met him in Lithuania.

'I'd got lost,' he says, 'when I saw Sylvie walking past. I thought he was this guy I was sharing a room with, so I dashed up and flung me arms around his neck saying, "God am I glad to see you." Then I realized I had the wrong guy, but we got talking anyway.'

The Lithuania trip was one of the ones that spawned more modern myths than most. There's the one about the group of young Latvians that became honorary Irishmen and bunked the train to join the party. It ended with the whole crew being chased through a forest by the Lithuanian army.

That's the point about all of this. Creating chaos on a Trans-European scale. And now the US, a whole new continent to go out and play in.

A little later I'm button-holed by Tommy. I've noticed him

around the place already. He seems to be taking part in about six conversations concurrently – advising, enthusing, eyes popping out from behind corkscrew curls, slender arms waving wildly from a green Adidas top – the tricolour on one sleeve and the stars and stripes on the other.

Adrian is unmistakably Irish, despite his years here. But Tommy, like Sylvie, has a London accent.

'We get a lot of stick from some of the Irish Irish,' he says, 'who'll say, "What are you doing following Ireland with an accent like that?"'

But nationality is more than just a matter of birthplace, it's a matter of culture.

'My mother is from Clare, she's the leader of the London Irish pipe band. So I've grown up with all of that. It's like the people in Glasgow whose parents come from Donegal. We might have English accents, but in our hearts we know we're Irish.'

If there's a controversy within the supporters, it has its roots in the questions raised over Jack Charlton's Republic of Ireland team. Charlton is an Englishman whose lack of repentance often borders on the jingoistic.

As a Leeds United supporter, I used to admire him when he wore all white with an owl crest, but when he took on his role as resident boor on the commentary team for the Home Internationals he used to make my blood boil, referring to 'the Scotch' and getting the huff when, after the first victory over England for years, Scotland had the nerve to do a lap of honour at Hampden.

He seemed unlikely as an honorary Irishman. And some of the cynicism in Dublin was compounded when he began to build a team using the FIFA ruling that players with grandparents born in a country are eligible to play for that country's team. Ray Houghton from Glasgow, Andy Townsend from London, Terry Phelan from Manchester.

If there was cynicism in Dublin, much of it dissolved in the euphoria of a run that took the team to the quarter-finals of Italia '90, albeit without winning a game in normal or even extra time. But it had its resurgence on this side of the Irish Sea when the steadfast growth of Charlton's team continued, while the luck that had seen the English to the semi-finals in Italy deserted them in qualification games against Norway and Holland at Wembley.

'The definition of being Irish now is anyone who's drunk a pint of Guinness,' one pro quipped in an oft-repeated line.

But the question remains, for the supporters as much as the team. What is the definition of Irish? The holding of the competition in America, where the Irish immigrant community is so strong, gives the question yet another dimension.

Eamon Dunphy, writing in the *Irish Independent* in an article which was reprinted in England a couple of weeks before the competition, took on the born and bred purists. There's more to national identity than birthplace, he argued. 'To be Irish is to possess a unique sense of humour, to be tolerant, to love a song, to face honourably life's vicissitudes, to be willing to play the game of life or sport, to win or lose yet have some fun.'

'Yes, but that's Eamon Dunphy,' said any of the Irish fans I spoke to, dismissively. Eamon Dunphy's standing in Ireland is best summed up by the scene in Roddy Doyle's *The Van*, where sausages are nicknamed 'Dunphys' because they 'look like pricks'. And of course he misses something out. To be Irish, as opposed to being British, means to be a Catholic.

The majority of Catholics in the North were behind the Republic that night in November, just as a large contingent of Glaswegian Rangers supporters would have been backing the North with a fervour about as far away from neutral detachment as you can get without actually having been brought up on the Shankill Road.

Of course there's always the exception. One such is Gary, a friend of mine I used to work with. As a Catholic, and one who sets great store on a Catholic identity, I had naturally assumed his sympathies lay with the Republic. Especially since I once saw him go off the deep end with a Rangers supporter.

Coming from Derry, Gary had seen the sort of extremist bigotry that Rangers are a rallying cry for at closer quarters. But all this made it the more surprising when I discovered that Gary follows the North.

'Not that night,' he says. 'I did want the Republic to win,

because the North were out of it. But usually I always like to see the North do well. They're all genuine Ulstermen born and bred.'

The unspoken implication being that the Republic belong to a broader, and therefore more dilute, definition of Irish.

On the other hand I see myself as Scottish, but part of New Year for me has always been to stand on a terrace, waving a tricolour and singing 'We're Going To Dublin In the Green' opposite a bank of Union Jack-waving edjits, singing 'God Save the Queen'.

Nationality is a complex business.

Sylvie knows exactly what I mean. He's wearing a rare Celtic away shirt. Born in England of Irish parents, he makes the trip to Glasgow regularly to see the Bhoys.

'My friends that I work with,' he says, 'really can't understand why someone who isn't Scottish and has no Scottish ancestry really hates Rangers.'

But of course it's about more than that.

We compare notes on this year's New Year fiasco. For the first time in years, shortage of money prevented me from making the trip. Initially I couldn't face the prospect of not seeing the match, so I sent my brother-in-law a blank video to tape the highlights from Scotsport. He lives so close to Celtic Park that if only his flat were three floors higher and he had a camcorder I could have had the whole match. Not that I wanted it, as it turned out.

I was in London, listening to the radio as the score flashes came in: 'Celtic 0 Rangers 1,' then a few minutes later, 'Celtic 0, Rangers 2'. Sylvie was there.

'We hadn't even got into the ground until ten minutes were gone and there was the scoreboard facing us, with that score on it. We just couldn't believe it, so we couldn't.'

Sylvie's conversation is peppered with Celticisms like that last inversion. At first they sound rather ill at ease in a rounded, Home Counties accent. But I know very well that they're not necessarily self-conscious. When you're brought up in a different country, you develop an almost bilingual facility. There are certain words and configurations you'll use only at home, or with people you know will understand them – they become like a code or a badge of recognition.

'But everyone thought, Ah well, we've lost this one, we might as well sing our hearts out, which is what we did.'

Strange how there's nothing like a defeat of a certain scale to pump up the volume of the support. It's the recognition that what goes on on the pitch is beyond our control, but the amount of noise we make is up to us.

Since that all-time low in the fortunes of the club, things have picked up a little. Fergus McCann has arrived, promising to bring the club into the modern age, and then there's the emergence of teenage winger Simon Donnelly, the son of an ex-Rangers player.

'We've got a song for him,' says Sylvie, who travelled up to Old Trafford to see him score two in a 3–1 defeat of Manchester United. 'It goes, "His dad's a Hun/But he isnae one/Donnelly, Donnelly."'

Celts versus Huns. Glasgow is one place where you can't keep politics out of sport. And it isn't the only one.

Rangers raise the Union Jack before every game. Their supporters' club bears a notice above the door proclaiming that anyone not willing to join in the singing of 'God Save the Queen' at closing time is not welcome to enter. The club stands for puritan values and conservatism, with a small and a large C. The Orangemen's March, which takes place in Glasgow, as it does in Belfast, every year to celebrate the crushing of Irish resistance at the Battle of the Boyne, is a great focus for Rangers supporters.

Celtic, on the other hand, a club based on a charity to help the underprivileged, embodies an enlightened Republicanism. That's why it's bigger than football.

One thing confuses me, and Sylvie too: how can Rangers fans join in the Separatist fervour that has traditionally surrounded the Scottish international team? After all, The Corries song 'Flower of Scotland', which has become the unofficial national anthem, is an unashamed paean to independence from England, with its references to 'We can still rise now/And be the nation again/That stood against them.'

'It's really puzzling,' says Sylvie, 'that one week they can be at Ibrox singing "God Save the Queen" and the next at a Scotland match singing "Flower of Scotland".'

It's a complex business, nationality.

Our answer comes a few weeks later in an interview with one of the Rangers Inter-city Crew (the scumbags who slashed Sunderland fans last year after a 'friendly') in the *Daily Record*. Calling himself 'Barry Britain', he says '[we] wouldn't open our curtains to see Scotland.'

So that's why no one turned up when they moved the Scotland matches to Ibrox.

Sylvie and I take a seat with Adrian, and I'm introduced to Kevin who was born in Kildare but moved over here with his parents. He has a strong Irish accent, but his younger brother Conn, who I meet later, sounds English. We discuss the idea of club versus country. An English friend had said to me a few days before: 'It's never a conflict for the English. Given the choice, ninety-nine per cent of Englishmen would take their club winning the European Cup above England winning the World Cup again.'

Of course he had to slip the 'again' in just to get at me. But obvious as this might be, it hadn't occurred to me before that this is why England's support seems to be so different from the people you used to stand and now sit next to at a club game.

'The thing is,' says Adrian, 'in Ireland the teams are so small that really the international team is the nation.'

He met an Irish Liverpool fan, though, who went for the return to European Cup glory fantasy option rather than the even more fantastic notion of an Irish triumph in the States. He was genuinely shocked. 'Really, I think that's sick, to have no feeling for your country.'

Of course, sometimes your club is a country to itself. But more about Celtic later.

The evening wears on and so does the Guinness. A screen is lowered from the roof and they begin to screen the Ireland/Holland match. We discuss the draw for the first round, which puts Ireland up against Italy, Norway and Mexico. They're already using the term 'Group of Death'.

Everyone has a superficial confidence, but it's down to Adrian to express the only real doubt.

'Packie Bonner,' he says.

Sylvie and I both wince.

'I just have this feeling he's going to let us down.'

There's a rebel move afoot to force the club to stay in Orlando itself, rather than out in the holiday resort of Daytona Beach. A guy with a thick Scottish accent is collecting signatures.

'If we get enough people saying they want out, they'll have to arrange something,' he promises. 'Daytona Beach is the families, Orlando is the pussy.'

Adrian is not so sure. Sylvie is more concerned with trying to talk the others into a jaunt over to New Orleans between matches.

'C'mon, you don't want to stay in Daytona Beach, Daytona Beach is Keifer Sutherland in vampire drag,' he says, referring to the movie *The Lost Boys*. Movies are our way of navigating our imaginations around these places that we've seen but never been to.

I thought New Orleans was the vampire city, all decay and voodoo.

'Yeah, but New Orleans is jazz,' he says.

We all travel to America as to Oz with these myths in our minds, and, like Dorothy, the lion, the tin man and the scarecrow, we will all find what we were looking for, but not necessarily in the way we expected.

We spend a while intoning the magical names: Santa Fe, Phoenix, Death Valley. Then we're interrupted by a cheer. Holland 0 Ireland 1. We return, not quite to earth, but to a different cloud.

Half an hour later, the lights are dimmed, some dance music comes on and the room starts to fill with dry ice. I take my leave of the crew like I've known them all my life and walk out into some misty summer rain, feeling like my honorary Irish status has just been confirmed.

22

After a few pints of Guinness, reality loosens its grip, but Willesden Junction railway station at precious near midnight wouldn't seem real if you were stark raving sober. It floats in the rain in a cloud of dim electric light. There are only two figures standing on the platform – two boys with English accents who've come all the way from Cambridge for the meeting. Of course they're going to the States too; suddenly the whole world is going, heading out for the biggest party of our lives. The train arrives and sweeps us off majestically a little closer to the promised land.

But when I get there, how am I going to get in? If you wanted to get tickets from the FA you had to apply before any of the qualifying teams were even settled. And I'm not much good at arranging my social life two years in advance.

Mysteriously, face-value tickets seem to be no problem if I want to book a package deal which promises me a five-star hotel, a courier to and from the games, etc; all a snip at three thousand pounds for a ten-day stay and two matches. Or I can have one Semi-Final, the third-place play-off and the World Cup Final (just in case you should think it was any other final) for a mere five thousand pounds. And should I think this was a tall price to pay, even to stay in one of F. Scott Fitzgerald's old haunts and attend a match watched by one fifth of the population of the entire planet, the hand-out informs me that this is only part of the fun. There's a whole package of tricks lined up for me, including 'the Oscar ceremony'.

Now you don't exactly have to be a celluloid junkie to know that the Oscars have already happened for this year and the movie industry is not about to bring them forwards by nine months to tie in with the World Cup, so which particular Oscar ceremony they're talking about is anyone's guess. Is it a video, or an interactive computer programme by which you get to choose your own private awards? Like in my case I get to assassinate Whoopi Goldberg just after the realization sinks in that she is not being ironic with that 'Y'know we are amazing' speech. Hmmmm, tempting, but then five thousand pounds is a lot to pay, even for a vicarious pleasure of these proportions.

The only way to get tickets without all of this is to go to an agency, and that means paying big prices. For Italia '90 the tickets were going at around the £60 mark. This time I'm quoted around £300 for any game involving Ireland or Italy. Strangely enough, some of the later games are less expensive, partly because the teams playing won't be settled until the first round is over. But for the Final I am quoted a figure of around one thousand pounds.

Why so much more?

'Oh, there's a lot more interest this time around,' says the agent in his patented Cockney wide-boy persona, 'lot more interest.'

Even with England not qualifying?

'Oh yeah.'

Is it possible that since Italia '90 brought back memories of 1966 and all that, we have developed from the stage of being football partisans and emerged as soccer sophisticates? Channel 4 Italian football came along and now we're all as cosmopolitan as A.C. Milan, as keen on Maldini and Baggio as we are on Gazza and McAllister.

It's possible. On the other hand, maybe market forces are pulling a giant con trick on us (No!). If they tell us there's a demand often enough we'll get to believe it, and if we don't snap up that three-hundred-quid ticket pretty sharpish then someone else will be in Giants Stadium soaking up the noise and watching Gary Kelly doing battle with Roberto Baggio while you'll be in a bar somewhere craning your neck up at the screen and cursing the fact you can't see the full majestic geometry of the game. So by far the most sensible thing to do would be to hold on to my money and wait for the prices to drop.

But what if it does sell out?

Marking down the most essential games – Ireland v Italy, the second-round game in Chicago, the Quarter-Final in San Francisco and the Semi-Final in LA – I dial a number and read out my credit-card number and that's it, it's done. I have just spent over one thousand pounds on four football tickets or rather on the promise of four football tickets.

'They'll be delivered to your house the week before you travel,' the agent tells me.

It's a dizzying feeling.

So if the Irish population of London was looking forward to the World Cup with gleeful anticipation, what about the Italians?

Considering its influence on the cappuccino culture of the capital, the Italian community is hard to find these days. Much of Soho is still Italian owned but the clientele has changed. Bar Italia, one of the original bits of the section, is still here, with its personally monographed portrait of the real Rocky in pride of place behind the original 1950s Gaggia, but they no longer show the Italian football matches on satellite.

'Too rowdy,' says Antonio, the manager. Apparently it was putting off some of the café's newer customers. For the World Cup itself they'll just have to put up with it, but for the moment Antonio is keeping what passes for peace amongst the hubbub of this nighthawks' caff.

There's also the Café Espresso on Marylebone Road, where the matches still get shown, but while personally I can put up with places run by psychopaths, outrageously rude and inefficient psychopaths are something else.

To find the real Italian London nowadays you have to go behind closed doors. St Peter's Church on Farringdon Road is one of those buildings that you've walked past a hundred times without noticing. A stone echo of Florence amidst the pigeon shit of Dickensian London.

Outside on a Sunday at twelve, the dark-shaded limousines pull up to take away the sleeker families after Mass and slick-haired youths surround girls who stand with one dark-stockinged leg on the ground and the other bent with the foot resting against the wall, like dark flamingoes. The priest is addressing a twelve-year-old boy outside, saying something to his parents like 'Ah, hasn't he grown,' which, like everything else, sounds better in Italian.

To find my way into the social club I elect to take the side entrance which leads me first through the youth section, across a roof with a view across to Bloomsbury and back to the Old Bailey, and into the Salle Rossa.

I'm told it's quiet around here for a Sunday. 'Probably 'cos of the sunshine,' Michael tells me. 'Usually it's packed. I don't know where everyone is. They're probably all out playing football,' he laughs.

Even so, there's a volume and passion to the conversation that makes it seem fuller than it is.

Michael looks about seventeen or eighteen. Born over here, he speaks with a London accent, although he's bilingual in English and a Southern-dialect Italian.

When asked how Italian he feels, his reply is symptomatic.

'When Italy win the World Cup,' he says, 'it's brilliant.'

An event like that unites the exiles across the generations, unlike any other.

'I remember the last one, in '82, when Rossi scored. It was the first World Cup I remember. It's funny, you can measure your life out with World Cups, can't you? Every time one comes around, you can remember what you were like, what you were doing, when the last one was on.'

He looks distant for a moment, and so do I. I remember the last one all right. The first match I watched was Scotland v Costa Rica. So profound was my disgust at Scotland's dismal performance, it felt at the time like the last football match I would ever watch. I got married that summer, and we went on honeymoon to Berlin. They were taking down the Wall at the time, which ruined the special atmosphere the divided city used to have. Still, they seemed quite keen on it in the East. In the West not everyone was so sure.

'Berlin is a happening town again,' said the East Berliner who saw us running up Unter den Linden, Frau pale in her scarlet chiffon dress and me overheated in my grey suit, and stopped to give us a lift to the church for the blessing we'd arranged.

'English?' asked the man by the sausage stand with the second-round programme in his hand. 'No, Scottish,' I replied, indignant. It was the first time I remember that my inquisitor didn't warm to the reply. Of course we hadn't qualified, although I didn't realize until later how close it had been.

The second match I watched was England v Germany, which was projected on a big screen in the Nuremberg-proportioned square by the former Eastern National Gallery, a mile or so up Unter den Linden from the Brandenburg Gate. The German skinheads behind me saluted victory as Waddle's penalty sailed over the bar. I've never been so dubious about seeing England losing.

Michael has a different memory. He was here at St Peter's that day, and remembers Italy playing Argentina in the other Semi-Final, a game which went to penalties too. As I'm replaying Berlin, he recalls Serena placing his kick, and the ball sailing with disastrous certainty towards the saving hand of Goycoechea.

This time it will be different. That much he knows: what he doesn't know is whether different means better or even worse.

Ironically it was Costa Rica that Italy played in a warm-up match the day I went to St Peter's Social Club. It was all over by the time I got there, but the members had been dodging in and out of Mass to watch it. The result was more creditable than Scotland's effort – but not by much, a slender 1–0 victory.

Giovanni, wearing the vivid red shirt of Caliari, hasn't seen much to inspire him.

'The whole performance has been disappointing in the warm-ups,' he says. 'The display against Finland was, like, sad.'

The team have managed a series of their specials, 1–0 wins, all of them against fairly lowly opposition. Like most of the pundits, Giovanni feels that manager Sacchi's attempts to replicate his success at A.C. Milan without the Dutch strike force of Van Basten, Rijkaard and Gullit is like remaking the Marx Brothers films without Harpo, Groucho and Chico, and with Zeppo playing the lead.

'If he's not careful,' says Giovanni, 'he could end up coming home after the first round.'

Anyone who followed Milan on Channel 4 during the 93/94 season would know what he was talking about. Without their flair players, their style was to let the opposition knock their heads against the solid brick wall of defenders Baresi and Costacurta, sneak in and snatch a goal on the break, then sit on the lead for the rest of the game. It was about as exciting as waiting for a piece of spaghetti to fall off the wall. I'm sure I'm not the only one who found myself opting for the infinitely less chic Division 1 action on ITV, which was a bit like turning to an old episode of *The Sweeney* after a particularly cliché-ridden Italian art movie and having to admit, despite yourself, that you'd rather watch banal, hell-for-leather action than banal torpor.

When it came to the European Cup Final in May, I sat down to watch more with a sense of duty than anything else. A year before, a match between Barcelona and Milan would have had anyone anticipating a scintillating dash of colour, intricate angles and artistry. This time round the last thing we expected was actually what we got.

Without the two centre-backs Milan were obliged to make more of an effort in other parts of the field. They were a revelation. Massaro, who had always looked solid and unexceptional, suddenly displayed a flair and skill you would never have suspected of him.

Giovanni agrees, but still with a sense of trepidation. He's reluctant to see Massaro, at thirty, as the great goalscorer Italy need. He's also worried about how the diminutive Signori will fare against the towering defences of Ireland and Norway.

He claims not to be looking forward to any of the games. I give him a quizzical look.

'I'm not, honestly,' he says. 'I'm not.'

With Scotland out already, I feel this great sense of relief. There's none of this fear for me, none of the searching through history, wondering will it be the same this time, or will some unknown quantity make the difference, what was I wearing the last time we had a good result, and so on.

'I think Ireland prevented Italy qualifying in the '58 World cup,' says Giovanni, attaching a mystical significance to this event which took place before either of us was born.

But then of course Italy knocked out Ireland only four years ago. Giovanni doesn't take much comfort from that. Everyone knows that this time it's different. Then the Republic were out to play with the big boys for the first time, and reaching the heights of the Quarter-Finals they looked down and felt dizzy. Going out to the home nation, the giant Italy, was making a stylish exit. This time round it's different – Roy Keane has grown as a player, and bagged a Championship and a Cup winners medal in the process, McGrath is always a presence on the pitch, no matter how many times he's absent off it, and then there's McAteer and Gary Kelly, too young and talented to believe in fear.

'You look at those players,' says Giovanni, 'and you know, they're all just incredibly fit.'

The stalwart Premiership players against the foppish dandies of Serie A.

'I'm worried about it, really I am.'

He tells me he's going to be in Italy for the Ireland game, just by coincidence. But for the rest of the games he'll be here at the club, and hardly notice the difference.

Born in England, he has the usual dilemma: over here he's considered Italian, over there he's English. But when it comes to international football, his identity is resolved into pure Azzurri blue. At the moment though, with England out and Italy still up there to be shot down, this only makes him feel more vulnerable.

'If Italy lose to Ireland,' he says, 'I know my life won't be worth living at work for a few days.'

He watches England play on TV, looking out for the players from his English club, wanting them to do well.

The Irish writer Roddy Doyle talks of a different process:

'We love English club football in Ireland,' he says, 'but when a player from your club pulls on an English jersey, love turns to passionate hatred.' I tell Giovanni about this and he smiles at the recognition, admitting he's felt the same thing on occasions.

Channel 4's coverage of Italian football has made Giovanni

feel closer to Serie A. 'Yeah, I mean from an early age, I've always bought the *Gazzetta*, you know, the Bible. But obviously, getting it on the telly converts you, because you can see the people whose names you've been following.'

But then suddenly something that is individual to you becomes the property of everyone. Inevitably the strongest image he attaches to Italian football is from childhood, before there were faces to those sacred names in the *Gazzetta*.

'My mum's family is from Sardinia,' he says, 'so my uncles are all Caliari supporters, and I remember it being a family ritual that we'd all pile into the back of his Fiat after Sunday lunch, and he used to pick up the Italian world service with the results on it.'

Like so many others it was the sound of this strange but wonderful-sounding place far away, beaming in over the static. The disconsolate sounding 'nil' that could make you feel sad. The level 'one', indicating the draw, which was just like nothing really, as against the solid tone that meant a home win or the lilt in the voice that indicated the away win (Do they do that the same in Italian? I forgot to ask him), and can make you feel happy right through the beginning of the week.

And yet he's still never seen Caliari live.

'I haven't had the chance yet. We would have gone over if they had got to the final of the UEFA Cup this season, but Inter knocked them out, so that was it.'

With something that's been so important, perhaps there's almost a reluctance. Like a voice over the telephone, a football club that you've never seen has a mystique that has never been made into flesh.

So this is quite an amazing place, I say, changing the subject for a moment. To think this has all been here and I've never known.

'Yeah, it's great. I live very close so it's a good central meeting place. Usually we'll meet here before going on anywhere else, because everyone knows where it is. It's a good link with Italy, the attitude, the feeling, the atmosphere, and when the football's on it's just manic.'

He keeps up with Italian football more than Italian politics, and displays the fabled Italian reluctance to discuss the way the two have become intertwined in Italy. The most successful football chairman, Milan owner Silvio Berlusconi, is now President, with a right-wing alliance held together by the international team's rallying cry – 'Forza Italia'.

Italy is a country, like England, racked by internal division and a big north/south divide. Except that in Italy it's the north which is the prosperous region, constantly resentful about its resources being drained by the more primitive south.

Giovanni, as descendant of Sardinians, has a particular perspective on this.

'The Sardinians just hate mainland Italy,' he points out. 'Like the Sicilians, they have their own culture which they feel mainland Italy doesn't understand or wish to appreciate. Consequently they want to be autonomous.'

Football, of course, becomes a focus for this inter-regional rivalry; with Caliari taking the hopes of all Sardinians with them when they set out to do battle on mainland soil in Serie A. But international football cuts across such divisions. The moment when all Sardinians, all Sicilians, and all Neapolitans feel unreservedly Italian is when the international team steps out for an important match; a fact which has clearly not escaped Berlusconi, who by stealing the cry that unites these contradictions has captured the magic that can, for the moment at least, hold together a nationalist right-wing agenda with the regionalist interest of the Northern League. Forza Italia indeed.

This power of football to unite is being strengthened by the policy of Arrigo Sacchi, the previous manager of A.C. Milan and now the Italian Coach, to have the national team playing in a variety of centres around the country. Presumably he sensed the danger when Maradona made his well-publicized but largely unsuccessful attempt to rouse the Naples crowd behind Argentina in that Semi-Final.

Since the last campaign, the team has been moving around; 'even to quite obscure places like up near the Austrian border,' says Giovanni. 'And that makes them feel a part of it.'

It is a model that Scotland made a half-hearted attempt to embrace when they held the game against Switzerland at Aberdeen; the one game of the qualifying campaign whose atmosphere was anything other than an embarrassment. England for their part have held steadfastly against the tide of public opinion and signed a new deal with Wembley, a venue easily romanticized by people who have never been there or who watch games from press boxes.

Sacchi has done what Danny Baker suggested England should do when he said the Norway match should be held at St James's Park, Newcastle. 'And we should make a public announcement beforehand saying "Paul Gascoigne is going to walk out on that pitch for the first time in years, and we are not going to be responsible for the noise."'

In the case of Italy, it has no doubt aided the cause of Berlusconi, the only politician, fortunately, to have tapped the awesome and sinister power of football.

If the fans at St Peter's are concerned about their team, though, it has not stopped them considering what will happen if they reach the Final. Particularly since the date coincides with London's own Italian fair, when the whole of Farringdon is closed off and the saints are paraded through the streets.

'There was almost trouble when we first noticed the clash,' recalls Giovanni. 'But then we realized that with the time difference the kick-off would be eight o'clock at night over here, so we'll have time to finish the parade and get back here for the game.

'It'll be madness if Italy make it, I tell you, total madness.'

I went to St Peter's initially with the idea that I'd find someone who was making the trip out to the States. But nobody who hangs around here could afford to make the trip, so they'll all be watching most of the matches at the club. But for some reason that was all the more powerful. Every time I saw Italy play, I thought of St Peter's – I could visualize the heads held in hands when they conceded, the unbridled joy breaking out when they scored. That's the thing about football: it begins as a magical incantation of names on a Saturday or a Sunday afternoon, and, as you go on, more and more faces become associated with those names.

The second meeting of the RISSC is in Harrow, which is not a particularly popular choice, being even more of a suburban wasteland than Harlesden. The Railway Hotel is an absurd mock-Tudor building set by a flyover. It seems all the more surreal to be contemplating New York and the epic clash with Italy from this standpoint.

I arrive about an hour late. Adrian, Kevin, Sylvie and Conn are standing on the edge of the crowd by the bar.

'You've not missed much, like,' Kevin tells me, indicating the packed room where the mayhem that's passing for the meeting is taking place.

All the talk is of the latest miracle result, the Republic's triumph over the World Champions, Germany; the first time that Germany have been beaten on their own ground for six years.

Jack Charlton is making light of the matter, afraid that their comfortable position as underdogs might be eroded if all of a sudden winning becomes something that is expected of them.

Kevin, who emerges as the realist of the group, is following the Charlton rubric. 'Germany were unlucky,' he says. 'On another day they could have won two or three nil.'

But the fact is that they didn't, and a six-year unbeaten record is not something you're about to cast away just before you go out to battle with the world. But there's an undertow of nervousness about the way he says 'They're a good side – very good.' It's as if this time round it might all end in tears.

Adrian isn't so reserved.

'It was brilliant!' he says, shining again. 'Just brilliant!' Gary Kelly had scored the second goal, the first ever of his career, and run up to celebrate right in front of them. Kelly had never thought that he would be sticking the ball in the back of the net in the Munich stadium, and Adrian had never thought he would be watching him. He is the group's enthusiast.

Sylvie wants to relive the result of the Scottish Cup Final with me. Rangers 0 Dundee Utd 1. One of the few scorelines that Celtic fans have had to celebrate this year, but better than nothing.

In Germany he found another group of kindred spirits.

'There's this team who are twinned with Celtic,' he tells me. 'They're Catholic, and, like Celtic, the fans are all really left wing. So they all turned up wearing Celtic strips, and supporting Ireland.'

It's a worldwide brotherhood.

Kevin is not so sure.

I try to explain how a Scottish Celtic fan can feel an affinity with the Republic, despite Irish roots that are buried generations back.

'I don't know,' he says, 'I think you're just one thing or the other. If you're English, you're English. That business you were talking about about Rangers fans wanting to be part of Britain. I mean what does that mean? Britain isn't a country.'

And thereby hangs a hundred tales and quite a few deaths to date.

Still, there's nothing going on but the mêlée. So we have another round. But we're starting to get a bit worried. Is something going wrong?

Then Tony, the president of the club, introduces the travel agent. A hush falls. She has a pony-tail, a Hermes scarf and a nasal drone of a voice.

'Ours is an international company and one of the biggest travel agencies in London. We have been dealing with your club for some time now and I pride myself that we have always delivered satisfaction.'

The whole room shuffles a little.

'But our expertise has always been in arranging flights and accommodation. We have no experience, and we have never had any experience in booking tickets for games.'

The room takes in a breath, looks at the next person, decides not to even think about it, swallows a gulp of a drink and waits for what she has to say next.

'When we first made enquiries about this trip, we were assured by a contact, who is a major power in world soccer, that tickets would not be a problem.'

I am terrified about what she is going to say next, and it isn't even my tickets she is talking about.

'Then at a later stage when we went back to them with numbers, we were told that they did not have tickets for us and they would not be able to deliver any.'

Only the shock prevents the room from exploding. But she is holding it together. This is a bravura performance.

Her tone rises slightly.

'At this time I have to say that we were no longer thinking of trying to make a profit from the deal; we were only concerned with keeping our good name with you. So we went to a travel-agent contact in Ireland who are acting as the official World Cup agents and were successful in securing tickets from them.'

At this point everyone realizes that they have omitted to breathe for a few minutes.

The rest comes quickly. It is bad news, but compared to the scenario that had briefly been opened to the room it's nothing.

Originally the plan had been to stay in New Jersey for the days in New York. Then it was changed to a hotel in Manhattan.

A good move, I had told Adrian at the time. In New Jersey you'll be in a state of hotel arrest. Now they were shifting back to New Jersey.

'It's a different world out there,' one guy mouths to his mate, dismayed.

I try to be encouraging, meanwhile congratulating myself on deciding to travel independently.

Of course I still haven't got my tickets.

In the midst of the mayhem no one in my group has heard that the match tickets are actually here tonight, until Adrian notices a second queue.

'What's this for?' he asks one bloke.

'Tickets,' comes the reply.

'What, airline tickets?'

'No, match tickets.'

Suddenly it all seems real.

He returns to the table with an envelope, which is torn open.

'I can't believe it!' Adrian shouts, making a kind of high-pitched squeaking noise, which does a very good job of communicating his excitement.

They all just hold the tickets, just hold them. Then they all start making funny noises and holding the tickets out to one another.

'After all that time, and all that money,' says Adrian. The importance of the money has now diminished to the width of these red, yellow and white slivers of cardboard.

'Jeez, I hope your tickets are all right,' says Adrian, seeing me looking on. 'I've heard some horror stories already.'

He means it well, but the worry must have zapped visibly across my forehead.

'Don't do that to the guy,' says Kevin.

'Oh look,' says Adrian, turning the ticket over to find nothing but a block of adverts, 'there's no map on the back. It's not the same without a little map on the back.'

And of course he's right. These details are important to the fetishism of football – the power this mere strip of cardboard has to call up the excitement and the atmosphere that it represents the gateway to.

After the ticket flurry quietens down, Kevin explains to me his other reason for being cheerful.

'They told me the last time that I'd paid a hundred pounds too much, so they gave it back to me tonight.'

Are you sure you didn't?

'No,' he says. 'I'm a financial adviser. I keep accounts for a living. I've been all through the figures. It must be some other poor bugger's hundred quid!'

Life seems good as we walk out to a sky the colour and the temperature of a pint of Guinness.

Three days later and still ticketless, bearing the faithful promise of the wide boy and the number of his office in Los Angeles, I say goodbye to Frau at the airport. It's not until I see her standing waving at passport control that it registers. She's staying here, I am going on.

As I'm walking down towards the gate I become aware that I am being followed by half a dozen skinheads.

Did England qualify after all? No, they're speaking German.

'New York?' asks the stewardess. Sorry, flight attendant.

'No, Chicago,' they reply.

See you later, boys, somewhere else in World Cup City.

2

The Emerald City

Travelling to a city you've been to before is like visiting your own past.

Has the place changed? How much is left of the city you used to know? Will you still like it? Will it be embarrassing to have to think back like that?

New York, huh? Oh yeah, we go way back. I sometimes think it might have been more of a thrill if, like friends of mine, I had discovered the world's ultimate city first as an adult. But that is making the mistake of thinking that there's anyone who hasn't been to New York. No matter what age you are when you finally see that skyline for real, you've lived it already in your dreams. Or in the movies, which is more or less the same thing.

Every visit is always a Return to New York.

On the tiny movie screen flickering away at the front of my section of the plane is the opening scene of the Coen brothers' *The Hudsucker Proxy*. A New Year in vintage New York. Snow falls, like it tends to do in movies.

The film looks like a typical Coen brothers comic book tale – and I mean that as a compliment. With their scrupulously storyboarded yarns (*Blood Simple, Raising Arizona, Miller's Crossing, Barton Fink*) full of visual surprise and photographic virtuosity, the brothers have brought the mythology of Americana entrancingly to celluloid – the open road, the trailer park, the late-night neon sign, the Irish versus the Italian gangsters. They know that these are more modern icons than clichés and they have recast them anew. There could have been few better choices for an in-flight movie. All the same, I think I'll save it for the cinema, and just let the flickering image supplement my own film show.

I first came to America in 1969, as a young boy. My father was a scientist and was doing research on viruses that had not at that stage become famous.

We started on the West Coast and moved East – the reverse of the present journey. It seemed that we followed the shadow of a riot all the way across. I remember distinctly the glee with which the Chicago taxi driver showed us the charred remains of buildings struck by the radical leftist terrorist group, the Weathermen. 'You guys be careful in this town,' he said as he left us standing outside the hotel.

This was fun, I reflected as my parents turned that clenched bone colour. Guns and stuff.

By the time we got to New York we caught up with the cloud of chaos, although from Central Park the echo of the events at the Stonewall Bar in Greenwich Village was a faint one. Twenty-five years later (in a few days' time) hundreds of thousands will be parading in the streets to commemorate the night that started gay liberation.

It is a surreal juxtaposition of typically New York proportions that the biggest celebration of gay culture and the biggest festival of football in the world should be happening in the city in the same two weeks. New York may not really be a melting pot, but the temperature was certainly going to be high enough. Another long hot summer, to be sure, but the days of frontiers are over with.

It was in New York that I first decided I was a Catholic. We were living on 5th Avenue, at the corner of Central Park, a few minutes' walk from St Patrick's Cathedral.

One day, because I had nothing else to do, I went in.

I had never understood religion, or the need for it, until then. My mother's family were Free Presbyterians, a Scottish sect who are every bit as mad as the Mormons, but in different ways. In later years her sister, my aunt, would stomp into the living room as we were watching the Saturday night Dracula movie and proclaim that it was one minute past midnight, thus it was the Sabbath and the television was going off.

Wee Frees, as they are called in Scotland, take the commandment 'Remember the Sabbath day and keep it Holy' to absurd proportions. Doing absolutely anything normal on a Sunday is strictly *verboten*, thus turning what is under any circumstances a dull day of the week into something of mind-stultifying tedium analogous to an alternative universe where Sheffield Wednesday and Arsenal are still replaying the 1993 FA Cup Final.

In order to limber up their boredom thresholds, the Wee Frees attend services in totally bare whitewashed rooms of the type that are used for keeping prisoners in states of sensory deprivation. The high point is supposed to be the sermon, a mad, interminable rant only mildly illuminated by some well-worn fire-and-brimstone imagery and characterized chiefly by a lumbering attempt at logic that even a nine-year-old could discern as veering between the deranged and the inept. But the really funny bit is the singing.

One guy gets up on his feet and moans for a bit, his voice wavering as though he's trying to hold on to some vestige of a tune, like a drunk trying to keep the bottle in focus for long enough to reach for it. The tune was always 'Amazing Grace', although I didn't know this until a couple of years later when Judy Collins ruined my enjoyment of the Sunday afternoon chart programme for a number of successive weeks. Then the whole bunch of them join in, creating a sound that calls to mind the image of the full moon over Battersea dogs' home.

Anyway, the point is that St Patrick's Cathedral, which was the first Catholic church I'd ever been allowed within half a mile of, wasn't like this. It was cool and dark. The gleam of candlelight on gold immediately appealed to me. So did the pictures and the statues with their mannered representation of agony and serenity.

My mother, who loosened herself from the Wee Frees only to land in the welcoming arms of the Happy Clappies, would argue with me about these being 'graven images'. But anyone who doesn't understand the power of artistic interpretation doesn't have a grasp of metaphor, and that's a severe handicap in dealing with religion.

Some years later I was invited on a full tour of Durham Cathedral, along with the candidates for artist in residence in the building. You got to see everything that way, even the long, narrow corridors of roofways where the tourists don't get taken. Just the sheer size of the building can be literally breathtaking, but it didn't compare to that first time I walked into St Patrick's. Protestant cathedrals always strike me as being empty by comparison, as if it is assumed that God prefers unfurnished accommodation.

Now you may feel, if you will forgive the infernal imagery, that this was a bit of a case of jumping from the frying pan into the fire. And if I had been brought up as a Catholic I might well have found that they share a reasonable number of the daft ideas that the Wee Frees have. But I wasn't, so Catholicism to me is whatever I want it to be – I can take the bits I like and leave the rest. There is nobody to stop me. As a friend of mine says, we might as well have fun with gods; after all, we invented them.

You may also wonder what this has to do with the subject of this book, in which case you are probably neither Irish nor Scottish. Because at this stage in my life I had yet to form any firm footballing allegiances. I had supported Celtic when they played in the European Cup Final, a feat which was made easier by the fact that we had been living in England at the time. 'Congratulations,' my friends said to me the next day at school. As the only Scot I was considered to be closely involved in their triumph. 'Thank you,' I said.

I had a vague affection, the ironies of which will become apparent, for Manchester United, because, like every other male of my age at that time, I wanted to be Georgie Best. But the only team I had been to see were Greenock Morton, which was a fair way to spend a Saturday afternoon, but I knew at the time it wasn't real football – just as I knew that compared to New York, Glasgow wasn't a real city.

When I decided to become a Catholic, I pitched in my lot irrevocably with Celtic, thus causing a degree of acute family embarrassment that I had to confess (figuratively speaking, you understand) was one of the additional pleasures.

'Look, would you hide this thing, your uncle and aunt are coming around,' my mother would say, waving my Celtic scarf at me. My aunt wasn't actually in the Orange Lodge, the club for Protestant bigots, but her father had been and she would still examine all produce in the supermarket carefully to ensure that it wasn't from Eire before buying it. My mother used to dread them discovering that my bedroom was festooned in green and white; I even had a small Irish tricolour on the wall.

I had a fellow fan in New York in the shape of Patrick, an Irishman who was a trainee priest at the cathedral. Slightly amused by seeing a nine-year-old spending so much time in the place, he asked me one day where I came from. When I said Glasgow he started up a conversation about Celtic and that was it. Now every time I called in to light a candle, a ritual whose significance was entirely lost upon me but which I enjoyed all the same, I would stop off to debate theology and the form of St Jimmy (Johnstone) with Patrick.

I wonder what happened to Patrick. Did he ever make it to the priesthood? Was he still in New York? If he was he would be there, somewhere in the crowd when those boys in green walked out into Giants Stadium.

Most people in Glasgow allow their religion to decide their choice of football team. I have always been proud of the fact that I chose both of them myself. Neither have I ever regretted these decisions, despite the fact that the annual triumphs that I celebrated throughout my life suddenly came to a halt after 1988. The more I found out about it, the more I knew that I was on the right side and my Orange aunt and uncle were on the wrong side. In the real world there's more to it, of course, but I still think that holds true.

The Return to New York had begun a couple of hours earlier, with an absurd pantomime.

'Hands up who wants to smoke!' the flight attendants had run around shouting, calling to mind the classic song introduction by post-punk band The Birthday Party – 'Hands up who wants to die!', or, in this case, 'Hands up who wants to compete for the chance to be shepherded into the four smoking seats at the back of the plane.'

Half of the smokers don't speak English and don't know what's going on until they try to light up. Paddy from Dublin and his English wife, Sue, who have secured two of the smoking seats, spend half the flight playing musical chairs with various nicotine-starved smokers.

Now I'm as intolerant as any other contact-lens-wearing-ex-twenty-a-dayer, but there must be a better way to do this. I make an 'isn't this ridiculous' gesture to the dapper black guy sitting next to me.

It turns out he is on the front line of the war currently being fought between the health lobby and the tremendous wealth of the tobacco business. He runs a video company, which operates like a news agency, circulating stories that have a positive spin for his client, a cigarette manufacturer.

As we're talking, the screen comes down and starts showing a short programme introducing the latest in computer technology – the plane is split between those who are interested, those who know it already and those who don't care. Respectively, the bourgeoisie, the aristocrats and the proletariat of the information revolution.

Michael belongs to the aristocrats. Much of his work involves the treating of images on computer.

'Once I had to change an ad we did and put some black faces in there because the client hadn't thought about it at the time.'

How did you feel about that?

'I had a problem with it,' he says, calmly and logically.

'But it's amazing what you can do. We had a copyright problem recently. We used some source material that some guy claimed copyright of, and I actually could not remember what was real and what had been altered in the video.'

Is it live or is it Memorex?

'Exactly.'

Science fiction has prepared us so well for the possible developments of the future that we have been remarkably blasé about some of the developments of the last ten years or so. With the advent of President Clinton's Information Super Highway, and the acceleration of development in technology that is currently taking place, we may not be able to remain so for long.

'It's like the development of a child,' says Michael, 'where it takes a long time for it to learn to hold something, to stand, to walk, to talk. During the first twelve years of a child's life things happen relatively slowly. Then it hits puberty and a series of complex changes takes place in a very short space of time. That's where we are with technology at the moment.'

So computer culture is just about to hit adolescence. Hold on.

Meanwhile, at the back of the plane there's an impromptu gathering starting of the Boys in Green.

'How long are you out for?'

'Where are you staying?'

And, most importantly, 'Have you got tickets?'

There's a fair number, including Paddy, who haven't. They're on the way out, anyway, thinking if they can get one for a reasonable price then fair enough. If not, well, what the hell. America! It'll be great craic all the same! Suddenly, altitude, anticipation and complimentary drinks are working their magic chemistry, and the excitement really takes a grip of my stomach for the first time. In a few days' time Ireland are going to be playing Italy, in Giants Stadium in New York. And I'm going to be there!

Of course I haven't got my ticket yet, but is a little thing like that going to hold me back? Look! What's that on yonder cloud? It's World Cup City coming into view.

I am tempted to make the same sort of silly noises as Adrian and his pals when they touched the tickets and began to believe it for the first time. But, although I'm sure that the rest of the gathering would have joined in, I make them to myself instead.

The day I arrive, the *New York Times* runs an article about a virtual reality exhibition. It makes a distinction between the virtual reality that people would like to see and the relatively primitive nature of what really exists. 'The virtual reality that everyone wants . . . is . . . an environment that is indistinguishable from real life, except that it is weirder.'

Welcome to World Cup City.

I know that to avoid jet lag you're supposed to avoid alcohol, but for a virtual experience, you can't beat knocking back a few double gin and tonics before arriving in the steam-room heat. I've been here quite enough to be blasé by now. But I'm not. Even a tacky tourist trap like Times Square can make my heart skip a beat, just the sheer scale of it – those great monoliths of neon rising up out of the evening mist, and the noise, the sheer adrenalin-surfing rush of the place.

There's a strange disturbing beauty about the New York architecture, captured in works as diverse as Robbe-Grillet's novel *Project for a Revolution in New York*, in which the city itself is the villain in a carnival of sado-masochism and murder, or *Ghostbusters*, which plays on the gothic quality of some of the city's buildings.

I look out of my hotel window. On the building opposite, alongside the more predictable lion heads, there's a row of what appear to be oyster shells, opening up to reveal mouths. And in the background is the Empire State Building, which I've always felt has a distinctly sinister quality, particularly at night when its subtle illumination glows with a ghostly light.

First night out I walk virtually the whole of Manhattan, trying to pick up the beat. From midtown up to Grand Central and across to Times Square, then all the way down Broadway. Trying to find the building I used to live in on 17th Street. It's not there. Either it's been knocked down to build a school or memory is playing tricks on me. Was it 16th I lived on? I thought that Cajun restaurant was on 17th, not 16th. Cities are like that; their fire escapes contain and confound our memories. They can change while we sleep. Then sometimes we are shocked, coming back after years and finding a corner that's like a bubble in time.

At least the Tasca D'Oro is still on 7th Avenue – the first

place I discovered New York coffee with its thick heady perfume that gilds the throat on the way down.

And on down to the village, along Christopher Street, a place caught in the middle of two contradictory emotions – the pride is big in Gay Pride as the movement reaches twenty-five. But there's a sadness that hangs around the place too. It's quiet around here, not just because it's summer, but because there are more ghosts around Christopher Street than the rest of the city, and there's an underlying anger that some are trying to stoke. 'Stonewall was a riot' says one of the posters, calling for a repeat performance. Nineteen sixty-nine was a hot summer. In 1994 the television tells us 'the mercury is breaking through ninety again' and warns us that medical advice is to take it easy. We'll see.

Over to St Marks and I allow myself to stop for a beer, to cool down. In the authentic fifties setting of the Holiday Bar, Pelé in New York Cosmos strip looks down beneficently from the walls as the Polish barman is complaining about his customers. 'I heard your voice last night,' he berates a tall guy with a moustache, built like a construction worker, 'all the way down Second Avenue. Four o'clock in the morning. My night off and still I got to hear your voice!'

'Hey, look, I'm sorry,' says the guy, laughing into his moustache. This barman's temper is a constant source of amusement in the Holiday.

'You're sorry! I tell ya, alcohol is OK for people who are intelligent. You – you're stupid.'

He throws his towel across the bar and milks the laugh, even allowing the traces of a smile to show around his lips.

Plus ça change, plus c'est le même New York.

By the time I head off back uptown, every bar I pass is packed and everyone is facing the television screen. The opening ceremony is not until tomorrow, and anyway I can't imagine it garnering this sort of interest.

The bars are so full, there's people standing out on the sidewalk and looking in the windows.

What's going on? I ask one of them. He looks at me as if I'm stupid, then realizes it's just that I'm from another planet.

'It's the Rangers,' he replies.

The Rangers are New York's jinxed ice-hockey team. They haven't won the Stanley Cup, the sport's biggest prize, since 1940. That makes any of the big trophy-shy soccer teams look like Liverpool in comparison. This is just one of the two massive sporting events that are currently dwarfing the World Cup for media coverage in the city. The other is the National Basketball play-offs in which the New York Knicks, who haven't won the competition for twenty years, are playing off against the Houston Rockets.

Coming from a capital city like London, whose sporting loyalties are so divided, it's difficult to imagine how big these events are. The Knicks and the Rangers are playing for New York in a way that Arsenal or Tottenham could never even play for the whole of north London. Madonna has been pictured at the Knicks games, Woody Allen has written in the *New Yorker* about his longstanding devotion to the team. And tonight the whole city seems to be looking out for the Rangers. By the time I get back uptown I'm almost caught up in it myself.

A cab screams to a halt in front of me and a woman steps out wearing denim short-shorts.

'What's the score in the game?' she asks, in a tone like there's been an accident and she wants to know where she can call 911.

I think she's talking to me and make my 'I'm a Martian' hand gesture.

It turns out she was asking the guy behind me. 'Rangers are up 2 to 1,' he says.

Further round the corner a black guy comes at me out of the shadow, fixing me with a mean stare.

'What's the score in the game?' he asks.

Rangers up 2–1, I come back.

'Yeah?'

Yeah.

I begin to feel my antennae retracting, and while my shirt is still green at least my face isn't any more.

There's no way of adjusting to a city quicker than sharing in its devotion, and under normal circumstances I would have been pleased for New York. But there's just one problem about all of this. It's Rangers.

I know this is a different city and a different country but the team is in red, white and blue. What's more, there's a vogue in Glasgow for American shirts. They go for the New York Rangers; we of course go for the Boston Celtics. When you've had people wearing New York Rangers shirts standing the other end of a ground from you singing all those fascist anthems, it's a bit difficult to get excited about whether the real team is going to end a losing streak – even a fifty-four-year one.

I don't, however, do what I automatically would in the case of Glasgow Rangers and become an instant honorary card-carrying supporter of the opposition. I'm not about to go into one of these bars and start shouting, 'Go Cannucks!' anyway, so instead I head for Paddy Reilly's bar on 3rd Avenue, hoping to have a couple of quiet drinks before going back to catch up on some sleep.

Inside Paddy Reilly's the Guinness is at least as good as you'd get in the Portman, which, for outside of Ireland, is very good indeed, and a banner proclaims 'Welcome to Big Jack's travelling Army'.

I settle down and read the *American Irish* magazine on the counter, which features an exclusive interview with Guildford Four member Paul Hill. Hill is in the process of making a film about his life, beginning where *In the Name of the Father* finished off. There is an unspoken undercurrent of resentment that Conlon should have become the focus of public attention around a case that took twenty years of his life too.

The Rangers game is on the TV but the sound is down. An American walks in and, seeing this, gives the bar staff a look like they're stark raving bonkers, then leaves.

There's one American Irish and one Irish barman.

'The BBC been in?' says the American, casually.

'Yeah,' replies the Irishman, 'they went away. They'll be back later.'

'Oh yeah,' the American says to me, 'there's been plenty of film crews around.'

'It's going to be a wild night tonight, you should stick around for it. We've got one of the guys from Black 47 coming down to do his World Cup rap.'

You've got *who* doing *what*?

'Black 47, they're this really hot Irish American band at the moment.'

Curiosity as to what a World Cup rap is gets the better of exhaustion but there's two hours or so to go before the band takes the stage, and two hours even of Paddy Reilly's Guinness might just kill me off altogether.

So I head off back to the hotel for a couple of hours' rest.

When I get back to the bar it's still quiet. I take a seat while I still have the chance. They tape a Reserved sign to the table next to me. Slowly people begin to arrive. Some of them have got that airline pallor to them – that 'isn't it really six o'clock in the morning?' look, faces falling into the beer.

Then a group of boys in the colours comes in looking like they've either been here for a couple of days or they have stronger constitutions than I have. They're just settling in to the drinking and the singing when the party arrives to claim the reserved table. It's four willowy-legged women who have the supermodel look off to a tee. In fact one of them looks the spitting image of Naomi Campbell, really the dead spitting image. I wonder . . . nah!

But there are looks flashing across in her direction a little too regularly as she and her friends sit there demurely sipping pints of Guinness. Then the girl on the other side leans over and says, 'You see the black girl there – that's the girlfriend of Adam Clayton from U2.'

She's a little more than that. This girl is so famous even the football supporters know who she is, and it doesn't take long before one of them ventures across and indicates a box camera sheepishly.

For someone who makes a living being photographed, she's

surprisingly co-operative. The camera flashes and there he is, captured for posterity, sitting in a bar in New York with his arm around one of the world's most famous models.

It's like the latterday American Dream that is dreamt in places like Connemara. The Promised Land where the streets have no name and the bars are filled with supermodels.

The band come on stage and open with a mix of Irish reel, keyboard and guitar. Technological jiggery normally comes across like Jeff Goldblum's first experiments with teleporting the monkey in *The Fly*, where the machine delivers a lump of blood and twitching nerves because it doesn't understand the love of flesh. Perhaps it's the jet lag or the occasion, or the Guinness, but this sounds good to me. On violin is an Irish American who can skip across the strings with the best of them. On tin whistle is another Irish American wearing . . . a New York Rangers strip. This is serious culture shock. The next song is dedicated to the Rangers' triumph and has a break that goes 'Let's go, Rangers', which is enthusiastically received by the Americans in the place. The boys in the colours are looking as bemused as I am.

'So the Rangers did some business today,' says the tin whistle man. 'But there's something else going on. The Republic of Ireland in the World Cup.'

Cheers from the bar.

'So now we're going to get into a soccer mood. Whatever the fuck that is.'

And so follows the famed World Cup rap, which has a break that goes: 'C'mon c'mon you boys in green/c'mon you Boys in Green.' Which he exhorts us all to join in with.

But the boys in green aren't accustomed to delivering rap versions of their favourite chant, so they render it with the tune instead, which creates the impression of pandemonium rather than unison. But it all resolves into a contented drunkenness, in the state of which I stumble out on to 3rd Avenue.

Goodnight, World Cup City.

I wake up and realize there was something that was supposed to happen yesterday. I can't remember what it was, but have the dim recollection that it didn't. I stand very still for a moment and catch in the mirror a reflection of the peculiar stupidity of the terminally jet-lagged. I knew I shouldn't have had those drinks on the plane.

Now let's see. Computers, Hudsuckers and proxies . . . Oh God, tickets.

I ring up the number of the office in LA, which is run by a man called Roger. He speaks in the same Cockney accent as the London agent.

'Which matches were these again?'

I am beginning to get more than a little nervous about the fact that I have to go through this ritual every time I ring up. A state that does not diminish when I am told that my tickets have been sent to the wrong city by mistake.

'It's all right,' the voice on the phone assures me, 'I've got a man in New York at the moment. He can get a ticket for the Ireland/Italy game to you, then we'll work on the rest. I'll get him to deliver it to your hotel.'

I don't sound convinced.

'I'll tell you what,' he says. 'I'll upgrade your ticket. I'll get you a Category One; you've paid for a Category Three.'

To be strictly accurate, what I've paid is somewhere near fifteen times the face value of a Category 3 ticket, but under the circumstances, this offer seems fairly reasonable. A little placated, I go out to buy a cable to allow me to plug in my lap-top.

In the computer shop the salesman, a Chinese American called David, asks me what I'm doing out here.

'Oh, World Cup?' he says. 'No one here cares about the World Cup.'

This is active disinterest, where someone wants to let you know that *they* don't care. The other usual American responses are: genuine uninterest (where they change the subject), feigned interest and genuine interest.

In a lot of ways active disinterest is the most peculiar phenomenon. OK, so I wouldn't expect you to know Gary Kelly's birthday, but why make such a big deal about the fact that you don't care?

This reminds me of when I was on the staff of the *New Musical Express* in the eighties.

'Oh, I don't read the *NME*,' a certain type of person would tell you. This was always someone who used to not only read it but probably memorize half of it and quote from it at length, often in lieu of having their own opinions. They were under the mistaken impression that their decision to cease reading the publication somehow said something about them. It made them older and more worldly wise, they thought, when all it really meant was that they read something with more pictures in it instead.

Active disinterest is usually a sign that 'something else' is going on. In the case of the Americans and the World Cup, the something else is a faction within the American press who have reacted to the World Cup not with cynicism – that I think we could understand – but with genuine hostility. What is this unwanted invasion of an alien culture? runs the line. We're not interested in this!

There are two types of response to active disinterest. The first, which is by far the most tempting, is a conversion of your own disinterests to active ones: eg, well, fuck you, no one in the rest of the world would call a sports team the Knicks.

At the other extreme is the understanding approach. Like what would we be like if they moved the Superbowl to London the same day that Manchester United were playing A.C. Milan in the European Cup Final?

Throughout the tournament I repeat this question, just to remind myself that I've always hitherto agreed with Colin McInnes – being anti-American is a dead loss.

But what provokes active disinterest? A lot of it, I suspect, is rooted in the insecurity of the 'expert'. Staffers on the sports sections of the papers suddenly find that this strange sport, with its unfathomable offside law, is coming to town in such a big way that it demands major coverage. They themselves are unable to provide this, and have to stand by and watch while other 'specialists' demand *lebensraum* in their precious column inches. And what happens if it catches on! Better stomp on this one!

David, for one, has bought the line. But when he sees I'm not impressed, he tries to make a hasty conversion to feigned interest.

'How far can those professional soccer players kick a ball?' he asks.

Oh, that's not really the point, I try to explain. It's the skill.

'Skill?' He looks at me with a blatant lack of comprehension.

Skill, I repeat, executing a Cruyff turn with a screwed-up piece of computer paper.

Now he looks at me as if I'm a total nutcase. I rack my brains for a statistic.

There was a Scottish player called Peter Lorimer, I tell him, whose shot was measured at 70 miles per hour.

A pitifully out of date fact, but I gave up memorizing stuff like that the first time I got served in an off-licence. It does the trick, though. His face breaks into a broad grin.

'Man, that's fast,' he wonders.

I take my time getting back to the hotel. When I arrive, I arch my eyebrows hopefully at the receptionist. He shakes his head. Still no ticket.

This time I take the subtle approach.

'Where the fuck is it, then?' I bawl down the phone to LA.

The short answer to this is that it's at the New York Palace, a plusher hotel, a little further up Park Avenue. So I get the name and telephone number of the 'man in New York'. He's called Michael and yes, he has the same accent as the other two.

'Yeah, yeah,' he says, 'it's a Premier ticket, isn't it? I'll bring it round to your hotel.'

But I figure, having already ascended from Category 1 to Premier in the last twenty-four hours, I'd better go and get it myself. After all, I don't particularly fancy an executive box.

'You stay right where you are,' I tell him.

On the way up, I pass a menswear shop whose window display

is decked out with World Cup footballs. These footballs are decorated, supposedly with the flags of the nations that are competing. Much to my surprise, the flags include the Union Jack, which indicates that a team known as Great Britain will be taking part. Well, that's something to look forward to.

As I'm sitting in the lobby of the New York Palace, waiting for Michael to come down with my ticket, I look around at the gilt and mirrors and old-style *Age of Innocence* elegance. This, I reflect, is where I'd like to be staying if I could afford it. And if I had secured a face-value ticket I probably could have done. Instead I'm contributing towards Michael's bill.

I recognize him immediately as he comes out of the lift. Tall, pale yellow sports shirt, slightly tanned, looks civilized enough but would be able to handle himself if the going got rough. He shakes my hand firmly and hands me an envelope. I feel like a drug addict securing a fix, because when I see that World Cup hologram glinting on that strip of cardboard, all the gilt and mirrors seem to lose their glitter.

'We'll be sitting next to you at the game,' he says. 'Roger and me.'

On the way back I decide to stop in at my neighbourhood bar, Desmond's Tavern on Park Avenue South, for a celebratory drink.

It's quiet tonight, and Tony, the Irish American, is holding court solo behind the bar. He's been out here for twenty years, working first in the shipping business, and then when the docks in New York, as in London and Glasgow, died off with the advent of container shipping, he became a bartender, a vocation he performs with the requisite mix of wisdom and paternalism. Within half an hour of my arrival he has to chase out a nutcase who bursts back in every few minutes to deliver another few lines of an apocalyptic sermon before getting chased out again. Obviously a Presbyterian upbringing.

Then a woman with dyed red hair comes in and screams at one of the drinkers at the bar, who adopts a phlegmatic silence. Then she storms out again.

'Who's your friend?' asks Tony.

'Don't ask me,' says the man at the bar.

'Jeez,' says Tony, turning to me and blinking through fishbowl specs, 'it's one of those nights.'

This stretch of Park Avenue, an office strip by day, becomes an island of prostitution late at night. Usually you don't see the hookers unless you're coming in well after midnight, but occasionally one will flit in and out of Desmond's.

But the only street trade we're interested in is the one in World Cup tickets.

'The prices have been coming down,' says Tony. 'Last week they were still asking about five hundred dollars. Now they're down to two hundred, and they'll come down further when the scalpers {the American word for touts] get nervous.'

So already the tickets have fallen to around half of what I paid. But it gives me a warm glow to think that I've made my score, I don't have to be out there asking around.

An Irish American princess comes across to the bit of the bar where Tony and I are talking.

She wants to know about tickets.

'He's got one,' says Tony, indicating me. 'You could sit on his lap.'

They don't come that cheaply, I come back.

Tony calls across Johnnie, an English boy who's a regular there.

Is he the contact? I ask.

Tony, with a single facial expression, manages to convey that as far as she's concerned he is, but then she looks like she has more money than sense. Somehow he seems to know that I'm a deserving case, and therefore not fair game.

From the conversation between the girl and Johnnie, it emerges that she's training to be an actress. Johnnie is clearly a little envious of her youth and opportunity.

'You know,' he says, 'when I was a kid they wanted to send me to the Royal Academy of Dramatic Art in London and my mother wouldn't let me go. She said I wouldn't make it. And it was the biggest mistake of my life, because I would have made it.'

56

She nods sympathetically; the bars and restaurants here are full of stories like that. How the big time passed me by.

Johnnie heads back across the road towards the restaurant where he works.

'See you later, Don,' he says. Two nights out and I'm one of the locals now.

In walks an Irish party, and Tony nods to me.

'There you go,' he says.

Eddie from Northern Ireland isn't going to any of the matches, he's just out staying in the Bronx with his son, just for the craic.

His son works for Immigration.

'Oh yes, the Bronx is still a big Irish area,' Eddie says, 'there's a big grapevine. If an apartment comes free and you know there's an Irish person looking for one, it doesn't get advertised, you just tip them off.'

'What are you called?' he asks.

Donald.

'Ah, Donald where's yer troosers!'

This is one thing I don't mind about living in England. Eddie is referring to a song by Andy Stewart about a Highland boy who goes back to his roots and decides to wear a kilt around Glasgow, thus occasioning the cry 'Donald where's yer troosers?' People in England are too polite to mention it.

Eddie and his family have been around the corner to see a play about the Westsiders, the first Irish Union in New York.

'So you're a Celtic boy?' says Eddie.

We discuss the changes at Celtic, and I express my reservations about Lou Macari. I'd like to see them winning cups again, but not at the expense of adopting the sort of puritan route one tactics that Super Lou became renowned for at Stoke. Brady may have made a couple of dodgy deals, but on their day they were playing beautiful football under his guidance.

The conversation turns to New York, and Eddie asks me what I think of it.

I tell him I think that if you like cities, you've just got to love New York, because it's the ultimate city. It's also underestimated for its beauty.

Eddie agrees.

But what's really amazing is just how quickly most of what you see around you has been built. It really comes home when you read Henry James or Edith Wharton that, in the nineteenth century, almost everything above what is considered today to be 'downtown' was virtual wilderness.

Martin Scorsese was clearly fascinated by the same thing. When you see *The Age of Innocence* you know, by the way he has lovingly recreated the image of the house by Central Park, standing on its own, without another building in sight.

'D'you know something else,' says Eddie, 'it was all built by Irishmen too.' He laughs. 'I'll tell ya, that would make a book for you.'

And if only I'd been there, it probably would have done. From wilderness to this in maybe twenty years. It still seems like a miracle in gilt and brownstone.

'Whadya think of this stuff about it being dangerous, then?'

I suppose you have to acknowledge that statistically it's true, but I've never felt unsafe in New York, the way you can in certain parts of London. Although I'd already discovered that 8th Avenue can be pretty unpleasant now that the sleaze has moved around the corner from the better-lit Times Square.

What do you think, Eddie?

'It doesn't compare to Belfast, that's for sure.'

He tells me he's been out to one of the beaches today.

'And we were told to be careful about the taxi drivers out there. But I wasn't thinking. This guy says did we want a ride, so we got in. We'd gone about a mile down the road and I realize that this character isn't a taxi driver at all, he's just some auld drunk. He's not got a clue where he's going – he does about five U-turns around petrol stations, knocks off a fire hydrant, taking half of his motor away with it. Then he asks a policeman for directions. He had some nerve, anyway. Then he finally gets us back to the Bronx, and we've been driving for about an hour. I says how much. He says ten dollars. Ten dollars! A real cab might have cost us fifty.'

Dangerous? Life out here's a party, a weird one, but a party all the same, full of madness and bargains. Or perhaps we've just been lucky.

'Jeez, will you look at this,' says Eddie, paying for a round of drinks and picking up the pile of dollars he's left on the bar, becoming familiar with the local custom already. 'There was one guy where I live in Belfast, he came out here, and when he got back home he starts leaving his money on the bar like this. He goes "That's what they do in the States." Course the first time he goes to the bog, he comes back and it's all gone. He got out of the habit quite quick after that.'

We're joined at this point by a used-car salesman from Northern Ireland who's in a category I call intriguingly obnoxious. He starts out telling us why he doesn't play rugby any more.

'I had a cruciate ligament injury, an Achilles tendon injury, a patella injury . . .' It goes on for about ten minutes, a carefully memorized recital of basically how he broke every bone in his body. Then he's on to the household implements he's managed to score for nothing by doing deals with his customers.

'I've got a fridge freezer, a washing machine . . .' Again it goes on for ten minutes or so, finishing up with 'but I had to buy the microwave.'

So how did you book your passage out here?

'I bought up my customers' air miles at a bargain rate.' I thought it might be something like that.

I make to leave, but Tony won't hear of it.

'Have another one on me,' he says. 'What's that, Jack Daniel's?'

Go on, then. I've got my ticket, all's well with World Cup City. I can always sleep tomorrow night.

Sleep, I am to discover, becomes a precious commodity in World Cup City.

The next morning Frau rings me up with important news.

'Lou Macari's been sacked,' she says.

This causes mixed feelings in the family. On one side there are the reservations expressed above. On the other is the fact

59

that Lou Macari plays a pivotal role in our memories. Our first date was in an ice-cream parlour in the Scottish coastal resort of Largs, where both our families were spending the summer. We were seven years old. The place was called Macari's and was owned by Lou's dad. A big picture of Lou in a Celtic strip looked down on the diners. My Orange aunt used to refuse to patronize Macari's despite the fact that it was the best ice cream in town and there's not many Irishmen named Macari.

We had both just finished our sundaes when up walked the man himself.

'It looked like you enjoyed those,' he said. 'Would you like another?'

He put another ice cream in front of each of us and ruffled my hair. Normally I punched people for doing that, but this was Lou Macari. I made an exception.

'He was a nice man,' says Frau. 'Remember he bought us an ice cream?'

I begin to feel slightly guilty.

'He had bandy legs, of course,' she continues.

The O.J. Simpson case broke more or less the day I arrived. By the Thursday it had begun to pick up its crazy momentum. First we heard about Nicole Simpson's death, then that blood traces had been found, next that the blood type matched the Juice's juice.

That day I wake up to hear that O.J. is on the run. The television landscape is filled with his figure, the giant whose gentility was under dispute. In the *Independent* the week before I left, there was an excellent article speculating on the candidates for the hero of the World Cup. Who would be the Pelé, the Cruyff, the Ardilles, the Rossi? The last line was stolen from Paul Simon's 'Mrs Robinson' – 'a nation turns its lowly eyes to you'. One of those flashes of insight that burst across the maudlin sentimentality of much of Simon's output, that line does seem to capture something. In the song it refers to Marilyn Monroe's husband, the hero of the New York Dodgers, Joe DiMaggio, but it conjures up a certain sadness at the heart of the love we have for great sporting superstars. Our disappointment is repetitive, but nonetheless tangible as we are inevitably let down, either by the decline of their magic potency on the field, or by proving in their off-field behaviour that they are 'only human, no more, no less'. What was so shocking about the O.J. Simpson saga as it unfolded, apart from its extraordinary public dimensions, was that, if the allegations are true, this great sporting hero had at one point in his life been actually less than human; he had become obsessed. The point about sporting heroes is that they are the obsessees, not the obsessed. We want them to be divine. For them to be human is just about excusable; for them to sink lower than that is either unforgivable . . . or it's a conspiracy.

Where have you gone, O.J. Simpson? A nation turns its lowly eyes to you. What's that you say, Mrs Robinson? The jolting juice has left and gone away. Hey, hey, hey. Hey, hey, hey.

With all this going on in the background, could we really search for a World Cup hero with the same earnest?

Amazingly, the wounds of disillusion heal before they have been made.

With O.J. added to the Rangers' victory celebrations (a ticker-tape parade up Broadway) and the ongoing Knicks series, the World Cup was reduced to a thirty-second item showing Italian and Irish fans being greeted by their American relations at the airport. But if the visibility on the television was restricted, even in a city the size of New York the presence on the streets was unmistakable.

From my midtown location you couldn't walk for five minutes in any direction without seeing a group of green shirts. But the blue of the Azzurri was less in evidence.

Little Italy is not the place to go and look for Italians these days. It's been shrunk by the continuing expansion of Chinatown and transformed by the gentrification of the Lower East Side. I have a lead on some places in Brooklyn to head for, but the receptionist at the hotel advises me to steer clear at night. This is probably out-of-date information – much of Brooklyn and Queens are now colonized by refugees from SoHo and the Upper West Side, the erstwhile bohemian hangouts that priced out the bohos. But it's advisable not to take a risk when you're still acclimatizing to a city. Besides which, Little Italy always warrants a visit just to walk around the set of one of my favourite movies, Scorsese's *Mean Streets*.

Watching *Mean Streets* now is like watching a historical document. It seems remarkable to think that when it was made in the early seventies, the world it contained could still be traced around the streets of the Lower East Side. As recently as the early eighties, Little Italy still had the feel of the 'neighborhood' that is referred to so often in the movie. Now Elizabeth Street, where Martin Scorsese was born, is a line of chi-chi bars.

From the film's content it perhaps shouldn't be surprising that the Italians have become assimilated in a way that the Irish have not. Charlie, Johnny Boy and their gangster companions have taken their Sicilian mores along with them, but they are making a visible attempt to establish themselves as Americans. Their toast to 'The Queen!', in imitation of the Anglophile ruling class of America, is partly ironic, but only partly.

Of the hall of fame of Italian Americans on the wall of Sal's Pizzeria in Spike Lee's Brooklyn movie *Do the Right Thing*, it's difficult to think of one that seems more Italian than American. Frank Sinatra, Joe DiMaggio, Al Pacino, Robert De Niro – all of them seem like cornerstones of American culture.

It's difficult to think of an Italian writing a line like 'Wherever we go we celebrate/The land that makes us refugees', as Shane MacGowan of The Pogues did. And that from someone who was brought up and educated in England. Where the Italians take Italian habits with them, the Irish take Ireland with them. The figures in the Irish hall of fame tend more to be Irish ones like Behan or Joyce, two Irish exiles who rarely wrote about anywhere else. It was Joyce after all who defined the sensibility of the perfect exile – one who takes his country with him, out into the world beyond its narrow confines.

Black 47, whose tape I listen to on the way down, have produced a series of songs that provide a perfect American Irish parallel to the London Irish paeans of The Pogues, full of memories of Wexford Town and thoughts of the Kingsbridge Road and 'Dear old Donegal', as well as a commemoration of Irish freedom fighter James Connolly, and an angry testament to the year of the 'famine', the Black '47 from which the band take their name. Above all there's the sound, that atavistic pull of the Irish fiddle playing a reel, a skill that these American-born players have been brought up with.

The soundtrack to the lives documented by *Mean Streets* is all-American do-wop counterpointed by the satanic English R & B cavalcade of The Rolling Stones' 'Jumping Jack Flash'. Perhaps it's appropriate that I went to Little Italy looking for Martin Scorsese's ghosts and instead I found . . . another bunch of Irishmen.

Walk down Mulberry Street and suddenly you know the World Cup is happening. The streets are decked with pennants. On closer inspection the tricolours are in the Italian red, green and white – but the sodium lights give the red an orange cast, making them look at first glance like the Irish colours of orange, green and white.

At one of the bars an Irish group are shouting over to an Italian storekeeper who is standing outside his shop.

'Hey, where are all your colours? These are all Irish!'

He points out their mistake.

'So where are the Italian boys wearing them?' they ask.

He holds his hands out in a shrug. It's a good question, which is to be answered in the next couple of days. Meanwhile, the storekeeper, not wanting to disappoint them, disappears for a few minutes.

Someone comes along trying to sell tickets with some patter about wanting to see the match with his family.

Two hundred dollars is the price, which doesn't seem bad. But there are no buyers.

'I won't pay any more than face value,' says one lad, who introduces himself later as Dermot. 'If you do that then people will get away with it.'

63

There's an indefatigable logic there. But what if it does sell out?

'C'mon and join us,' they say. 'Pull up a chair. What's your name?'

Donald.

'Ah, Donald where's yer troosers?'

'Sorry, I bet you've heard that one before.'

Only once in the last twenty-four hours.

'So, that sounds like a Scottish accent,' they say.

Celtic supporter, I say, by way of explanation.

Dermot holds his hands wide above his head and cheers. Another of the party, sitting in the corner, raises his top lip and snarls.

'This is Cathal,' says Dermot. 'He's a Rangers supporter. There's only three Rangers supporters in the whole of Cork, and they all drink in my pub, just to piss me off.'

Cathal sniggers.

'Mind you,' Dermot says, 'I don't think he can name a single one of Rangers' players.'

'I can't,' says Cathal, 'but it does piss you off, doesn't it?' He makes a snarling face again.

Dermot raises his eyes heavenward.

Dermot and Cathal are the double act who make most of the noise; equally outgoing but gentler in manner is Eldon. Eldon is already lower down in the hierarchy out here because he wasn't in Italy in 1990. 'But,' he says to me later, 'I've re-mortgaged my house to come out here – isn't that enough?'

The quieter members of the party are Paddy and Patrick. Paddy wears a sombrero in Irish colours. 'We've just met these guys tonight,' he confides in me quietly. 'I don't know, they seem a bit wild.' Patrick is getting into the spirit of things though, and ordering another round.

As we talk about our favourite subject, the question is raised. Is Graeme Souness a bigot?

'No way,' Dermot and I chorus. 'He may be a lot of things but a bigot isn't one of them.'

Remember, I point out, he was the one who signed Mo

Johnston. I pause to spit before uttering the name, as is customary. Mo Johnston was the first Catholic to sign for Rangers, although he had announced, twenty-four hours earlier, that he was to return to Celtic. Shortly afterwards he refused to play for Scotland. Hugh McIlvanney calls him one of the 'new breed of players who put personal wealth and advancement above any feeling for place'; a footballing yuppie. But all the same, he's a powerful argument in Souness's defence.

'I don't know,' says Eldon, 'I just think it was strange that when he came to Liverpool the first thing he did was sell the three Catholic players – Saunders, Staunton and Houghton.'

Yeah, but he'd bid for Houghton while he was at Rangers.

Eldon still isn't convinced.

'I'll tell you who's a bigot,' says Dermot. 'Terry Butcher!'

There's no argument on that one, after all, it's all documented in Pete Davies's portrait in *All Played Out*, his otherwise excellent book on Italia '90. I say otherwise because there seems to be a trace of approval in Davies's description of Butcher as the man who throws Simple Minds tapes out of his car window because he discovers they're Celtic fans, and who sings the Rangers anthems of religious intolerance in the shower after England matches. But perhaps I do Davies the disservice that Eldon does to Souness. I'd like to think it was irony, but, like Eldon, I'm not so sure.

Then the storeholder from next door comes back out wearing an Italian shirt.

This brings out first cheers and then catcalls.

'Schillaci was lucky!' they shout, referring to the goal that put Ireland out in the Quarter-Finals in Italy.

A TV camera comes around and a chorus of 'C'mon you boys in Green' starts up to the tune of 'Those Were the Days'. Playing the agent provocateur, I can't resist starting up a round of 'Are you watching, Engerland?' which is taken up enthusiastically, much to the amusement of passers-by and the surrounding clientele, this being the first time they've heard that stalwart taunt.

If this was England we'd be surrounded by lowered eyes and an atmosphere of nervous tension. Here we're the centre of attention. People come up and want to introduce themselves, they want to know what part of Ireland everyone's from.

Dermot, Eldon and Cathal are from Cork. Paddy and Patrick are from Dublin. Most of the curious have names as Irish as Sean O'Casey and accents as American as the Brooklyn Bridge. More times than not they have antecedents from one of the two areas.

'You're going to get what the Germans got,' they begin to chant, turning their attention back to the storekeeper.

'Yes, but this was a friendly,' comes the sound of a clear voice from another table.

Up goes a cheer.

Michael and Jochen, from Hamburg, are staying in New York for a couple of days before driving to Chicago to see the German team in their second match.

'C'mon, pull up a couple of chairs, boys!' goes the cry. Now we have a real posse going. More beers!

Eldon has discovered that one of the pennants above our table has the Union Jack on it, and is protesting vociferously to the waitress.

'But you are all British, aren't you?' asks Jochen, who looks like a ringer for David Seaman.

There is a short silence followed by a very loud and very sharp intake of breath.

Jochen has a wicked smile underneath his 'tache that also calls to mind that great Lad amongst goalkeepers. But in the heated exchange that ensues there turns out to be some genuine confusion.

'It's like calling you Austrian,' Eldon remarks.

'I am Austrian,' says Jochen.

Fair enough, then.

Then he grins.

Bah! Let's go to another bar.

So we do, up the street to Mare Chiaro's bar, with the inexorable force of a few beers inside us and the World Cup coming closer by the second.

As we go, Eldon is still explaining to Jochen about the red

hand of Ulster, the symbol of Unionist resistance which adorns the Northern Irish flag.

Every second song on the jukebox in Mare Chiaro's bar is Frank Sinatra, which is explained by the pictures behind the bar showing Frank with the owner, and Ronald Reagan and Madonna. Quite a Holy Trinity. But the third song is Martha Reeves & the Vandellas, with that rasping bass brass sound that you can feel in your stomach like excitement itself, counterpointed by the high, clear sound of the three girls singing.

It's one of those times when music and moment combine to create an alchemical explosion.

By the time the first line comes around we're all ready. Nobody says anything but everyone starts right on cue:

'Calling out around the world,' we fling our heads back and sing as if, through the open door of Mare Chiaro's, the world might hear, 'Summer's here . . .' with a vengeance 'and the time is right' we smile as we sing the title line, punching the air as we do so, 'for *dancing in the streets.*'

When a song has fallen victim to an inept cover version, as this one did (the perps being those ridiculous old tarts Bowie and Jagger), you tend to strike it off your internal jukebox. But when you hear the original again it's like hearing the song for the first time, and you can be astounded by the power it packs. So it was that night. Although the circumstances may have contributed.

But it was something everyone in the bar could feel, the sheer electricity of Motown for which we were the conductors.

In New York City they'd be dancing, in old Chicago, up in San Francisco, down in LA they'd be dancing. We didn't yet know who 'they' would be, but they'd be dancing, dancing in the streets. We knew this for a fact.

'And win, lose or draw we'll be dancing with them,' says Dermot, and it's true.

Again there are smiles from all quarters. Two American boys come over to sit with us.

'Are you a football fan?' Dermot asks one of them.

Nope.

'What, then?' Eldon wants to know. 'Basketball, baseball?'

Not really a sports fan. Both of them just want to sit with us, be a part of the energy. The posse is under its own momentum now, picking up new members all the time.

So what are you, I ask, another beer inspiring me to take on the voice of an auctioneer. German? Italian?

'Half German, half Russian,' one of them replies.

OK, we've got three from Cork, two from Dublin, one Glaswegian, two and a half Germans and half a Russian. Any more bids, please, any more bids, please?

'I'm a quarter Russian,' says the other.

Anything more to declare?

'A quarter German and half Polish.'

So three from Cork, two from Dublin, one Glaswegian, two and three-quarter Germans, three quarters of a Russian and half a Pole get into a convoy of cabs and head on uptown to the Blarney Stone. The night opens up to allow us passage.

Every bar in New York claims Irish roots, but the Blarney Stone, a chain of plain, chrome-fronted places, does so more convincingly than most. There's a good pint of Guinness on tap and The Wolfetones on the jukebox.

Named after the leader of the United Irishmen Wolfe Tone, one of a tradition of Protestants like Charles Parnell, who campaigned for a United Ireland, The Wolfetones were one of the early models for The Pogues. It was with a collection of rebel songs borrowed from The Wolfetones repertoire that The Pogues first appeared, under the name of The New Republicans, at Richard Strange's club Cabaret Futura.

You'll often hear people say that the chant 'Ooh-aah Paul McGrath' is based on 'Woops Upside Your Head' by the Gap Band. In fact, it's based on a rebel song sung by The Wolfetones, whose chorus is 'Ooh-aah up the RA' – the RA being the Republican Army. The chorus rings out in the Blarney Stone that night, but the one that really opens the throats is 'The Boys of the Old Brigade', which has become an anthem of the Irish World Cup escapades.

When The Wolfetones sing 'Where are the boys who stood with me/When history was made?' they're talking about the 1916 uprising, which led to the declaration of the Irish Republic. When they join in, the football fans are serenading Kevin Sheedy's goal against England and David O'Leary's penalty against Romania.

Tonight it's ringing through the bar and all the way down 8th Avenue.

Michael and I are talking at the bar with an old man from the North with a mouth like a geyser. We stand slightly back in an attempt to avoid the shower of spittle his every utterance is wrapped in. He's sitting on a stool in a semi-daze, just happy to be here. You can feel in the air what it means to these people – you can almost imagine that history really is being made. And in some way, I suppose that it is.

Michael deals in stripping down old factories, so as a result he's spent a lot of time in the old East.

'It's difficult,' he says of reunification, 'but it is our country and it should be under the same government.'

The old guy nods his head, like he knows what Michael means.

Then we turn around and Jochen and Cathal are standing forehead to forehead.

'Wind yer neck in!' I shout over to Cathal.

He doesn't look amused. Neither does it seem like the time to enquire what this dispute is all about.

A few days later I see Cathal again and ask him.

'He just thinks that everyone hates him, because his dad fought for Germany during the war.'

That's the problem with history. People tend to disagree about it.

When I arrive back at the hotel, there's a telephone message for me.

'Basia rang – dying to see you.'

Basia is a girl I used to share a house with in Acton. Taking the model of measuring your life out by World Cups, I think back to Spain in 1986. Despite surnames like O'Sullivan, Ogilvy and McLean, the rest of the house were English and more interested in the cricket. Basia was born in England too, but her parents were Polish. When talking to her mother on the telephone, she used to be able to switch into Polish at sensitive moments. A useful facility when you share a house with four people.

She was still on a high from Poland's performance in 1982, when they finished third. But it was a disappointing World Cup for both of us. Scotland were virtually out after losing 1–0 to Denmark in the first game. I threw my lot behind Poland and we both sat and cheered them on against England. But they lost 3–0.

Basia! Bloody hell. She'd heard I was in town purely by coincidence – an acquaintance of Frau's who I'd contacted turned out to be a friend of Basia's. That's the thing about New York. It's tiny.

The next day I ring Frau.

'Aren't you watching the first game?' she asks me.

In the midst of the chase for tickets and the search for fans, I've forgotten the actual games. But then it's easily done when the news channel has switched over to live coverage from the Rangers victory parade, which is taking place on Broadway, a hundred yards or so from where I'm sitting. The commentators make no attempt at objectivity.

'I've been a Rangers fan for so long,' says one of them, apparently fighting back the tears, 'and this day means so much to me.'

Despite advertising cable TV on its brochure, my hotel does not have the sports channel ESPN, which is the only English-speaking network broadcasting the majority of the World Cup games. But it does have the Hispanic channel, which is pandering to the football fervour of the indigenous community with the sort of blanket coverage we might expect in Britain. So I watch the second half of Germany v Bolivia in Spanish. Letting go of the one tenuous link that connects me to the US (i.e., that we speak approximately the same language) only increases the foreign feeling that's creeping up on me in the wake of the jet lag.

The first half had apparently been the traditional epic bore of opening matches. Perhaps all the objective reporters had been lulled to sleep by this time, or perhaps it was my feeling of dislocation, or the controlled hysterics of the Spanish-speaking commentator, Andres Cantor, but the bit I saw looked like it had been edited for MTV; they had scarcely finished showing action replays when there was another chance at the other end.

For a moment the Germans are living dangerously, and an opening-day shock looks like a possibility. But then the offside trap is easily beaten by Völler who pushes the ball to Klinsman, and for the first time I hear Cantor go mental.

'*Goooooaaaaaaaaalllllll!!!!!!!*' he bellows.

'*Goooooaaaaaaaaallllllll!!!!!!*'

'*Goooooaaaaaaaaallllllll!!!!!!*'

Of course you've heard this sort of thing before – usually with some smarmy English commentator doing his bumbling attempt at urbanity and sniggering up his sheepskin about how these hot-blooded foreigners get so excited about football. But none of that prepares you for the sheer exhilaration of hearing it live and for real. It sounds like total dementia, but that's the point. That is the best way to represent the sheer madness of the moment when the ball strikes the back of the net.

The sooner we get this man beamed over on satellite the better. More power to his tonsils.

Later on, I decide to seek out some company for the Spain v Korea game and head over to Desmond's.

Tony is behind the bar again.

'We've got basketball in the back and football up the front for us,' he grins, indicating the packed back room with his thumb.

'Us' constitutes Tony, in the moments he can squeeze between serving pitchers to the Knicks fans, me and a guy from Honduras, who is perched at the end of the bar.

Spain take a 2–0 lead and look fairly comfortable, then begins one of the fightbacks for which you love this competition – a combination of sheer determination, luck, some skill and the

71

passion that only a newcomer to the world stage can summon up in the early part of the first round.

First the Koreans get a free-kick on the edge of the area and a freak deflection takes it past Zubizarreta. Now their blood is up and you can see them almost literally increase in stature, taking the game to the shell-shocked Spanish.

'Hey, could we put the basketball on this TV?' says a guy behind me.

'Basketball's in the back room,' says Tony dismissively as the Honduran and I protest.

'Sorry,' says the guy, looking at us like we just asked who O.J. Simpson was, 'I didn't realize anybody was watching this.'

You bet they are. The South Koreans come back again and again and finally break through. The equalizer is a well-taken goal too, threaded past the advancing keeper, and we all at once burst out in a laugh that is not just derision but an expression of respect for the sheer guts of the South Koreans.

In a bar in New York City a Honduran and a Scot slap palms in celebration of a goal scored in Dallas by a South Korean. For tonight at least they are the favourite minnows of everyone outside Spain.

Later on that night, I meet Basia for a drink. She takes me to a place called 188 Houston, which is usually a music bar but has been taken over tonight by Knicks fever.

The Knicks will win this game, to put them 2–1 up in the series and in sight of the NBA Championship, but this will be dwarfed on TV by the news that breaks as we watch in the bar, dumbfounded.

O.J. Simpson has been found, and that now famous scene of him driving up LA Highway 405 in the white Bronco is being broadcast live on one of the six television screens in the bar. At first people are looking from one TV to another, trying to follow the chase at the same time as keeping up with the score in the Knicks game. Then, obligingly, Channel 4, which is broadcasting the Knicks game, puts an insert of the O.J. chase on the picture, so now everyone can do both at once.

The great running-back is making his last great run for touch. The cameras are on him again and like the old days he's holding them with action, not stinking up the place with a lot of talk. The LA public who have seen this on TV leave their homes to line the highway.

Go, O.J. Go.

After the initial amazement, watching what is after all a slow drive up the motorway – even with a famous passenger holding a gun to his head – palls as a form of entertainment.

'If he shoots himself we can always watch the action replays later,' says Basia, proving that she's been here long enough to be as cynical as any native New Yorker. As we leave 188, the final whistle goes in the basketball. The Knicks have won, and are within one game of the NBA Championship. Soccer will be taking back seat for another week.

'I'll show you another place. This one will give you a laugh,' Basia says, leading the way across the road to the Temple Bar.

'They do a wicked Martini,' she giggles.

I recall my most vivid image of the time we shared the house together. It was just before the start of what were to become our infamous house parties and one of our fellow inmates had produced a bottle of champagne for a toast, prior to the first guest arriving.

'I know!' Basia had said. 'Car Crashes!' She had given the same giggle then, before scuttling off and returning with a bottle of well-chilled Polish vodka. We drank the lethal cocktail and shortly afterwards mayhem ensued.

'Plus ça change,' she says. Funny you should say that.

Back in the Acton days, Basia was a small bundle of muscle, as was the vogue in those days. Here in New York she hasn't grown any, but the muscle has fallen away, leaving a haunted, hungry look that I seem to see on so many New York women.

What is this, the percolating down of the superwaif? I ask. Basia works in the fashion business.

'No, it's genuine starvation,' she replies. 'All those women you see have such frantic work lives, they never get a chance to eat.'

She's now totally legit out here. Her Green Card came through the lottery. Most white Europeans tend to be successful through that route, I'm told, although Basia's boyfriend Sean, who set it up for her and some of her friends, wasn't. He still exists six months at a time.

I tell her I'm envious, having decided against staying in New York in '86 because at the height of yuppiedom the pace was too frantic, the real-estate panic too destructive. Then of course the London I'd elected to return to got almost as bad.

'I do love it out here,' she says. You know that when someone puts the 'do' in there's something wrong.

'But you'd be amazed what you begin to miss. I've discovered that so many of my friends are English or Scottish and, like me, living in exile out here. It's quite sad in a way, but it happens because you all share the same references, and other people don't understand them.

'There's one friend of mine . . . We just spend all the time saying the name of obscure bands from the mid-seventies to one another and then collapsing with laughter. Everyone thinks we're totally batty, but it's like you cling to that recognition because basically you're existing in a world that is strange to you. You'd be amazed at the things that you start missing. Like English television. I know it's such a cliché, but the television here is crap. I really would love to come in tired one day and be able to switch on the English television news.'

The loneliness of the long-distance exile.

'But look at this place,' she says, getting over the outpouring of *Heimat* sickness, and delighting again in the surroundings. 'Isn't it hilarious!'

The lighting is controlled gloom, with a dim spotlight directed down at the table, so you sit in a pool of light amidst the darkness. The waitress brings me a large basin of gin on a stem.

'These are the two sides of the café and bar society,' she says. 'One Eight Eight is the social side, and this is the seduction haunt. You can tell looking around these tables that all these people are ready to go home and fuck each other's brains out.'

If this is the case, mind you, they don't seem too eager about it. By the time we leave it's about three o'clock in the morning, and they're all still there, leaning through the pool of light towards each other.

'Oh God, at least it's Saturday tomorrow, I can sleep,' says Basia as the cab drops her off at Gramercy Park.

But I can't, I reflect, as I speed on back to midtown, not for as long as I'd like to, anyway. I realize that for the last hour or so I have not repeated my mantra.

Tomorrow I am going to see the Republic of Ireland play Italy in the World Cup.

As I get out of the cab a rotund black woman, squeezed into a mini-skirt, asks me if I need a date.

I've already got one, I reply, much to her confusion.

I lie down and get one and a half times through the mantra before falling asleep.

The day finally arrives, wrapped in surreal sunshine and bearing a dry throat and a headache. After mooching around the outskirts of World Cup City, today is the day I am to enter the citadel.

Only this sense of purpose keeps me upright as I head off to 8th Avenue.

Cathal, Eldon and crowd had promised that if I could get up to their hotel by twelve they would make sure I got to bunk on their courtesy coach to the ground. But the whole of 8th Avenue is a veritable car park of courtesy coaches, with queues of green-swathed people each uttering the secret password that will allow you to be whisked off to Giants Stadium, and without which you are stuck on the sidewalk.

So I give up on that and head down to Port Authority Bus Terminal.

I haven't had breakfast so far, but I thought I could live without the greasy burgers from the stall outside the terminal. I suspect that the food at the ground, as is traditional, would be as bad, but at least the hunger might have penetrated the delicate state of my hangover by that time.

There are tickets openly on sale and already the price has dropped way below what I've paid. So much for the stories, which had circulated at home for weeks, of them being impossible to come by for this game.

Frau has even been talking to a journalist who, quite seriously, repeated the story that the Irish tickets were being controlled by the IRA and the Italian ones by the Mafia. A rumour which, by its very existence, speaks volumes for the strength of the relative myths of these two nations.

As we queue for tickets for the coach, they want to check game tickets. A brave attempt to cut off the customer supply for the scalpers, which is, nevertheless, doomed to failure from the start.

In the distance I can hear the familiar ring of the Celtic anthem: 'Oh it's a grand old team to play for/It's a grand old team to see/*And if you know your history* . . .'

And here in the confines of a foreign bus terminal, I sense an old familiar feeling rising in my stomach. Normally pre-match excitement makes me feel slightly sick. Today, perversely enough, it makes me feel slightly less so.

The trip to Giants Stadium through the swamplands of New Jersey seems to take no time at all. Have these people never heard of the way a traffic jam adds to the sense of anticipation? But in the acres of car-park land that surround the towering edifice of the ground there is already a substantial gathering.

From the coach set-down point you have to pass through a covered bridge that looks like a piece of junk some sentimental American picked up after a pre-war refurbishment at Anfield. As someone discovers that age-old football secret of just how loud a few hundred voices can sound in an enclosed space, a question booms out.

'Where the fuck, where the fuck, where the fuck are Italy?'

There are a few variations – a Newcastle shirt, several Man Utd shirts, and just to cheer me up there's four lads in Leeds Utd strip. But the rest is row upon row of green and white, scores of Celtic hoops offsetting the solid green of the Republic of Ireland Opel shirt.

On the other side of the bridge, in the shadow of the stadium, the atmosphere is just beginning to dawn. Picnics are being set

out, football games are underway. There are small crowds clus-
tered round TVs on which the final few minutes of the USA v
Switzerland match are being shown. But there's not the slightest
trace of a hot-dog van.

I wander around for fifteen minutes or so, past the sort of
razzmatazz that you might expect from an American event. A
Budweiser cool zone – a giant inflatable cube with pipes spraying
down dry ice. A soccer shooting gallery – another giant inflatable
cube with a plastic image of a goalkeeper at the far end at which
you kick a football, attempting to land the ball in the circular
holes in the fabric. But no hot-dog vans.

I have about as much spare weight as the average stick insect,
and by now I'm beginning to feel distinctly faint and thinking
how good those burgers smelled outside Port Authority. Then
the USA match comes to an end, a tie, as they say out here, and
I realize that inside the tent behind them is a buffet. Yes, that's
right, a 'buffet'.

The notion of trying to put a buffet on at a Man Utd/Leeds
game does a sort of crazy Three Stooges meets *Apocalypse Now*
dance in front of my eyes, which by this stage are those cartoon
bloodshot numbers with pinprick pupils the shape of frankfurters.
Not even the price, an outrageous $20, can put me off. By this
stage I have no alternative.

So I stand in the queue for approximately an hour. The heat
is unbearable, it's like meltdown in a tent. A rock band comes
on on a stage behind me. I can't remember their name, all my
mental effort is focused on not falling over, but their workaday
set seems to get people warmed up for a party.

Then all of a sudden there's a chorus of boos and an Italian
tricolour is paraded through the sea of green. A cry of 'Italia,
Italia' goes up, only to be drowned by the overwhelming sound
of 'C'mon you boys in green'. It's like being in the middle
of a city centre when everyone around you starts singing in
unison.

Finally I get to the food. Hot dog. Yup. Pastrami. Yup. Pizza.
Yup. Fried Chicken. Yup. Salad. If you can fit anything else on
the plate. Second helping. Yup. Sod it, if they are going to

charge me enough to feed four people, I am going to eat enough to feed four people, and in my condition it isn't going to be difficult.

Feeling vaguely *compos mentis*, I begin to look around me for the first time in an hour and a half. What strikes me above all is the number of families I can see, all swathed in green. The point is, I suppose, that you don't have to be a football fan to be here. Just being Irish is enough, but even that isn't essential. Later I discover Frau has watched the game on television, this being the first football match she's seen live since sneaking under the turnstiles to watch Celtic play in the days of Kenny Dalglish. There is an atmosphere here you can breathe; you'd have to be dead not to be moved.

For some reason I want to linger outside for a while, to delay as long as possible the moment of entering the stadium and seeing the pitch. If my subconscious reason is to maximize the drama for myself, it certainly works.

An escalator takes you up to a concrete parapet and then through to a shaded section. So this is where they sell the hot dogs from! I walk around for a while before I find the gap into the sunshine that represents my gate. I stop for a minute and take a deep breath . . . It's just as well I do, because when I finally walk into the stadium I feel for a moment like I'm suffocating. I don't know why it should affect me so powerfully – I certainly wasn't expecting it – but this is just *incredible*.

The shadow of the periphery only emphasizes everything further, because you find your gate, and the pitch is there and you step out into this massive great amphitheatre of light and colour.

It may not make it as comfortable to sit in, either in the broad, glaring sunshine like this or presumably in the sleet of the New York winter, but as a spectacle a stadium of that size, that sheer height without a roof, is matchless. Unlike a Scottish or an English ground where the stands disappear into gradations of shadow, here you can see everything, and the whole place has just been turned green, gold and white. There are small groups of Italians here and there, but that's it. There must be fifty, sixty thousand people wearing Irish colours. Jeez, I hope the last person leaving Ireland remembered to cancel the milk.

I'm not Irish but I feel, not just for a minute but for the whole duration of the match, like I'm about to choke up. I can feel that twist in my throat, and sometimes my sentences seem like they're going to get strangled by emotion half-way through. And it's not even my emotion – it's just there in the air around you, as tangible as the heat.

I make my way down to my seat, which is almost on the pitch, and the opening ceremony begins.

On TV I hate this bit when a bunch of kids come on to the pitch and wave a lot of flags around. But in the midst of all this, it's all quite affecting. It's also choreographed for a channel-switch attention span. Each section lasts just enough to milk the moment, before it's whisked away.

The tannoy announces two World Cup stars of the past, who turn out to be members of the US squad from Italy, which wasn't quite what we were expecting. So when he introduces one of the International stars of entertainment, we're all keyed up for someone fresh from the chicken-and-chip circuit. But instead we get Liza Minnelli. Everyone makes 'OK I'm impressed' faces.

'She's looking good, isn't she?' says the man behind me. Quite how he can tell from a distance of half the length of a football field is beyond me. But her gestures are overblown enough to reach at least to the top of the first tier, without the aid of the television screens.

Her song, mind you, seems like a strange choice. 'If not Tomorrow then the Day After That' has never been a rabble-rouser. I would have expected a version of 'Cabaret' customized to indicate that 'Life is a Soccer Game'. Although had she been gifted with second sight she could have dedicated 'Goodbye Mein Lieber Herr' to the German team, 'I Love You, You Pay My Rent' to the many backers of the Colombian team, or perhaps 'Maybe This Time' for the Brazilians. Failing all of that, I'm sure most of us would have settled for the obvious choice of 'New York, New York'.

'The Americans know how to put on a show!' comments the

man behind me. It never ceases to amaze me not only how quickly a cliché can be formed, but also, once it becomes received opinion, how many people reiterate it as if it's something they just thought up.

Well yes, it's big and brash and haphazard around the edges, and that's exactly what we expected, isn't it?

Liza with a z gets zip time to bathe in the applause – to be frank, there isn't all that much because the song has dragged on for so long to such little consequence that a lot of people have lost the excitement of seeing her in the flesh, or at least in the distance. This doesn't stop her holding her arms wide, bowing profoundly from the root of the neck, or waving to the crowd, even though some long-haired disaster who looks like he's been spruced up in a Tyneside Ladies' salon has now taken up the stage and the screens to belt out the appallingly sentimental theme tune 'Gloryland'. When I get back I will discover that this is Daryl Hall, a man given shelf space by otherwise taste-ful people. But at the time I think simply this is not a World Cup for high culture. Toto, I don't think we're in Europe any more.

In a waft of aftershave and a chink of Rolexes, Michael and Roger, the ticket agents, arrive to take up the seats next to me. Even they are wearing green in honour of the occasion.

As the teams take the field, I look up into the heights of the stadium and watch all the colours come out, imagining what it must feel like to have this volume of support behind you, especi-ally so far away from home. They line up for the national anthems in front of us, and the whole place is singing 'You'll Never Walk Alone'.

In front of me, Sean from Dublin is wearing a multi-coloured Ireland In The US shirt and a pair of shorts. He has come to the game with his wife, Maria, his American cousin, Seamus, and Seamus's wife, Marion.

'I'm useless at these things,' Sean tells me. 'I just get so nervous – Look at that.' He holds out a trembling hand.

Seamus, who looks like a road sign for an American Irishman – tall, red haired and square featured, wearing a golf cap, decked out in shamrocks – says nothing. He doesn't have to. He just looks up at the flags as the Irish national anthem is sung, and looks at me and we both just laugh and shrug. No, neither of us has ever seen anything like it.

'C'mon you Paddys,' says Roger, attracting a few quizzical stares. Roger is over six foot and built in such a way that quizzical stares don't bother him.

'I'd love to see them do it,' he says to me. I look around yet again and imagine what might happen in this place if Ireland score first.

'So, he's allowed to handle the ball, is he?' asks an American as the ball comes back to Packie Bonner.

'Boy, these guys can kick!' he wonders at Packie's long punt upfield.

And of course everyone knows what happened next – Ray Houghton's run across the penalty area and the shot lofted towards the goal.

Everyone I speak to later was in a different area of the ground and saw it from a different perspective. We will all recount our own action replays to each other, again and again, never tiring of it. But the one thing we will all agree about is that the ball seems to hang in the air for ever. From my angle Pagliuca seems to think he is closer to his line than he really is, and his disorientation causes a spacial distortion. He reaches towards the ball as if it's going over comfortably, and I'm already 'ooooh'ing for a close thing, but then he and I realize simultaneously that the goal is a long way further back, and we both watch – the two of us plus eighty-odd thousand others, as it swoops down. The nets are square hung, rather than having the customary drape at the back, which means that the ball has further to travel. It feels like there is time to observe all of this before the small ripple that triggers an immense tidal wave of noise.

Seamus and Sean hug their respective wives, then each other. Everybody is hugging everybody else. Even a couple of Italians get hugged by mistake, but, despite their hang-dog faces, whose chins get nearer the concrete as the game progresses, they don't really seem to mind.

Somewhere in this stadium, Sylvie, Adrian, Conn and Kevin are going fucking mad.

The heat is almost unbearable in the stands. I can't even begin to imagine what it's like on the pitch. In addition to the temperature there's a thick layer of humidity that makes the air seem solid and gives a pastel hue of unreality to the whole procedure. But even that can't obscure the electronic scoreboard which reads: IRELAND 1 ITALY 0. The photo-processing labs in Dublin will be sick of the sight of that scoreboard in a couple of weeks.

There isn't an Irish heart that doesn't skip a beat more than once, but, all the same, Italy never seem to threaten. Signori is ploughing a lone furrow in front, but dealing with the two Irish central defenders is like trying to plough through concrete. The two half-chances that come his way in the first half find him lacking in the balance and surety we expect from Italian forwards. McGrath's vision is paired perfectly with the pace of Babb, and both display a skill on the ball that belies the 'meat and potatoes' reputation of the Republic. Despite the poise of Roberto Baggio on the ball, he spends much of his time with his back to goal, McGrath breathing down his neck. The Azzurri only really look dangerous when Dino Baggio runs from midfield.

Up front the Irish are playing a similar game, with Coyne holding the ball up and waiting for support from midfield. The difference is that the Irish rush forward with a force and intent which seems to have even the unrufflable Italian centre-backs looking shaky. Houghton is floating two inches above the pitch, jinking and running at the defence. Keane never allows a 40:60 ball to be won with any comfort and gets into enough positions to cause more trouble than he actually does, while, with the exception of one run right through the centre of the Irish defence, it's Irwin and Phelan who are looking more like attacking full-backs than the legendary Maldini.

In the second half, Italy begin to come into it, but once again the Irish defence looks not just solid but deft, and it's Ireland that have the real chances. Keane blasts one over the bar. Houghton is beckoned to the touchline to be replaced by Jason McAteer. But in a preview of one of the puzzling aspects of this World Cup, McAteer is not allowed on the pitch, although Houghton has taken his seat on the bench. So Houghton comes back on, and this time the fingertips of Pagliuca prevent him from getting a second. Then Keane breaks through to the byline and cuts it back for Sheridan, who hits the bar.

McAteer meanwhile has finally been admitted to the game and is turning the Italian defence at will. We're inside the last fifteen minutes and the realization is beginning to seep in that the anticipated equalizer is not going to come. It's going to be glorious victory, not an honourable draw.

As victory begins to take shape, it becomes all the more precious. Suddenly nothing else will do.

Seamus expresses the opinion that any more than five minutes of extra time will see him needing medical attention. Nerves are stretched to the sound of screeching whistles, and then it's over.

Everyone finds an Italian to shake by the hand and assure that we'll see them in the next round. There's an aura of disbelief that settles in the fine mist.

Roger and Michael make their way out, all camaraderie and promises that they'll see me all right.

'We'll get you the best tickets all the way through,' they promise.

In front of me the man in the styrofoam Uncle Sam top hat, decorated half in the tricolour, half in the stars and stripes, opens his arms wide and points his long ginger goatee to the sky and shouts: '*Un-beeeeelieeeeevaaaaable!*'

Ten minutes after the game is over they're still there, cheering, shouting and singing.

Outside, a group of Italian fans from Venezuela are dancing a jig with the Irish fans and after waiting for three quarters of an hour to file into the old wooden bridge over the freeway, it begins to echo to the sound of a chant, gaining volume by the second:

> 'We're going to have a party,
> *We're going to have a party.*'

*   *   *

Back at the Blarney Stone, I run into Patrick, and we watch Romania putting two of their three past Colombia. For some reason I can't quite fathom, Patrick salutes the goals with a cheer and a shout of 'C'mon the Europeans!' turning round to me and saying, 'This is going to be our year.'

Slowly, tired disbelief gives way to wild celebration:

> 'Where are the boys who stood with me,
> When *history was made?*'
> 'We are green,
> We are white,
> We are *fuckin' dynamite.*'

In the middle of it all is a tiny Brazilian, a four-foot ball of muscle, who's dancing a samba around a bottle of Budweiser.

'He's amazing,' says one guy with a Lancashire accent. 'He knows everything about football. We were just talking to him and he was talking about Premier League games between Wimbledon and Blackburn that we couldn't even remember.'

So I talk to him and his mate for about half an hour, just the usual chat about the Irish performance, was he going to play Kelly in the next game, should he drop Phelan, etc.

'Well, being a Man United fan . . .' one of them says.

I suppose I should confess I support Leeds, I say.

And the atmosphere changes like I'd just grabbed his beer bottle from him and shattered it on the bar.

'*Woooooooah!*' he shouts.

At first I think he's joking, and partly he is, but there's an undertow of genuine malice.

'Hey!' he shouts over to his mate. 'He's a Leeds fan.'

'I'll tell you,' he says to me, 'you should save your confession for St Patrick's on Sunday.'

I'm beginning to wish I'd done just that. There's a tension building up, particularly between Leeds and Manchester United, which is beginning to suggest that the dark days of the seventies could be due for a revival. I had hoped that in a different context it might be possible for members of the opposing faction to treat it like it is, a joke. But obviously it was a forlorn hope, so after trying to put a brave face on the Cantona jibes I move off to talk to somebody else.

The rest of the bar is still one happy throng of camaraderie. There's an American Italian and his girlfriend, who went along to root for Italy but just got carried along here on the green tide. There's countless American Irish who had little connection with the World Cup until today but who have been drawn in by the party.

I start a conversation with an American ex-under-19 player: one of the standard conversations out here, like will soccer ever really catch on as a professional sport in the US?

'The thing is,' he says, 'they're trying to start it on a city basis, but that's not how it's going to work. The way to get soccer off the ground here is to start with the ethnic base that you have – like have a Mexican team, an Irish team.'

It might not do much for the image of America as a melting pot. But he's right, it would certainly have some of the fervour that football needs to survive.

I leave the Blarney Stone rocking to the sound of The Wolfetones and walk back to midtown.

At Madison Square Gardens there's a massive salsa concert going on. The Hispanic community is out in force. Amongst the gold dresses and the tacky gladrags there's a sprinkling of Brazilian shirts.

A sad-looking figure in a Colombian strip comes towards me.

'Hey, you guys really did it,' he says, seeing my Irish hat. 'You know what happened to Colombia tonight?'

In what I will later regard as an ominous portent, he puts his finger up and mimes a cut-throat action, with sound effects.

At Desmond's Tony greets me with a handshake, and I spend the rest of the night with two Irish journalists talking about Celtic, the South and the North, the revisionist movement,

Scotland and Ireland, the Jacobites, Culloden, the Highland Clearances. It's getting to be that time of the morning.

As I get back to my hotel there's a guy in an Irish shirt, speaking to the receptionist.

I give him a high five as I ask for my messages.

'Is this the friend you were looking for?' the receptionist asks the guy, not realizing that all over the city complete strangers are greeting one another with such gestures.

'Nope,' the guy says, 'but he knows about it.'

The lights are all on until the dawn makes them obsolete, that night in World Cup City.

3

In Giants Stadium No One Can Hear You Scream

New York wakes up to a city scattered in green and white ticker tape. I have a dry mouth, a raw throat and the sound of 'The Boys of the Auld Brigade' ringing in my ears.

I try ringing the London Irish again. Adrian answers in a croak.

'We all just got in a couple of hours ago.'

It's twelve o'clock.

'We're going out to Queens to watch the Norway/Mexico game. Do you want to come?'

It's a long round of bars and football games. Life is hard in World Cup City. We arrange to meet at Port Authority at two.

'And if we miss you . . .' says Adrian, 'well, we just won't.'

Adrian puts the phone down to snatch a few more hours of sleep and I head off downtown to meet a New York friend for brunch.

The humidity that has held a damp sheet between the city and the sun has been burnt away this morning. It's clear and blue, and the heat hits you straight across the neck as you exit from an air-conditioned building.

The tables outside the Time Café on Lafayette Street are deserted. Even with the umbrellas up, no one is brave, or foolhardy, enough to risk the noonday sun. The silence of the exterior belies the bustle that's taking place inside.

'Is this warm enough for you?' asks Lynne. It's the standard New York greeting at the moment. Just a glimpse of my Ireland World 1994 (yes, that's right, spot the deliberate mistake) baseball cap is enough to elicit it from a complete stranger.

I smile weakly and say, 'Just about,' as usual, because it doesn't seem to offer much potential for a witty response. I keep thinking of the last line of Lou Reed's *New York* LP: 'Like my good friend Donald says: "Stick a fork in their ass and turn them over, they're done."' But most people might get the wrong idea.

Like Lou Reed, Lynne has lived with the city all her life. A good friend of John Cale's she was around for the Exploding Plastic Inevitable and is currently involved in writing the history of Andy Warhol's Factory, the history of a subculture that works its way through the very structure of New York.

I tell her how little I seem to be picking up of the mood of the city. The last time I was here it was a few weeks before the anti-yuppie riots in Thompkins Square, and the groundswell was already detectable in the air. This time round the heat surrounds a strange vacuum.

'It's vacation time,' says Lynne. 'Most New Yorkers, if they're not physically away, are on vacation in their minds.'

But the all-abiding feeling currently is nervousness, she says. Particularly since the election of a right-wing mayor, Rudolph Giuliani, who ran on a law and order ticket. The gay community in particular detects some of the advantages it gained from the previous administration being swept away.

Giuliani appeared at the opening ceremony of the Gay Games and has taken out advertising space to broadcast a message of tolerance on the subway system. But at the same time his administration is packed with religious fundamentalists who are virulently anti-homosexual.

The incident that precipitated the downfall of the previous mayor, the black and left-wing Dinkle, underlines the tension that the city was built on and which continues to be a part of its uneasy construction. At Crown Heights a young black child was run over by a Jewish motorcade. Dinkle was slow to make his appearance at the scene and was seen as ineffectual in the eruption of race hatred that followed.

There is a strong undertow of anti-Semitism to the black Muslim movement, which the incident brought to the fore.

Lynne, a Jewish liberal, visibly shivers as she recounts the aftermath. Being in favour of the black cause is one thing, hearing shouts of 'Kill the Jews' is quite another.

'The Thompkins Square riots are still very much a flashpoint,' Lynne says, 'but a lot of the anarchist principles that surrounded all of that have given way. Now we have these people called squatter punks. They're all heavily into body piercing, and they're really quite nasty.

'The other day I had a couple of them sitting outside my apartment and this old man walked past, just minding his own business. One of them turned to the other and said, "Shall we murder him?"

'And there was no trace of irony as far as I could make out. It was really quite unpleasant.'

The conversation turns to sport. I try to explain to her just what it was like being at the game the day before. But I can tell I'm not being successful.

In one of her books, she explores the territory of nationalism and how our relation to a country is illusory. As a supporter of the New York baseball team the Mets she says, 'You can feel a sense of allegiance to your team that you could never do to your country.'

So I try to give the sense of what it might feel like to be Irish, from a tiny country of four million people, and to walk into Giants Stadium in New York, on to the world stage, and see the flags of your country dominate this enormous space. Well, let's say it's lost on a left-wing American.

'Yes, nationalism,' she says vaguely. 'Sport is like the last refuge of that stuff.'

Like the last refuge of the scoundrel. But then to a left-wing American, nationalism is automatically right wing. If you're Irish, or Scottish, or Nigerian, it's a different matter.

So I tell her about the reaction of the Italian fans. Obviously,

I say, they were a bit subdued, because they were well beaten.

'Even though it was only one point?' she asks.

Somehow the word 'point' could never suffice to describe a goal in football. A point is something you pick up, almost without thinking about it. A goal in the World Cup is something you sweat blood to achieve. The game can brood for an hour, longer, then finally it comes like a summer thunderstorm to break the heat.

It's just something you either understand or you don't.

But then I don't understand baseball. Surely it's about as exciting as watching paint dry. I tried watching a game on the television, but it made cricket seem interesting by comparison.

'I think you need to get an idea of the scale,' says Lynne. 'You need to go to a game. There's a heraldry to it with these giant men in white uniforms, and the floodlights and the green pitch and the white lines. You could get quite fetishistic about it.

'But when you're there you realize the sheer physical size of it – just how far someone is hitting the ball to get a home run, how far they're running to steal second.'

It's ironic that this all seems to fit the national stereotype that Europeans have of Americans – that scale and might are valued over subtlety and skill. So from the real New York, I take a subway uptown and back to World Cup City.

Port Authority Bus Terminal, for those who've never been there, is rather like Hell with air conditioning – a multi-floored world to itself.

The boys come off the bus looking shiny with the afterglow of victory. Adrian in shorts and a Striker T-shirt, Kevin in the Celtic away strip, Conn the dandy in a blue buttondown shirt and an Ireland In The USA waistcoat. There's a new-found confidence that replaces the trepidation of the first meeting.

'They're a good team,' Conn says of Italy. 'It's just that we're a better one.'

This is their moment, the early peak of the campaign.

'Sylvie's still in New York,' says Adrian. 'We're meeting him at the bus stop.'

'He'll be here in about five minutes,' says Adrian. 'He'll roll up carrying a can. Every time I've seen Sylvie since we landed he's been carrying a can.'

Then in the distance there's a flash of green and Sylvie lopes into view. Now it's time for swapping stories of where the emerald tide took us last night.

'We ended up in a field in Brooklyn,' says Adrian.

Now that's one I haven't heard yet.

'We were up at some of the Upper West Side bars,' says Sylvie, 'but they were too small and full of drunken Dubs pushing you around. What can you expect from Dubliners?

'So we heard about this rave that was supposed to be happening out in a field in Brooklyn, and we talked the hotel's shuttle driver into taking us out there. But we got there and the place was deserted. I think it might have been raided by the cops.'

So there they were in the surreal New York heat of the first night out, standing in the black of a disused baseball pitch in Brooklyn, pissing into a hedge, feeling just fine.

'You've got to admit,' says Sylvie, who encouraged the excursion, 'it was different from just spending a night in the bar.'

The others agree, if not with the greatest of enthusiasm.

Sylvie didn't go back to the hotel with the others, instead he crashed out with his cousin Sean in Brooklyn. Sean, a cameraman, had spent the day shooting a commercial with Charlie Sheen in one of the parallel worlds to New York City.

'You know he got paid six million dollars for a day's work?'

Nice if you can get it.

'Video directors,' says Adrian. 'You don't meet them in Kildare or Glasgow, do you now?'

But you can't go out of your front door in London without tripping over one.

'Well, you might where you live,' he comes back.

So there's Sylvie, still in his green Opel strip from the game, waking up in the middle of an Italian area of Brooklyn.

'Most of them were fine,' he says, 'although I did get a mean look in the corner deli this morning.'

'That wasn't the strip,' quips Kevin, holding his nose, 'it was the fact you slept in it.'

We walk down from the gate of the air-conditioned bus station to the Subway, and a wall of heat.

We're heading out for Woodside in Brooklyn, which is one of the Irish strongholds in the city. The Subway train emerges from the tunnel and into the open air, and you feel the relief of pressure that you do in any city as you reach the fringes.

The place we're going to is Centrefields on 46th Street. According to the media there were fans who'd come out without a ticket, and, balking at the scalpers' prices but unwilling to make the trip out to Meadowlands in the hope of a late bargain, had watched the game there. 'Great craic,' they'd said, 'worth the trip out, just to be here.'

But Sean, not realizing this, takes us to the centre of Woodside. Adrian had said earlier, 'Isn't this our stop?' but we had been following the native. So we look for the nearest bar that is showing the game.

The first place looks like the party is still going on from the night before. They are playing Eddie Floyd's 'Knock On Wood' and two girls in the Opel green shirts are dancing on the bar.

'Do you think they'll turn it down for the game?' we ask one another.

We try asking the barmen but don't get much in the way of a sensible answer, so we leave.

As we are prevaricating in the street, a hunched old woman comes past.

'You Irish,' she says, 'you think you win the World Cup already. Never!'

'So we'll be seeing Slovakia in the final then, will we?' shouts Sylvie after her.

She did indeed sound Eastern European, but she takes great exception to this, stopping in her tracks and raising a gnarled finger. 'I am German!' she insists. 'Get one thing right, can't you!'

'Germany, Slovakia, Hitler Youth, it's all the same,' says Sylvie.

The woman just carries on mumbling as she hobbles away. 'Ireland, think you win the World Cup, you're dreaming!'

So we try another bar, but they're watching the baseball, and Adrian is getting seriously aerated at the prospect of missing the kick-off.

'I'll tell you,' says Sylvie, 'he gets badly stressed out that boy. If there's anyone that should take some Valium it's him. Wherever we're going, he always wants to be there yesterday.'

We decide to take a cab over to Centrefields. Sean and his sister Jennifer, Sylvie and I jump in the first one, leaving Adrian pacing the street with Kevin and Conn.

'So you lads were at the Rosary Bowl yesterday, then?' asks the barman, a thick-set guy with a handlebar moustache.

Eh?

'Ireland versus Italy,' he says, 'the Rosary Bowl.'

Oh, very good – Rose Bowl is the venue of the final, so Rosary Bowl for this, the Catholic Caucasian Cup Final.

We were there all right. This is to become a question that we'll all be asked for some time to come and when asked 'What was it like?' we will hold one hand in the air as if to grasp the memory of the sight of that amphitheatre decked in the colours and say simply 'Unbelievable.'

'Yeah,' says the barman, 'I live in an Italian area. I heard the score just before I left for work and I was going past this café where they were all watching it, so I stuck my head in the door and shouted "Hey 1–0, you guys" and did this—'

He motions squeezing his cock like a hooter.

'And they were all shouting "Hey, motherfucker!" and chasing me down the street. It was really funny.'

Another hot day in the melting pot.

'So what'll you have, you guys?'

We order a round of Buds and settle down at the bar to watch what the next two opponents have to offer.

Not much, is the conclusion. Norway are playing a typical European waiting game, the sort of tactics you'd expect Ireland to employ, keeping Mexico outside of the penalty area. Mexico's strikers, Garcia and Rodriguez, are limited to shots from outside the area that we all agree are never going to trouble Tottenham's Erik Thorstvedt.

Or Packie Bonner? There is a certain nervousness in making an assertion like that. And then late in the game a breakaway goal with an impressive finish from Flo makes temporary Mexicans out of us.

A draw would leave Ireland two points clear at the top of the group. A 1–0 win like this would tie us up with Norway and throw the whole thing wide open again, leaving us to project the indices of future possibilities once more.

'But if Mexico beat Italy and Italy beat Norway—'

As we speak, an amazing sequence of scrambled clearances keeps the ball out of the Norwegian net. For half an hour or so we continue debating the possibilities.

'But if we beat Mexico, then it's all over.'

'Yeah, but we knew that anyway.'

Welcome to the Group of Death.

After the game we head round the corner to get something to eat while watching Cameroon v Sweden. Just as we're leaving they're showing the last few minutes of the Knicks game, so we stop to watch. With a minute to go, Houston are up. John Starkes, the Knicks' leading scorer, has the last shot. He can take the ball into the area and go for a two-pointer which will take the game into overtime, or take a pot from outside, hoping for the three points that will take the NBA Championship there and then.

He goes for glory. The shot hits the rim and bounces out. The nation, or at least New York, turns its lowly eyes away.

We head back into town.

I suggest a trip to the Blarney Stone. Large, spacious, Wolfetones on the jukebox. Sold.

As part of the background to the place I tell Sylvie about my meeting with the Cork and the Dublin contingent.

And then there's Cathal who's a Rangers supporter.

This had seemed funny to me, but Sylvie is not amused.

'Really? That's sick,' he says.

It's just as a wind-up, I reply.

'But it's not funny. He should read up on it a bit more, find out what it's all about and what that means.'

As if to emphasize his point, as we exit the Subway we are confronted with a neon news-strip which confirms the rumours we had already heard. Six shot dead in a bar in County Down while watching the game.

Americans I've spoken to, like the video director on the plane, don't understand that every time you have a death in Northern Ireland, it isn't necessarily the IRA. But they aren't alone. Even the British media, which is well aware of the number of Loyalist killings it reports, persists in implying that the IRA lays down arms and presto! we have peace in the North.

It is often assumed that the Loyalist terrorist organizations were formed in the seventies as a reaction to the IRA. Indeed, at least one of the recent television programmes on 'The Troubles' gave that distinct impression. But if, as the song goes, you do know your history, the Northern Irish state was actually created by anti-democratic military action on the part of the Loyalist Ulster Volunteers in 1914. When they talk now about democracy, they are talking about the freedom of the people of Northern Ireland to come to conclusions that suit the Loyalists.

Implicit supporters of Unionism often quote the fact that the British military presence in Ireland was called in originally to protect the Catholic population, as if to imply that the Nationalists have been failing to display due gratitude ever since. But they fail to think the matter through to its root cause. Like why did the Catholics need protection in the first place, and who from? If you conclude that the IRA is wrong, it does not necessarily follow that Unionism is right.

This implicit bias in observers who claim impartiality finds its way into football writing too. Pete Davies in *All Played Out* criticizes the Republic fans for singing rebel songs, but fails to point out that the Rangers songs he refers to on more than one occasion are based on religious intolerance and support for

Loyalist terrorism. Simon Kuper in *Football Against the Enemy* makes the same mistake.

Perhaps now they might take notice. It's not just the IRA who kill people.

Walking up 8th Avenue, we have a moment's spontaneous silence, then break into heated discussion.

'The thing is,' Sylvie says, 'there's also an assumption that Gerry Adams can just say to the IRA, "OK, we're laying down arms now." There's got to be a complex power structure in an organization that is only partly legal. You can't just get all those interest groups to agree to such a radical move in no time.'

Sylvie is unusual in having an active interest in the subject. When I'd tried broaching it with Patrick, one of the Dubliners, the night before, suggesting that the IRA and Sinn Fein are more separate than is suggested – that the lines of accountability are not direct between the political and the provisional wings, he just came back with the line: 'Ah, they're all the same.'

He'd gone on to say: 'We don't want the North anyway. Their social security payments would just ruin our economy.'

But such a pragmatic view, grounded in what is after all undeniable economic fact, can exist at the same time as the romance, as he proved that very second by turning away to join in with The Wolfetones.

I kid you not, the very line in the song was 'When being a lad like you, I joined the IRA', which, despite his disparagement of a matter of seconds before, Patrick joined in with in a full-throated voice. This isn't the real IRA, this is just the IRA in the songs, the ones that look with heroic gaze to the flag and are frozen in the action of pointing forwards, not the ones that have been tangled in a complex and limb-strewn struggle.

In the Blarney Stone it is the evening after the night before. The Man Utd fans are still there. They raise their glasses to me across the bar, but there's a distinct tension in their faces.

'He's one of your lot,' I say, indicating Sylvie, who is a Man Utd fan too; as if to say, if he can be my friend then you can as well. But their expressions don't soften and they make no move to come over.

That famous quote from Bill Shankley runs around my head again, resonating as it always does, with ironies:

'Football isn't a matter of life and death – it's more important than that.'

It is to come back to me again and again in World Cup City – and it will mean a different thing every time.

One of the guys I'd been speaking to the previous night is still there. Well, by the looks of him he's been there ever since. There's a drink in front of him, but his head is down on the table and he's out for the count.

Another one is still dancing around the place, the lone reveller at the end of the party.

'Y'know,' he says to Sylvie, 'last night a nigger comes up to me and says do you want some crack? I says I'm having some already. He says twenty-five dollars a bag. I says you'll get a lot of beer for that.'

And it looks like he's had double that by the way he's swaying. He exhorts us to sing along as 'Celtic Symphony' comes on the jukebox.

Later on, Adrian is holding this moment for all it's worth, just in case something comes along later to shatter the feeling.

'At the moment,' he says, 'I feel like we could win the World Cup. We beat Germany and Holland and people said They were only friendlies, now we've beaten Italy in the real thing. It might all end and we could lose the next two games and go out, but even if that happens at least Jack Charlton has given us the dream. For a few nights we can believe that we can win it.'

Sylvie, Kevin and Conn are standing by the bar talking to a sophisticated-looking blonde woman and her escort, who have clearly come down on a recommendation to see the wild Irishmen in the flesh. So Adrian continues.

'But then if we win it, we've got Andy Townsend coming to pick up the World Cup and doing interviews afterwards in an English accent.

'I can say that to you,' he says, looking over towards Conn and Sylvie in particular. 'I couldn't say it to the lads, but do you know what I mean? I hope if it happens Charlton will just make Paul McGrath captain for the day.'

I leave them at Port Authority to dream on for one more night before heading down to the heat of Orlando for the high-noon confrontation of the Group of Death.

New York is to become a quiet place for a week or so.

I yawn and look at my watch. It's half-past twelve. I remember it's my birthday.

The following day we're into the full madness of the round of 24. This is binge time for the football addict, watching each new team and each new configuration of a familiar team attempting to map out the three-dimensional geometry of how they play this mystifying game.

It has always annoyed me that watching football is considered somehow more passive than other forms of televisual entertainment, like watching a documentary (which is good for you) or a play, or even a soap opera. Nonsense! Viewing football is about as active as watching television gets, it's just that the mental activity is bound up with space and time, rather than language.

I have my lap-top set up so that I can type up notes and watch the game on television at the same time. For a moment, when watching Brazil v Russia, I think of Jack Kerouac's inspirational delusion that he could blow a typewriter like Charlie Parker did a sax. Perhaps I could make words skip across the page like Bebeto. No, I'm not serious.

But nevertheless there is a sense of perfect rightness. This is just what I want to be doing right now, watching this game, and this is exactly the way I want to watch it – in Spanish. You don't have to understand a word of the language to be able to understand who's on the ball, or to read the very real excitement that the commentator reproduces. Most football commentary, as we know, is total gibberish, but the sound of excitement in a voice is part of the televisual experience.

At the launch of the anthology *My Favourite Year*, John Motson turned up.

'I hope he didn't read what I wrote about him,' at least half a dozen people said to me. But however disparaging they had been about him in the past, they all wanted to talk to him, because the sound of his epiglottis changing gear had been a part of each of their respective childhoods.

Andres Cantor's commentary is a tirade of dread and celebration that any fanatic would recognize – no matter what their native language.

'*Viene, viene, viene, viene,*' he repeats in rising tempo as Romario weaves his way through, when by all rules of gravity and physical contact he should be lying on the pitch. Then there's an expression of amazement tinged with disappointment, which eludes any possibility of phonetic transcription, as Bebeto's volley sears into the crowd.

In 1970 I, like millions of others, learned to love a team I had no connection with. But since then Brazil have never, for me, recaptured the spell they cast. But this time it's different and from the moment I see that poise and balance, that combination of elegance and strength that is contained in Bebeto and Romario, I can see the drama of this World Cup emerging. It's the romantic heart of Brazil against the clinical head of the Germans.

Romario touches in a corner at the far post.

'*Goooooooaaaaaaaal!*'

Was it a mastery of the infinitely complex art of the corner kick, by Bebeto, combined with a control over deceptive speed that made it look easy? Or was it just bad marking at the back post? Such are the profound questions the television viewer ponders with each successive replay. At the game you think only '*Goooooaaaaaaaal!*' or 'shit'; the pondering of subtleties is set aside in a box marked 'I must watch that tonight on television.' The mind of the football supporter on the couch resembles the dolphin much more than the potato.

Brazil add a second from a penalty, and seem satisfied with that, but the sheer force of their sweep forward suggests that, should the Russians get one back, they will just sweep forward again and regain their comfortable, two-goal lead.

If Ireland have emerged as serious contenders, Brazil give some idea of what they might be up against. Meanwhile I want to blow this thing like Andres Cantor. Yeah, baby.

Later on a friend from London rings. He's just arrived in New York and will be here for a few days.

'I'm just watching Holland losing one–nil to Saudi Arabia,' I tell him.

'Whaaat?' His astonishment is tinged with delight. Is this what we've all been waiting for? The first great shock?

It really looks like it. A shell-shocked Holland rally, but the Saudis come back again, looking stronger than ever, litheness replacing nervousness. Then it all goes mad. Holland dig their heels in, convinced that this just cannot happen. But the Saudis kick back and nearly score again as the ball sticks under a forward's foot, allowing the lone keeper to somehow scrabble it back as the striker loses control of what should have been a tap in.

Of course we know that Holland scrape it back. A draw seemed fair after Jonk's long-range shot, but the snatched victory, a simple header after a goalkeeper's mistake, was harsh on the Saudis. We know also that early conclusions can come back to haunt the prophet, but there is nothing to indicate that Bergkamp has either the personal magnetism, or the team around him, to bring the Dutch the trophy that Cruyff should have brought to them in '74.

No one has, as yet, added Holland to the list.

To everyone's surprise, Brazil are joined by Argentina the next day, with the word Maradona in brackets afterwards. The flashbulb of memory ignites on the mad face of the poison dwarf genius when, after pulling away from two Greek defenders and launching a shot from outside the area into the top corner of the net, he celebrates by racing towards the camera looking like he might tear it to pieces in the sheer photo-lust of celebrity triumph. I think of Gordon Strachan's candid reply when asked what keeps him playing – 'the fear of not playing'. In Maradona's face you can see he has conquered that fear. For now.

Go, Diego. Go.

Later that evening Spain tear at Germany with an irresistible force, although predictably the Germans manage to escape with a draw, while Nigeria prove, if proof were needed, that the African Nations Champions are more than just a trendy hype. The pace has been set, and it's a punishing one. On the three-dimensional chessboard within our minds we pit European determination against Latin flourish, and the strange and magical eccentricity of Africa. The juju beat plays the samba, the tarantella against the forceful thump of the bodhrán. Already punch-drunk and Jack Daniel's-smitten, even I can recognize that this is shaping up to be a classic.

I feel like I need to abscond from World Cup City for a night, to allow all this a chance to gestate in my mind. A contact who works in the music business here told me about a party that's taking place tonight at the Supper Club. She hasn't rung back with any details about an invite but I used to be a music journalist and crashing parties is second nature. Just in case my approach needs site-specific refinement, I call up Basia.

'Let's go for it,' she says. An hour or so later she arrives at my hotel, wearing a silver mini-skirt and a lime green top. The receptionist seems surprised and a little relieved when I say I'm coming down.

'He thought I was a prostitute,' Basia explains. A combination of twenty years or so's blagging expertise heads off in a taxi uptown.

The party, it turns out, is an awards ceremony to mark the tenth anniversary of *The Paper*, the trendy, downtown magazine. It's being held as a benefit for Quentin Crisp, they explain to us at the door, after apologizing profusely for not being able to find our name on the list, and could we possibly buy a ticket at $50? I'm still thinking how we can make a dignified exit when we're handed two passes.

'I'll call you at your office next week,' the PR woman says to Basia.

What happened there? I ask, concerned that she's going to get landed with a $100 bill.

Don't worry about it, says Basia, and we're into the world of free food, wine and Absolut vodka.

The compère for tonight is the singer from the B-52s, another refugee from World Cup City, who's flown here direct from the opening ceremony in Boston. He introduces a drag act done up in *Cabaret* gladrags who sings 'Goodbye Mein Lieber Herr' to Quentin, a (presumably unintentional) dose of black humour I couldn't hope to rival.

'Does any configuration of the words "hat" and "old" spring to mind?' asks Basia. 'God,' she carries on, 'I'm so sick of being a fashion business fag hag.'

The awards continue, largely to people I've never heard of, while Basia goes 'Oh God, not her' about some earnest fashion victim who seems to believe she's a writer, or 'She's really good' about a seventy-year-old woman who makes a Christmas tree look like minimalist chic. Most memorable is the ungainly little twerp who gets an award for writing a nightlife column (I might have suspected stamp collection).

'This doesn't make up for not putting me on the list of one hundred cutting-edge people,' he whines in the direction of the magazine's editors, in lieu of an acceptance speech.

'He's serious, too,' says one of his co-awardees. And he is.

'What do you think of the cutting edge?' the editress asks Quentin.

'Well, I didn't know what it was until you explained it to me,' he replies. True stardom always shows through the bullshit.

We take another cab downtown and meet Basia's friend Kevin in a bar. Kevin has been caught by the soccer bug already, and wants to talk to someone who was actually there at Ireland's famous victory. Then we head off to the meat-packing district on the West Side, previous home of infamous S&M clubs like the Anvil and the Mineshaft. Now the thing is tacky glamour – the place we're going to is apparently Madonna's favourite nightspot.

'What, this person?' asks the doorman when Basia indicates

who else is included in her guest listing. I look all too clearly like I've come straight from World Cup City.

Inside, there's about five hundred semi-naked muscle-pumped bodies crammed into a tiny space, with more arriving all the time. You don't have a choice whether or not to dance, you just get carried along with the crowd as they bounce up and down in a vague semblance of rhythm. But having my T-shirt soaked with the sweat of strangers is not my idea of fun, so I make my excuses and leave, happy to be back in the night and heading back to World Cup City.

The World Cup has already displayed all the passion, skill and diversity that we could have hoped for, and certainly there are signs of other Americans like Kevin who are beginning to notice. But there is another bit of business to be taken care of first. At least in New York nobody is thinking beyond the Knicks and the final game of the NBA play-offs tonight. No matter where you go, you can't get away from it.

'I like the Rangers,' says the young bank teller to the customer in front of me, 'but if I see the Knicks win the NBA, then I'll really be able to die happy.' He looks like he might be nineteen, at a push.

I'll settle for Ireland winning the World Cup, I tell him, as my turn comes around. I don't say Scotland, partly because I am now beginning to fall into character. It is easier to pose as a genuine Irishman than to go into a complicated personal history.

'That will never happen,' he says authoritatively.

'So how are Poland doing?' asks his friend who's putting the money in his wallet, to my right.

'We won't talk about Poland, if you don't mind.' I look down to see the consonant-packed name on the front of his till.

'Romania's looking good, though,' he tells me.

So I've heard. My friend Ian has already called to inform me that Ceaucescu's Babes (they really were the darlings of the former dictator) are picking up the cult audience in England. So I go back to the hotel to watch them being unceremoniously torn apart by Switzerland, thus disturbing the tentative balance that was beginning to settle on the early round. Hagi shows the grasp of the spectacular that has had the people back home talking with a long-range shot to level the scores at 1–1, but the game is most memorable for Sforza's surging run and perfect cutback for Knup to score the third.

'Respect Switzerland' says a banner in the crowd, and we have to.

In Desmond's that night there are two TVs set up in the back room. At first both are tuned to ABC for the USA versus Colombia; two televisions showing the moment that most transformed the profile of the World Cup in the States, as a cross comes in and Andrés Escobar directs the ball past his own goalkeeper.

Two nations go mad, simultaneously, for different reasons, and with very different consequences. Andrés Escobar – a nation turns its no-longer lowly eyes to you. Then comes Ernie Stewart's quite beautifully taken chance, sliding the ball past an advancing Cordoba, putting Colombia out of the competition, the United States irrevocably on the world soccer map and as a result raising the World Cup from cult status to a place in the psyche of main-stream America.

The second TV is retuned to the beginning of the Knicks game, and it's a bit like the toasters competitions in Jamaica where one DJ would set up at one end of the park and another at the other, and the winner would be the one that the crowd gravitated to.

And the winner between the closing stages of the soccer game and the opening of the deciding game in the NBA Championships is . . . the soccer! This isn't as decisive as it sounds, of course, since basketball never really comes to the crunch until the fourth quarter, but all the same . . .

A great time-honoured chorus of 'Shit!' goes up as the Colombians get a goal back on one TV, followed by a cheer as the Knicks score on the other. Then we enter the twilight zone that is injury time on a one-goal lead.

'The Americans really don't understand all of this,' says

Kevin, who's come down to watch the game. 'They're used to games being timed really precisely, so you know exactly how much time is left.'

How much they're missing out on. That gut-wrenching feeling when the last few minutes of a game seem to drag on for eternity is an essential part of the thrill of football, because you know it can happen, even a two-goal lead can be miraculously overturned in seconds. Being on the losing end of a fightback from the death can be the most devastating feeling. On the other hand the snatched point can sometimes mean more than an unconvincing victory. And the whole point is that you never know how long the twilight zone will last. All praise to ambiguity.

But this time nothing happens. The States go in 2–1 winners, and all eyes turn, satisfied, to see the Knicks pull off the treble. First the Rangers, then an improbable US victory, and now all the weight of New York rests on the shoulders of John Starkes.

Back in the front room by the bar there's two Norwegian fans who have just checked in around the corner. They look typically Nordic, tall, blond and clear skinned, with an extra glow that comes from an early victory.

'We'll beat Italy too, then you [the Irish], will beat Mexico, and we'll go through together,' one of them predicts. For the moment, we are the killers in the Group of Death.

We have quite a posse here: there's my friend from London, Ziyad, and his friend, a Scottish Rangers supporter called Andrew, who lives in New York, and some of his colleagues. They're all astounded that not only do I know a good place to watch the game, without being crammed in with a couple of hundred frat-house types, but I also get 'buy backs' from the barman (roughly one in every three or four drinks comes free, an American tradition that's going out of vogue in Manhattan). For the basketball we're joined by Andrew's wife Julia and her friend Leanne.

Leanne, an English girl, is wearing what would be called in Scotland a tartan skirt. 'It's a dress kilt,' she says (it isn't but I don't bother to point this out). 'It's what they wear when they're going for it.' (I don't enquire quite what 'it' is that 'they' are going for either.)

It strikes me as symptomatic that Julia and Leanne can feel a part of the American sport, but not of the football. Partly this is explained by the American attitude towards sport which is much less gender specific than it is in England. Although it is changing slowly – like the majority of other readers of *When Saturday Comes* I have noticed more women at matches recently – football remains a largely male bastion in England. In the States it's different; the fervour that surrounds the Rangers and the Knicks affects women as much as men. More men and women play and are interested in sport here; physical culture is just much more central in the States.

The change in the gender make-up of the English football crowd will continue as the realization sinks in that football grounds are simply not the same intimidating places that they were in the seventies. But it will be a slow change, and the reason for this is as much to do with women as it is with men.

Sometimes conversation about football is greeted not only with disinterest by women, but also with active hostility, a hostility that has its roots in the feeling of exclusion, in the belief that there are codes they do not understand. This is not in itself surprising, but what is interesting is that the women who react like this are often the ones who will say 'Mind your own business, girl talk' as a way of keeping an item of conversation private, or who will make references like 'And then the men left and the conversation got really interesting.' If you ask how, they will of course reply, 'Oh, just girl talk.'

In other words, the resentment about football comes about because they don't like to think that there is a male discourse that parallels 'girl talk'. Football comes to represent more than just football and becomes what men talk about when they talk to one another. It's probably no more, and almost certainly no less interesting than the mysteries of 'girl talk', but it exists as something which by and large men have grown up with and women haven't. Women who want to have a monopoly on mystery will therefore brand the endlessly fascinating subject of who is the most talented midfield player currently playing in England (answer: Gary McAllister) as being banal boys' talk, to be derided in as loud a voice as possible, as opposed to intriguing girl talk, simply to be coyly hinted at in mixed company. While it carries all this ideological baggage, football will never be seen as what it is – just another game.

As the basketball gets underway, it becomes clear that John Starkes is having a nightmare. The Knicks chase bravely but time after time he misses the shots, and in basketball you lose a game by not scoring rather than win it by scoring (an intriguing reversal which, if you think about it carefully, makes it a more negative game than football – an argument which would be lost on the American sport bigots who lurk in sections of the US press).

A lone supporter of the Houston Rockets parades up and down the bar bellowing 'Yeeesssss!' every time Olajowon, the ex-football goalkeeper turned Rockets top scorer, sinks a basket. As the fan bellows, he reveals that he's lacking a front row of teeth.

'I wonder why?' Kevin ponders.

'It's like pantomime,' says Leanne, 'and he's playing the villain.'

The two coaches stand on the sidelines, glaring across at one another.

'There's a huge cult of the coach in American sports,' Tony had told me a few days before. 'It's all in the tactics in basketball and American football – that's one of the reasons they don't take to soccer so much; there's not the same sense of power and control.'

The Knicks coach in the end is a defeated man. You can see the agony etched on his face, but the beautiful loser is an unknown concept in American sport.

'What time's the parade?' Toothless Joe mocks the Knicks fans.

Do they have a reception for second place? I ask.

'No way!' comes the chorus.

John Starkes had a shot at hero. But he blew it. Tony Meola,

Ernie Stewart, Cobi Jones and Alexi Lalas were crowned in his stead. A nation turns its eyes to the set showing the soccer match.

The next day the TV says: 'Soccer used to be, to quote Dick Jones, "a bunch of Commies in short pants, chasing a ball around". But now that's all changed.'

There is a mythology that clings to Brooklyn much as it used to cling to the Lower East Side. Long after the Lower East became more the haunt of the off-duty performance artist than the gang member, the reputation clung. Perhaps partly because New Yorkers like to advertise the danger of their city as one of the features that sets it apart, and therefore sets them as residents apart, the tales of the taxi drivers who wouldn't go across the 2nd Avenue dividing line would be repeated long after the area had been colonized by sushi bars.

So it is now with Brooklyn. The line runs 'Don't go to Brooklyn after dark.' But the artists moved out of the Lower East and SoHo quite a few years ago; having made the areas trendy, they made them desirable and priced themselves out of the market. So a different crowd moved in, and the artists moved on to form the vanguard elsewhere; in Brooklyn, and even in Jersey City. Only the last one, at least the last time I was there at the end of the eighties, was still genuinely scary after dark.

What initially attracted me to Manhattan on my first visit there as an adult in the mid-eighties was how much of it, given the sophistication of the city, remained quite primitive. Most of those corners on the island have been chromed over now, but you still get the sense in Brooklyn that you could be walking back into one of the sets of the movies you'd grown up with. The old New York with its sinister fire escapes and glam gangsters.

When you think of Italian Americans, you think immediately of Francis Coppola and particularly of the less yuppie-spirited Martin Scorsese. But Scorsese's films are more than just portraits of an ethnic grouping, they form a very individual history of the city itself. The progression of his films illuminates the evolution of his vision of New York.

His first film, *Who's That Knocking At My Door?*, is characterized by a romantic vision of Manhattan, as seen by the Harvey Keitel character – the Italian boy from the other side of the tracks, or rather the Hudson, viewing the city as the promised land from the deck of the Staten Island ferry. Even in our cynical age, that journey, past the Statue of Liberty and into New York Harbour, has enough vistas of grandeur that like the Brooklyn Bridge it creates an aura of naïve idealism that can't fail to impress you, even despite the knowledge that it was never more than myth.

The young Scorsese was happy enough to echo belief in the myth. Keitel's Charlie in *Mean Streets* is the archetypal romanticized gangster – the numbers runner whose hero is St Francis of Assisi, who believes in Hell Fire and the Heaven on Earth of the American way. You take what is rightfully yours, but you look after your own – the creed he can't deny and ends up being killed for.

Taxi Driver has the same ultimately humanistic vision. Its hero Travis Bickle may be a psychopath, a Vietnam Vet burned out by acid and atrocity, watching the neon filth reflect back off a windscreen as blank as his mind, but he is also a latter-day saint whose mixed-up vision of the 'real rain' ends up bringing deliverance for Jodie Foster's corrupted innocent, the child prostitute. It's a unique vision that comes from the meeting of two minds, Scorsese's and Paul Schrader's, formed by opposite ends of the religious spectrum. Scorsese was brought up a Catholic, Schrader, the nearest that America has to a Wee Free.

For *New York, New York*, the most romantic of his movies, he went back into the past to cast a rosy-coloured lens over the heyday of the jazz age and the man who wrote the city's theme tune. It was a two-hour-long invocation of that classic piece of American cornball that nobody can quite deny.

And then something happened. From the misty Technicolor of *New York, New York* he moved to the bleak and brutal black and white of *Raging Bull*. Here was Scorsese's vision without the strange, transferred notion of salvation. De Niro's grotesque pugilist is a failure as a boxer, a failure as a human being, and is left with no hope by the film, only the knowledge, which he expresses in borrowed words, that he 'coulda been a contender'.

The King of Comedy, although it appears on the surface to be a shift into a lighter vein, is actually his most cynical film. It displays a modern-day America, obsessed with the notion of celebrity; not skill or talent, but celebrity itself. Despite the cliché that success comes with hard work, the film's message is that the drawbridge to fame has been pulled up and those on the inside have sophisticated surveillance systems to boot. The difference between those inside and those outside is . . . just that, one lot are inside, the other out. The only way to reverse this is insane and violent action.

Rupert Pupkin's methodology is roughly similar to Travis Bickle's, but where Bickle has a distorted conception of a cause, Rupert Pupkin's only cause is Rupert Pupkin. In telling the tale, Scorsese turns comedy itself inside out. The things we should find funny are simply excruciating, the things we should find disturbing, we find ourselves laughing at.

Scorsese by this time had become a recluse and this is a recluse's film. The message from the film's view of the city is: 'Don't go out there; the place is full of madness and people who wish cancer on you.' A long way from the view from the Staten Island ferry. *After Hours*, one of those films that made a brilliant five-minute trailer, compounds this opinion. You may live in a safe little world, it warns, but out there is a city full of weirdos, hanging one another up with chains and dressing up like Nazis.

The Colour of Money, unlike the Walter Tevis book it was very loosely based on, deals with the lack of place for talent in a world where the hustle has become more important than the skill it conceals.

Despite some fine moments in his very personal vision of *The Last Temptation of Christ* Scorsese's resurrectionary film was *Good-Fellas*. Here was the new cynical Scorsese going back over the territory of the old idealistic Scorsese. He begins with what appears to be autobiographical material – living in Brooklyn, the young Ray, like the young Scorsese, admires the small-time local gangsters from a distance. But Ray, unlike Scorsese, breaches the distance. At this point the resemblance stops. Ray is no Charlie, he has no concerns of the spirit or the soul, as the young Scorsese, called to the priesthood, did. The frightening insight of *GoodFellas* is that the 'honour among thieves' and the strict alternative morality that is one of the great myths of the Mafia is at best a cold-blooded and twisted code. At its worst it is simply non-existent, there is no more morality here than there is in mainstream capitalism, the one true tenet is that might is right, and the greatest might is of the racially pure cadre of 'made' men. Ray could never become a 'made' man because he is half-Irish. The coke-fuelled second half of the movie enhances a situation built on shifting sands of paranoia, where simple loss of temper leads to murder.

The reputation of the mob lingers on. A contact in England tells me his brother-in-law is an Italian American. But he didn't want to meet me.

'There might be Italian American things he may not want you asking questions about,' I was told.

In Bensonhurst in Brooklyn, one of the main Italian areas, you can still see the ghosts of *GoodFellas* even though the spirit of Charlie and Johnny Boy has long been chased away from Little Italy. Right opposite the Subway station is a taxi depot which is the duplicate of the one run as a cover in the movie, although the corpulent figures sitting outside are discussing nothing more threatening than the performance of Roberto Baggio against the Irish.

'He'll come through, I tell ya,' says one.

'He'd better,' the other replies, 'because there's no one else on that team gonna see us through.'

All these hopes hanging from a pigtail.

Bensonhurst had actually been my second port of call. I'd first come out of the Subway at Carroll Street, an area so Italian the older generation still don't speak English, as I'd discovered when I walked into the dry-cleaning store displaying the picture of Saint Roberto in the window.

The faces of the old couple light up as I point to it.

'Ah,' they say, 'Azzurri! Wait there a second.'

The man scuttles off into the back room. Perhaps he's gone to find an English-speaking son. But ten minutes later he comes back, looks at me as if he's forgotten what I'm there for, smiles and takes a seat in the back of the shop.

An attempted exchange ensues, at the end of which they invite me warmly to come back in half an hour. Since they're indicating the television that's standing in the shop, I guess that they're inviting me back to watch the game.

Refusing such hospitality is difficult, but instead I opt for the more conventional setting of the Café Sorrento in Bensonhurst to watch the game. The way down to the café is littered with the small surreal touches that you get off the more regularly beaten tracks in this city: 'Be proud – stay American!' says the sign outside the bagel shop.

Café Sorrento is opposite a large buff-fronted building that proclaims itself as the headquarters of the Loyal Order of the Moose.

But once inside you are in the polished chrome environs of a classic Italian café. There's a huge banner on the wall bearing the legend 'Forza Italia'.

Umberto Eco, a dedicated hater of football, had previously pointed out in an essay contained in his *Travels in Hyper Reality* that the revolution itself would have to be cancelled in Italy to make way for the Sunday televised football. But even he, a schoolyard wimp (as most footophobics tend to be), never suspected just how much of a reactionary force the sport could become.

But for the Sicilians who revolve around the Café Sorrento, Forza Italia represents support for the Azzurri, and not for Berlusconi.

I drink an espresso and feel that prickling at the back of the neck that indicates a place where they take their caffeine habits seriously. But there's still an hour before kick-off, so I saunter next door to get something to eat.

I expect a pasta bar of the type you used to get in London's Soho before gentrification. Instead this is more opulent than anything the post-Invasion of the Nerds Greek Street has to offer;

all polished floor-tiles and ballooning glassware, mirrors and even a fountain in the corner.

At first I'm the only customer but then, as I'm tucking into Fettuccine Marinara, two middle-aged women come in. One has her hair tied up and is wearing a blue sleeveless tank top and cut-off jeans, the other has dark dyed hair and is wearing a white dress with gold and pastel trimmings. They look respectively like mutton dressed as lamb and mutton dressed as a Christmas tree.

They conduct a conversation with the proprietor that revolves around his private life and veers between English and Italian. Finally Christmas Tree asks him in English:

'So, is Italy going to win today?'

He goes off into a wild, gesticulating speech in Italian.

Excuse me, I ask, after he's flounced off into the kitchen, but what did he say?

Christmas Tree looks at me coldly and makes out she can't understand a word I'm talking about. Those green antennae I haven't felt for a few days begin poking their way through the top of my head again.

Oh, forget it, I say.

But by now the proprietor is back.

'Is there a problem?' he says.

I have visions of being carted out of here in a meat truck at nightfall wearing a pair of concrete boots on my way to a swimming lesson in the Hudson. But finally they decode my accent and smiles break out all round.

'I just said, they'd better! Or it's back on the plane,' he explains.

Like I say, most things sound better in Italian.

Next door, things are warming up. For one thing it appears I'm not the only one out to capture the spirit of Italy in New York City. There's a fully fledged film crew set up in the Sorrento, who take a sweeping shot of the café, capturing me in the background.

I have already seen on my own TV shots of a vaguely familiar figure leading Dermot, Cathal et al in the chant of 'Are you watching, Enger-land'. Now I'm popping up in footage of the

Italians, like some strange Zelig-like figure. Had I anticipated this, I could have memorized some inflammatory chant in Italian.

Dino, a small, pudgy-faced restaurateur from Sicily, is sitting to my left.

What's going to happen, do you think? I ask.

'Italy will win,' he replies. 'There's no question, we have to.' His certainty wavers slightly at the edges.

Tempers meanwhile are running high. For reasons best known to himself, the bartender, a large nose attached to a tall figure in a white apron, is throwing salt at everyone. A Sicilian superstition, perhaps.

A huge cheer rattles the coffee cups as Roberto Baggio's face fills the screen. Sacchi is roundly booed.

Rosario, a rough-hewn figure with a wire-brush moustache and blue overalls and, given the heat, a bemusing woollen hat, sits down on my right.

'He's ruining Italian football,' he says. 'It's all this Sky football.' By which I take it not that it is being shown on Mr Murdoch's satellite channel, but that the ball spends more of the time in the ether. It strikes me as strange that the country we look to for the purist ethic should be having their own crisis of pragmatism at the moment. It also occurs to me that England may be one of the few countries in the world where anyone would buy the manager of the national team a drink.

The first chance goes to Italy and to Baggio, his shot going over the bar. The clientele scream in disbelief at the replay, as if they think it might go in this time.

'Mano! Mano!' they howl at a suspected Norwegian handball. The noise, concentrated in this small space with all its hard surfaces, is deafening. This really is like being at the game.

The Italian team also look highly motivated. They have already had more chances in the first twenty minutes than they did in the whole of the Ireland game. It's a do or die affair. The guy with the scarf tied around his head mimes biting off his finger as Signori sends another chance whistling wide.

In general the comments are delivered in rapid Italian, but

occasionally a snippet of English emerges like a Coca-Cola bubble in the Peroni.

'Piece of shit!' concludes a guy in a vest and front-to-back body hair after a long tirade at Casiraghi, who has been selected in a vain attempt to make the Italians look more decisive in front of goal.

The early blue tide has left no impression and now the Norwegians are coming back into it. Theirs is the first clear-cut chance of the game and hearts stop as Leonhardsen gangles in on Pagliuca, making to chip the ball over the stranded keeper. Pagliuca raises an arm and stops the ball, but he's a yard or so outside his penalty area and a terrible sense of dread descends.

No one bothers to protest about the decision as Pagliuca is sent off. No one in their right minds, and possibly only Alex Ferguson, would. It was a certain goal, stopped by an illegal action, and the fans skulk around like they know that only breaking the rules has prevented them going one down – it's an atmosphere of guilty relief.

There's a flurry of confusion on the field and, when it clears, Baggio is walking towards the bench.

What's going on? I ask Rosario.

He seems as stunned as everyone else. 'Baggio has a tendon injury and his fitness is in question,' he says. 'I figure if he's going to be playing with ten men, he wants ten who can run for ninety minutes. That's why he's done it. I don't agree with him, but . . .'

He raises his arms in that time-honoured gesture of the hopelessness of the long-distance football supporter.

One guy mimes throwing his scarf away. The atmosphere of the whole place can be summed up in that great incantation of defeat: 'Oh well, that's it, then.' Here they are, in the same city as the match is being played, watching pictures sent back to New York via satellite from Italy. All the same, there's that special frisson of knowing that Azzurri are in their town, but by the looks of things they're not going to be around for long.

Gianni sitting next to me wants to know if I'm Norwegian. With my fair hair and blue-green eyes, they know I'm not Italian.

Apparently there was the odd Irish American in here for the Italy match, so it doesn't seem so strange to them that a stray Norwegian should be wandering around Brooklyn today.

His parents are from Sicily, but he was born here. And, although he speaks with a fairly strong Italian accent, there are features that mark him apart. His clothes look more 'clean-cut', less 'stylish'. He tends to initiate conversations in English, even with the others. He also seems less sure of the rules of the game than the die-hard fanatics around him. But there's none of the crisis of identity here. When I ask him if he's Italian or American, he just smiles and nods.

'Italiano Americano,' he says, pointing to a badge with the Italian tricolour and the stars and stripes, two flags crossed.

The first half comes to a close to the soundtrack of a discontented murmur. The tension is suspended, rather than removed.

Rosario and I now have the chance to talk at more leisure. So we have the conversation about soccer and the US.

'Everybody loves soccer in this country. We do, the Mexicans do, the Poles, the Colombians, the Irish. It's only the American Americans who don't.'

From the perspective of the Café Sorrento, they are a distant race indeed.

With the start of the second half, the match seems to have boiled down to a dogged battle for a single goal. Within five minutes, Baresi limps off to general dismay. As far as I'm concerned this now means that they can't use Massaro, the one player who seemed to make a difference when he came on for the second half against Ireland. But then, twenty minutes or so later, there is Massaro on the pitch. Without the benefit of the blanket media coverage you might get at home, I was getting to know the rule changes as I saw them applied, and I gather from talking to people that in addition to the two standard substitutions it was now permissible to substitute your goalkeeper.

That still doesn't explain what Italy have done. There seems no way around the fact that they have substituted three outfield players. FIFA will later claim that, because one of the three brought on was a keeper, this was OK. Conviction or pragmatism? Imagine the headache of replaying the fixture. Norway will have to live with it, or, this being the Group of Death, die with it, as the case may be.

While I'm still trying to figure this out Signori sweeps the ball in and, against the Nordic Route One Giants, the masters of triangular passing score off the head of Dino, the other Baggio. Soda bottles shatter on the floor, impromptu jigs are danced, the bull horns that stand above the giant screen are taken down and ceremoniously kissed, then used to lead a procession that winds its way around the chairs.

After two and a half hours of exhorting a television screen to do as they wished, these supporters have finally got their way. Italy have scored their first goal of the World Cup. It was not momentous in any way other than the fact that it happened, it happened when the game was scoreless, and despite a scare when the Norwegians managed to bundle the ball into the net illegally, it is not replied to in the desperate final twenty minutes. Gianni has difficulty understanding that Norway have not equalized, but his fears are quelled impatiently by the rest.

'*Due, due,*' they chant hopefully, cheering every skyed clearance as the beautiful game is forgotten. It is only victory and survival that matter now.

The black cloud above the café has broken and a lighter mood has taken over.

'Who is that guy?' asks Gianni, of Sheffield United's centre-forward. 'Floo?'

'Flow,' someone else replies.

'Nobody famous anyway,' another concludes. The place collapses into contented laughter. Who are these Norwegians? Who cares? Even the bartender is smiling.

Italy have been tried and tested, and they have come through. This scrappy victory has taken on totemic significance. At the final whistle the whole crowd pours out on to the pavement. Cars are already roaring past with the Italian tricolour waving out of windows. Fire crackers saved from the Saturday before are set jumping at our feet, car horns blare and voices are raised in the chant of 'Italia', defiant in the breaking heat of early evening.

Three kids emerge from the video store next to the café.

'What was the score?' they ask. I tell them. Didn't they want to watch the game, I enquire.

'Nah,' they say, 'we don't follow soccer,' and they head back in, their curiosity satisfied.

I gamble that I know Rosario well enough to bring up the subject of Berlusconi.

'What do I think of him?' he asks. 'You mean football? Or politics?'

I make the wrong reply.

'I don't follow politics,' he spits. But then, eager to remain on cordial terms, says by way of consolation, 'Come on, you can take a picture of my truck. I have an Italian flag on the front.'

Outside, Dino is a little ball of contentment.

'I'm so happy,' he says. 'I'm just speechless.' He has already been interviewed by the TV crew and is beginning to sound like a professional already. 'We needed this game,' he continues. 'We'll win the World Cup now.'

From fears of a first-round exit to such confidence in a team that is still far from impressive. Such is the significance of a single goal in the Group of Death.

By now the slight suspicion towards me has dissolved in euphoria. People are seeking me out, introducing themselves, volunteering their thoughts on the game. The character in the vest, who introduces himself as Vicenzo, even wants to know what I think. It was a heroic performance, I reassure him. And, although it was scarcely dashing, it was heroic, with Italy ending the game with only eight men capable of running.

Back down towards the Subway, the road is a cacophony of car horns and a succession of black limousines with dark tinted windscreens fluttering the Italian flag as the sunlight turns liquid in Brooklyn.

Coming back into Manhattan, I stop off at Little Italy to see if there's a celebration going on, but there's little sign here that the game has even happened.

In Mare Chiaro's there's just two guys at the bar. One of them, the younger one, is accompanied by his blonde wife and is trying to talk the older, bearded one into joining the Masons.

'The Lodge I belong to is one of the oldest in America,' he says. 'We own the Bible that George Washington swore his inauguration oath on.'

A reminder that the Mob are not the only secret power group in America.

Outside, a black guy walks past trying to sell a garden hose. A garden hose!? In Manhattan? I don't know what planet this is, but it isn't World Cup City, Toto.

It isn't until I return to the Irish bars that I'm back in the realms of the Group of Death. In Fitzgerald's on 3rd Avenue I get involved with the barman John in explaining to a Norwegian American why the keeper was sent off.

The Wolfetones come on the jukebox.

'Oh ah up the RA, said oh ah up the RA!'

'What is it they're singing?' the guy asks.

John and I look at one another like, is this one really worth going into?

'Up your ass,' says John, in the nicest possible way.

'Really, is that what it is?' the guy asks. John nods. 'I thought that was it,' he says.

At the far end of the bar, I notice that a man with an American accent is wearing an 'Ireland, Independent and United' T-shirt, the first sign of the much-mooted romantic Republicanism of the Irish community here.

Behind the bar are T-shirts for sale, with the Statue of Liberty holding a tricolour bearing the slogan 'We are the Boys in Green'. All proceeds go to a fund to help Irish immigrants.

An Irish New Yorker had told me the night of the Knicks game that the myth of visible fundraising for the IRA here was just that, a myth. 'Although,' he added, 'sometimes you'll get a raffle in aid of a basketball team, and you'll wonder if that's where the profits are really going.'

So where are you going to be tomorrow? I ask John.

Tomorrow at 12.30 is Ireland's high-noon confrontation with Mexico in Orlando.

'I'll probably be here,' he says. 'There'll be a few of us in if you fancy stopping down.'

I tell him I might do that.

Back at Desmond's, the two Norwegians have lost the confident glow I saw before. Now they know it's a crunch game against Ireland the following Tuesday.

'We just hope Ireland beat Mexico,' they say, 'then they won't have so much to play for against us.'

Now it's getting serious. This World Cup City isn't big enough for all of us.

I go to sleep after watching coverage of a prayer for O.J. and hearing of the rape of an eight-year-old girl in Chinatown.

You know that something is wrong about a day when you put on the TV and it tells you a man has set his girlfriend on fire.

These surreal nuggets of atrocity are what you expect of the American media, but it still takes a few days to build up that blasé protection barrier. When the report comes on, I am for some reason slightly relieved to discover that what he actually did was burn her house down. She was in it at the time so the murder is no less brutal, but I am still unable to dispel the image of a trussed-up figure doused in kerosene.

The New York news programme reminds you of the difficulty of seeing the world from the perspective of a country this large, and this self-centred. When used to the sizeable sections of international news on British networks, you get taken aback to hear a section about 'the world outside New York', featuring only one item that isn't just from another State. The US isn't a country, it's a whole continent, a whole world to itself, a fact which is self-evident but no less of a revelation when you see it from the inside, with its own near-sighted vision.

From the love-sick arsonist we turn to an item on the 'America first' education programme. A move by the right-wing lobby to force ethnic groups to study American history before their own.

I put on my Ireland hat and head down to Paddy Reilly's, curious to see whether the Black 47 crowd will be gathering there.

'Cutting it a bit fine, aren't you?' says the Polish bank teller. 'Only fifteen minutes to kick-off.' New York always does that to you. Just when it seems like a great anonymous madhouse, you're struck by just how friendly it can be.

'Go Me-hi-co,' says a passing Chicano, giving me a flash of white teeth. Turning round to wave, I nearly stumble into a construction worker, who, blood gushing from his head, is being helped into an ambulance.

There's something wrong about today.

The first thing that's wrong is that this kick-off is just too damn early. Quite apart from the issue of the heat of the Florida sun, what about the poor spectator? I have never seen a good game that kicks off early. It is part of our genetic programming that football takes place at 3 p.m. or 7.30 p.m. Maybe 7.45 or 8 p.m. if you're pushing it. Personally I prefer evening games, because you have the whole day for the anticipation to build, but that may be because I associate the 3 o'clock kick-off with the mad dash up the M1 to Elland Road. But 12.30? Never.

To say Paddy Reilly's is quiet today is an understatement. There's a row of six or seven people at the bar, all drinking take-away coffees from paper cups.

'D'ya want a drink?' someone is being asked, as I walk in.

'Nah,' he says, shaking a heavy head, 'it's too early.'

This is no spirit for a game to be played in. There's something wrong about today.

'Hey,' says an older barman who's on the phone at the other end, 'c'mon down here and be part of the crowd.'

Are you talking to me?

He is. It seems some misguided soul back in England is ringing up to do a telephone interview with the hotbed of Irish support in New York, which consists apparently of me and a handful of half-hearted Irish Americans. Still, we muster a cheer between us.

'Now they'll hear it go silent,' one of them says to me.

'Yeah, but we'll still give them the idea that there's something going on,' another replies.

'Instead of the truth,' a third shouts down from the far end of the bar. 'Nobody cares out here!'

Nevertheless, a few more people turn up, including, almost inevitably, somebody I know – Tony Fletcher, one-time protégé of Paul Weller and founder of the magazine *Jamming*. Like I say, New York is a small city – or a large cluster of small cities all inhabiting the same space/time continuum.

I didn't know you were Irish.

'I'm not,' he replies, indicating his Crystal Palace shirt. 'But Eddie McGoldrick's on the bench and he used to play for Palace.'

That's the most obscure reason I've heard so far. But we football fans need to have our allegiances in World Cup City and we need to be able to justify them, as much to ourselves as to others.

If the display of support is muted in a slightly damp and surprisingly chill New York, it perfectly matches the performance on the pitch in the heat of Orlando where the heatwave is still at its zenith. It was easy to forget in the midst of the heroic performance at Giants stadium, but today you cannot miss the fact that Ireland are a team held together by rusty links. Townsend, Staunton and Houghton have all had injury problems this year, while Sheridan has scarcely played at all. Sheridan and Staunton particularly were carried along by the magical atmosphere of the Italy game, but today they're looking like they're playing underwater.

At first the pattern of the game is what you might have expected from the two teams' previous games; Mexico hanging back and relying on the long shot, Ireland looking to Coyne to hold the ball up and pressurize from midfield.

'The Irish keeper Packie Bonner has been under pressure for his place from Gary Kelly,' says the ESPN announcer. OK, anyone can make a mistake and there are of course three Kellys in the Irish squad, but one look at the match programme helpfully labels Gary of that ilk as 'defense'.

The more the first half goes on, the more it becomes clear that Mexico have got the Republic sussed. Instead of leaving defenders back to cover Coyne, allowing the midfielders space to run, they're more or less ignoring him and covering Keane, Staunton and Houghton instead. Even one on one Tommy Coyne just isn't much of a threat, while the almighty scrap in midfield is almost invariably going Mexico's way.

Garcia's first goal is a sickener, coming right on half-time, but only because Ireland seemed to be a minute away from getting away with it.

I decide to try out Fitzgerald's for the second half. There's no sign of John the barman, but the place is showing a respectable crowd. The majority of them are sitting back in the booths where they've been making a brunch of it – a sure sign that these are the well-habituated Irish. I take a vacant seat at the bar and the second half starts.

'Ach, no,' says the guy next to me, an unshaven figure with a straggle of sandy hair, 'ye'll no get through that.' The pattern of the first half is resuming as if Charlton's interim salvos have had no effect on the Mexicans' confident grasp on the game. Again and again it happens – up to Coyne, Coyne dispossessed, Mexicans break forward, looking sprightly, Irish defence lumber after them. Irwin and Phelan, both of them booked for the second time in two games, are living on their nerves.

Conversation seems preferable.

'Mike.'

Donald.

'Dundee.'

Glasgow.

Pleased to meet you.

Mike is out here lecturing semi-seriously in political science at NYU, and playing bass very seriously in a band. His classes have been starting fifteen minutes early, by common agreement, since the competition started, to allow him time to get to a bar for the kick-off of the afternoon game.

We start the inevitable conversation about Ireland and Scotland, Celtic and Rangers.

'Do you think anybody really cares about that religious divide in Glasgow nowadays?' he asks.

From the perspective of the Celtic end, it seems like they do.

'I know there's the songs and all that,' he says, 'but I don't think most of them take it seriously.

'I support Dundee Utd, but when I moved to Glasgow I started going to Ibrox – partly because a lot of my friends did, but also because there's a side to Celtic support that really gets on my nerves, even though I am actually a Catholic. You know, they're all romantic about Ireland and Catholicism, but half of them have never been there in their lives.'

People pretty much like me in fact, I don't think having been to Ireland counts me out. But in exile, differences in perspective seem minor. The fact is that we share the reference points, which, to me almost as much as to him, is a rarity. It's a perfect illustration of the point that Basia was making.

'I mean there's the real bluenoses at Rangers, but they're in a minority now.' He tells me about a friend of his, 'who is actually a real bluenose', who got sent over to Parkhead by his firm to repair the roof. 'And he said he was stapling this felt to the roof, to try and stop the leaks and he just goes, "This club is fucked."'

I tell him about the Fergus McCann takeover.

'Jesus, really? I haven't heard any of this out here.'

Meanwhile on the screen above us, Garcia scores his second goal.

'Oh look, that's it.'

Finally Charlton's bringing on McAteer, that's the only thing that's going to make any difference. We both agree: the only solution is to run at the defence. The absurd pantomime of substitution occurs again. Coyne has come off, it's quite clear that Aldridge is the man to replace him, but some git in a shirt and tie won't let him on the pitch.

Mike and I are rolling around laughing. Aldridge all but headbutts the guy, Charlton gives him a tonsil bashing. Despite this formidable challenge, the FIFA man is a model of unruffled officiousness.

Belatedly the Irish challenge comes to life. I make a quick

calculation. At the moment Ireland have slipped from top of the group to bottom, a goal back would raise them to third, above Norway, and would mean that a draw in the last game would probably be enough.

We realize there's still something to play for.

The great advantage of the armchair critic is that there's never anyone to call you on your mistakes. When you've spent all the game deriding Lee Chapman and he scores in the last minute, you can either just forget about it amongst the mayhem, or bellow: 'About bloody time, Chapman!' One way or the other, no one will take too much notice.

But when you get it right, the feeling of self-congratulation is incomparable. So it is six minutes from the end of the game, as McAteer tears off down the right and crosses right on to Aldridge's head. Campos? Not a chance!

Having masterminded this vital goal from the bar of Fitzgerald's on 3rd Avenue several hundred miles north of Orlando, Mike and I slap hands.

We resume our conversation, swapping stories about Billy Mackenzie, the supremely talented Dundee musician and singer, who happened to come from a family of local gangsters. Billy spawned a series of chart hits with The Associates in the eighties, and created his own special brand of total chaos wherever he and his entourage of mad pals and crazy whippets went.

'Aye, but did you ever meet his brother?'

Did I? The pair of them turned up at my flat one night with a bag full of apples they'd stolen from some gardens in St John's Wood, and a pair of irate Doberman pinschers on their tail.

Roland, Mike's American friend, is nonplussed by this.

'Did you two guys know each other before today?' he asks.

No, but you know how New York is a small place, well Scotland . . .

So we all head off to Boo Radley's together, a bar downtown where research has promised me a large Brazilian contingent, complete with samba drummers. The sun has burnt off the mist by now and we head out into the great noisy, shambolic city in search of a cab.

At moments like this it feels as if New York bars are deliberately close and intimate as if to emphasize the change of scale when you walk outdoors to the width of the Avenues, the sheer dwarfing height of the buildings and the hopeless disproportion of people to that suddenly endangered species, the vacant cab.

Then providence intervenes and a taxi screeches to a halt in front of us. A pair of Hispanic-looking businesswomen with power-padded shoulders flounce past us. Roland and I get into the cab while Mike gazes after them.

'I don't know what it is about New York,' he says, 'but there's a powerful lust factor here. I think it's the ethnic mix.'

Either that or the Heineken, I suppose.

The taxi drops us off at Waverly Place all right, but we're about 400 away from the number we've got for the bar, so we set off at a run.

'Jeez,' says Mike, as the air scorches our lungs, 'imagine playing football in this.'

And Orlando is hotter.

Roland falls behind quite quickly, but Mike and I are keeping pace. The air's so close, you can hardly squeeze a breath out of it, but Scottish machismo determines that neither one of us wants to be the first to flag. Through Washington Square, sidestepping the ghettoblasters and the hustlers. Pace for pace. Roland is somewhere way behind. Boo Radley's arrives, mercifully fifty yards closer than the passing-out point.

The bar itself is downstairs, off the street, and is reassuringly cool and gloomy. In the back is a giant screen, and the game is already underway.

Unusually for New York, there is no cover (or entrance charge) for these facilities. Typically, a giant screen means entry can be as much as $30 – the face value of a good seat for the first-round games.

We take a seat at one of the tables. Crayons are provided to draw on the paper table cover. Ours is already decorated with a lovingly rendered 'ITALIA'.

Samba drumming is accentuating the natural drama of the play, picking up with the Brazilian attack, but in the crowd around the screen at the front we can't see the source. Is it live, or is it Memorex?

'It must be taped,' Mike says. 'No one could keep up a rhythm that complicated for this long.'

And yet it follows the flow of the game too closely to be taped.

Moving from the Ireland v Mexico game to this is like entering an air-conditioned building out of the heat and humidity of the street. It feels like walking into a slightly different dimension. The local time is still 1 o'clock out there in San Francisco, but it is the comparative cool of Northern California, which is a factor but no explanation.

The technical skill on display takes you aback. Much has been written about the lack of a Brazilian midfield in this World Cup, but in the past we've seen Brazilian teams that rely too much on moments of mastery from the middle of the park while settling into a languid game plan up front. There seems nothing complacent about this team. Romario and Bebeto may not like being forced to play from deeper, but it is brilliant to watch as they alternate peeling wide or coursing down the middle. There's a devastating speed and accuracy to the way they play the simple ball, too. Much of the time there's nothing spectacular, just the pass you would expect from any European team in that situation. But Brazil play it quicker. Especially with the samba-drumming describing the rush of adrenalin you might feel as if you were watching a speeded-up tape. Except there's only one of the teams playing with this charged-up sense of accuracy and dynamic.

Cameroon's quirky charm seems lost in this company. The African pretenders are playing soccer's old masters and the Latin Americans are making it quite clear that the Championship of Romantic Soccer is staying right where it is for the moment. The force of the beat and the elegant control of Romario's first touch combine in the magical moment of the first goal, perfectly timed towards the end of the first half. And there will be no looking back; the party is underway.

A spontaneous song I haven't heard before, and won't hear

again for the duration of the competition, breaks out. Someone has probably made up this crude but effective conjunction of rhythm and melody on the spot, such is the spirit of improvization.

'Whoaahh wo wo wo wo, wo wo wo wo – Brazil.'

In front of us a man in a pink shirt and a Yankees cap is being kissed by a bevy of rotund women whose dance seems to defy gravity. Someone brings out a bag full of Brazil shirts and starts distributing them around the party.

It often puzzles me how anyone is rich or profligate enough to buy one of these things, let alone invest in duplicates to dress your friends in.

Roland, Mike and I just sit and eulogize.

'I'd like to see Cameroon get one, though,' says Mike. 'I want to see them go through.'

Whatever hope we hold out for this, we all know that one goal is not going to be enough to hold Brazil on this form.

There's a lull and nothing more than a hub hub, as everyone gets more drinks and recovers their breath at half-time.

Roland goes to the bar and returns with a pitcher of the strange and florid Boo Radley's own-brand beer, an example of the 'micro-brewery' American real-ale movement. It tastes quite unlike anything I've ever drunk before, but works its own magic as the game starts again.

Brazil sweep forward and another melody is picked up as a chant to go with the insistent pressing beat. The syllables are the familiar fare of the football chant 'Ole ola', this time, 'la, la, la, la' and the punch is still '*Bra-zil!*', but each time the tune varies, bringing a dimension of invention to the time-honoured tribal ritual.

The tempo rises and rises to a pinnacle at which Santos obliges by heading the second goal, remaining on a plateau for Bebeto's *coup de grâce*, rounding the goalkeeper and finding the net with a target the width of a dollar bill. And in the middle of this madness, this unbelievable spirit of celebration, two Scots and an American sit and applaud a large television screen.

By the time the celebrations around us have muted sufficiently for the celebrants to notice their surroundings again, we're just sitting there, looking football dazed. Ayilah sashays over.

'I'm sorry,' she says.

This reminds me of being in the house of a friend of mine who's a Tottenham supporter. When Rod Wallace scored his remarkable goal I forgot, in my delighted amazement, that the consequences of loss for his team were so much more than the rewards of victory for mine. His girlfriend, a Leeds fan, and I came down to earth to see him and his two friends sitting in a glum row. We did exactly the same thing; apologized, meaning it, but visibly still floating an inch above ground even as we pretended to sympathize.

Of course, there is one crucial difference here. Despite the depressing spectacle of Mexico v Ireland, now way back in the memory, we are not downhearted. We just happen to be the only three people in the room who aren't kissing somebody.

Mike voices the common thought in the nicest possible way.

'Do we look like we're from Cameroon?'

'I thought you might be Swedish,' she replies.

'No, I'm American, and these two are Scottish,' says Roland.

'You're Scottish!' she says. 'Well, you should be supporting Brazil; you guys love soccer – we play beautiful soccer.'

'No, I'd just like Cameroon to qualify. I don't like the way the Swedish play,' Mike explains.

'I want Sweden,' says Roland.

'Are you Swedish?' she asks.

'Three generations back,' he replies.

I thought you were Irish.

'My mom's Irish.'

Oh, OK. Keeping up with the national extraction of your companions can be a tricky business here in World Cup City.

'I tell you one thing, though,' Ayilah says. 'If Brazil got kicked out, I would root for Cameroon, because I think they play nice soccer and I love Milla, but heeey, I'm Brazilian!' She does, mind you, have an affection for the host country, unlike many British minorities, the Irish and the Scots above all.

She tells us she was born and raised in Brazil, but she's lived here a while.

I tell her she sounds like a New Yorker.

'If you were American, you could tell,' she says.

Roland concurs.

'But Brazil will win,' says Mike.

'Oh, I hope so,' she replies. 'I can see a final between Brazil and Germany.'

We vacillate between which version of the past is affecting us the most. The romantic victory of 1970, or the heartbreak of 1974 when Cruyff and Neeskins were unthinkably overturned by Beckenbauer and crew.

'The Germans see everything as a military operation,' Ayilah says, 'and skill doesn't always win. The Brazilians want to turn on the ball and play it out of defence, and all it takes is an unlucky bounce or an interception and they lose it.'

The mystery percussion man turns out to be Carlos Darci, a jazz trombonist daylighting on maracas.

'I like to do this when Brazil plays; it makes the team seem more,' he says. He's a Brazilian and has been in New York only a few months, coming here from a spell in Berlin. Now he's hot-footing home to warm up for a gig tonight in Sullivan Street.

'New York City's where you have to be for jazz,' he says.

He has been accompanied by Lydia, a Brazilian student, who's carrying a device that looks like an abacus with cymbals instead of beads.

'Oh, I have a whole collection of these things,' she says. 'I just pick one on the day of the game, according to my mood.'

Her naked midriff has been attracting the attentions of another Carlos, a dark figure with a shaven head, who hovers around during our conversation.

So is Brazil going to win? I ask him, feeling it might be prudent to involve him since Lydia is admiring my accent and beginning to make dancing motions around me while his eyebrows are getting lower by the second. I'm far enough away from home to be a novelty, but that can be a dangerous thing to be.

'No,' he says.

'*Noooo?*' Lydia is exclaiming in mock exaggerated shock, and it seems as if I might have stamped out a beautiful friendship.

Why not? I venture.

He says something in Spanish which Lydia translates.

'Because he's from Argentina,' she says. All the same, he forecasts an Italian victory. I leave them to argue it out.

As we go out, the man behind the bar says, 'I'll tell ya, Monday night American football won't be the same after this.'

Again Mike gives words to a common feeling between the three of us.

'I wish I was Brazilian,' he says.

Back at the hotel, Frau has arrived from London. She takes one look at the figure in the door with its baseball cap and T-shirt, the *New York Times* tucked under one arm.

'Are you sure that's you?' she asks.

Amidst the sea of nationalities, I have overlooked one thing. I have begun to look and behave like an American.

The next day is the day of the Gay Pride march.

I take a look at a bit of the first half of Belgium v Holland, but with both teams almost certain to qualify, it looks like an apologetic spectacle, so I take a trip down to Chinatown with Frau instead. Sharing a Subway platform with a hundred or so men with moustaches and women with cropped heads, we are conspicuous heterosexuals, for all the world to see.

Together we enter a dimension where glimpses of World Cup City are few, although we do see a Chinese boy walking past with an Italia cap.

Frau, like me, is Scottish but with a soft accent that's taken frequently for Irish. A firewood stockist she spoke to on the telephone once not only refused to serve us, but threatened to call the police if we came within a mile of his premises, apparently under the impression that either bombs are made of wood or terrorism is still living in the age of Guy Fawkes.

She has a French name, her mother's maiden name is Swedish, and her spiritual home is pre-unification Berlin. When she tries on an electric blue Chinese jacket in a shop on Canal Street, the assistants are visibly amazed. Her dark hair and pale skin and delicate proportions are instantly cast into an oriental perspective. Noticing this in the mirror, she begins to adopt gestures of a romantic China of the imagination.

Frau loves Chinese things but has never been tempted to go to the real, post-Cultural Revolution place.

'China for me is Fu Manchu, bandaged feet and Mother Gin Sling's lipstick,' she says. She has no wish to have this illusion tarnished by reality.

Watching the first half of Nigeria versus Argentina, back at the hotel, I realize how much of this imaginary dimension we take into a football match with us – we watch the Nigeria of tribal magic and bacchanalian drumming, the Brazil of sex and samba, the Ireland of the Romantic struggle, the Argentina that veers between Nijinsky and Machiavelli like the team's brutal yet creative country. Football fans are often quite conscious disseminators of the image: the Irish with their magnetic go-for-broke hedonism, their openness and hospitality, the Nigerians with their tribal dress and drummers, the Brazilians aware that their percussive celebration enhances even the electronic image of those wonder-ful yellow shirts. We are all making a movie, playing a game.

I cannot think of anything to say about Nigeria that is not bound up with my image of the African continent. When they play – despite the fact that they're playing a game that I recognize, a game I have grown up with, a game that is ingrained in my culture – I am aware, above all, of their otherness. They just don't seem to do anything quite how I expect to see it done, whether it is the individual components of the game like trapping the ball or laying on a pass, or whether it's the overall rhythm and progression of the ball. It's the direct equivalent of African pop music, the way it has adapted to the Western influences beamed over the radio waves but is unable to conceive of them except through the vivid colour of its own vision. As with music where things just come out sounding different, so an African team – and Nigeria look like the prime exponents of the African game – don't look like anything else in the world. That difference is as exhilarating in football as the first time of seeing Youssou N'Dour's band on stage.

I watch the perfect arch of Siasia's lob over the keeper for the opening goal and, along with the rest of the world, I see the confirmation of a promise that makes Pelé's prediction of an African side winning the World Cup look like a safe bet. Johannesburg 2002?

But then there's the Argentinians. In particular there is one Argentinian, and if this movie was plotted as the bright new star of Africa contrasted against Maradona's setting sun, then there was one key supporting role who wasn't content to take to the wings just yet. All I expected, all anyone expected from Maradona this time round was the odd touch, maybe a glance of the old magic. But he is playing like a man possessed. It is his partner in crime Caniggia, just back from suspension himself, who is bagging all the goals – the first, to equalize, high into the net from a rebounding free-kick, the second curled around the keeper, set up by Maradona's set piece. But Maradona's place in the headlines is fully deserved. It is he who is the inspiration of this rejuvenated Argentinian team, adapting his game to his slowing pace with a versatility we never expected, prodding the team forward with skill and vision, rather than leading from the front. It is either an inspired celebration of the life-force or a testament to the single-minded grip of power lust, depending on your point of view. But by half-time one thing is certain: just like yesterday, Latin America is rampaging through the promise of Africa.

Maradona has been dumped on the turf with bruising regularity, even if he's contributed by casting himself down every now and then. But we have also seen one of the glaring refereeing mistakes that are becoming a feature of the competition. Nigeria's defender Eguavoen fouls Maradona, but one of his team-mates, Sunday Oliseh, is booked by mistake. Moments later, he receives what should have been the second yellow card which would have sent him off. Didn't the linesman notice? Couldn't somebody have told him? Apparently not.

Down in Boo Radley's for the second half, there is nothing like the crowd there was for Brazil. Without Ayilah and her friends the place seems quiet, but Elisa makes up for it, stalking the empty floor in a realm of her own, shouting at the screen, her mini-skirt swinging. There's no doubting her perspective.

'Hey, *que pase?*' she demands of one Argentinian as he sends a chance flying over the bar. '*Veni, veni,* Diego', as the middle-aged barrel slips his marker and feints to the byline.

She and her friend Ayrton, a Brazilian, both work across the road at Panni et Chocolata. She has an arrangement with another Brazilian friend. When Brazil play she covers and her friend watches the game. When it's Argentina, like today, it's her turn.

But what happens if Brazil meet Argentina in the Final?

She looks at me with deep, dark eyes through her short curly hair. 'You can't be too careful with your friends,' she says. 'Your team being in the World Cup Final is a totally egotistical moment.'

There is hope for all, except the Colombians. But there are a lot of different dreams in World Cup City tonight.

You can be in my Final, if I can be in yours.

OK, but I want to win.

As I walk back to the hotel, I cross Broadway and the discarded drag of the parade. There's a chalk testament on the road to the Cleveland Gays. But the carnival is over; it was going on above my head while I was down in the darkened cellar of Boo Radley's watching the electronic likeness of a game going on in Boston.

From across the Avenue comes a distant, approaching sound of rap music. As it does, I make out the homophobic lyrics. A bunch of homeboys are on the prowl, looking for a stray queer.

'There's one!' comes a shout.

I realize at once that on a Saturday evening midtown New York is suddenly a ghost town. I'm the only one around. Then they see my Ireland baseball cap and pass by without making another comment.

They're only about fifteen or sixteen, so who can tell how seriously they mean it, but I am still glad that an item of my clothing can beam me into some parallel city to the one they're inhabiting.

The next day is the biggest ever in the soccer history of the United States. Admittedly that's a bit like a comparison with ice-hockey in Nigeria, but all the same, the odd dissection of John Starkes aside, the Knicks are history, or not as the case may be, and for the first time the soccer team are the centre of attention.

'Can lowly Romania stand in the way of a dream?' asks one sports columnist. Is he joking or has nobody told him that when you're talking of international spending power, Romania is lowly, but in World Cup City . . . ?

Actually the game is more evenly matched than any of the visitors here might have suspected, confirming my suspicions after the Switzerland game, that Romania's power is built around an unreliable engine called Hagi.

Although they manage to beat the US, the manner is not at all convincing, relying on a near-post fluff by the usually reliable Tony Meola.

But the game is more notable for the sheer weirdness of the media coverage. This is one of the few games so far that has been given full network coverage on ABC rather than the cable channel ESPN. Used to American sports where bursts of frantic activity are followed by long interruptions, they have devised a whole gamut of garish tricks, which only seem to get in the way. What they don't gather is that, in football, there are whole passages of seemingly non-eventful play, which are nevertheless vital to the all-important question of which way the power of the match is swinging.

Tony Meola goes down and we have shots of his father in the stand. OK, fair enough, but then as the game progresses we get a box, inserted in the picture, showing some jerk sticking a microphone in the man's face.

'What do you think of your son being injured like that?'

Quite understandably Mr Meola expresses the opinion that we should 'get on with the game'.

Undeterred by this brush-off, they wait a few minutes and when there aren't any goals, broken limbs, riots breaking out, etc., back comes the box. This time it contains a pre-recorded interview with Alexi Lalas.

Other highlights during the game include: an external shot of the stadium showing one of those giant inflatable things that spray carbon dioxide down on you – 'And the fans are in the cool zone,' says the commentator, not thinking to reflect on why, if fans they be, they are outside the stadium at all while the game is going on; an interview with Tab Ramos's father, who seems a little less concerned with watching the game than Mr Meola; and various statistics which actually obscure the action, sometimes at crucial points in the game.

'Oh, by the way,' says Tony the barman who's off duty today but around to watch the game with the rest of us, 'I've got a ticket for you for the Norway match.'

It turns out that the corporate packages have been selling like Colombia – World Champions T-shirts and have been returned to the stadia, selling for face value. Tony has a batch and there's one going spare.

'Don't worry,' he says, 'you're definitely going.'

This, I have begun to realize, is part of the thrill. The long hunt for the ticket, wondering whether it is worth paying two hundred for a sixty-dollar ticket, just to be sure, then securing one of the best seats for eighty-five dollars. Those magical words 'face value'. I've scored.

So what do you think of the result? I ask, after thanking him profusely.

'Oh, it's grand,' he says. 'My wife's American German, so I want to see her teams meet each other. She's been teasing me so much for being football crazy, because she only watches the two. If they meet one another, I can watch her decide who to cheer for.'

That evening, Frau and I head off uptown to the Algonquin hotel, the centre for the famous literary circle in the twenties. I think I'm going AWOL from World Cup City, only to discover that the bar there is staffed by Colombians, and in the dark wood, nineteenth-century surround they're watching their already eliminated team turn it on too late against Switzerland, thinking of what might have been.

On the morning of the Ireland v Norway game, I head round to Tony's apartment on 2nd Avenue. He is one of the upper class of the housing market, having moved into a rent-stabilized place with his wife before the rents started to go mad in the eighties. It is a comfortable and spacious apartment for central Manhattan.

'You weren't in yesterday, were you?' he asks.

I wasn't, thereby breaking my usual routine of stopping off at Desmond's at midnight or so. If I had missed a game during the day, Tony would play it back for me on video in the back room.

'Oh, we had a scene. Germany were playing Korea on ESPN and Spain against Bolivia was on the Spanish channel. So we were trying to do the usual thing of splitting the channels, one TV on one and another on the other – but it didn't work. Oh, there was all hell broke loose.'

I had watched the first half of the German match, seeing them going 3–0 up, and had switched over to see Spain beating Bolivia 3–1, missing another great Korean fightback, with Germany clinging on to victory, looking nothing like the composed and arrogant team of their public image.

Sean, a Tottenham supporter who's at college out here, is there too. Tony hands him a rosette in the Irish colours, and he looks at it, wondering if it's right to wear it. Eventually he hands it back.

'It's too hot for a rosette,' he says bemusingly, then later adds: 'After all, I don't have any Irish blood.'

Tony gives the rosette to me instead. I have no such worries.

Tony is waiting for a phone call.

'There may be some other tickets coming up,' he says. 'I spoke to a guy on the *New York Post* who's got some. We'll hang on and see if they're better than what we've got – we can always sell these ones at the stadium.'

Which seat will you be left with when the music stops?

When the tickets turn up they're not as good, so Tony and Johnnie wait on outside Port Authority to get shot of them while Sean and I, with Patrick from Dublin, take the bus out to Meadowlands.

On the bus, I meet a couple of Irish Americans who are going to their first soccer match.

'We just saw the Italy game on TV and thought "Wow, this is amazing, we have to get tickets,"' they say.

Like most of the Americans I speak to at games, they have played the game themselves.

'Before we got into beer and partying too heavily,' they confide conspiratorially.

One of them has an Irish tricolour, with a flagpole which, he will probably find, is inadmissible to the ground.

Did you put any tape on it? I ask him. Like Irish Americans on Tour?

'No,' he says, 'it was enough trouble making the thing in the first place.'

He'd stitched together three tablecloths, but had had to start again when his dad came home and told him he had the colours in the wrong order.

It's another blistering day at Meadowlands, but the strange dramatic prescience of the Italy game's thundery weather is lacking. The heaviness of that day is replaced by a lighter, more cheerful atmosphere, quite out of keeping with the last day of the Group of Death.

There is a more even showing of fans here today. Norwegians with Norse horns swarm around the place singing an adaptation of the Smurf song. I hear it often enough but can't quite be certain of the lyrics.

It sounds like: '(booming voice) Who are you in green and white? (Smurf voice) We are Irish – we don't fight.'

But I may have made up that rhyme. Whatever, if there is a warrior bravado present, it is an entirely tongue-in-cheek one, and the song is received by the Irish fans with a laugh, and an equally light-hearted chorus of: 'You'll never beat the Irish.'

I'm absorbing the atmosphere outside when Adrian and Sylvie wander past, looking intent.

'Did you see the Mexico game?' Adrian wants to know. 'Crap, wasn't it?'

How were the Mexican fans? I ask.

'Oh, they were OK,' he answers, 'but having been beaten by them you didn't really want to party with them.'

It's crunch time in World Cup City; the camaraderie of the early days is gone. We're all out here, but only some of us are staying.

Inside the ground I find my seat, although I have to edge past a cop complete with moustache and mirror shades to get to it.

Within a few minutes a fan wrapped in a tricolour is pulling at the cop's trouser leg from below.

'Hey, Justin!' he shouts.

'Hey, man!' says the cop. 'Where ya sitting? . . . OK, I'll be round to see you in a minute.'

Justin, it turns out, is an Irish American, like the mythological NY cop, and he made a lot of friends from the homeland at the Italy game.

Never, I reflect, thinking of England.

Some of the Norwegian fans have brought along inflatable models of the figure from Munch's *The Scream*. You don't have to be one of Munch's compatriots to feel that this represents the existential angst of the football supporter perfectly – that sickening moment when you realize that something so important to you is entirely beyond your control. The nervous figure with its mouth open in horror and hands raised to its head in anguish could be the symbol of the fans of either team as the game progresses.

Ireland has all the possession, but they're using it up playing square balls in midfield, and rarely venturing as far as the penalty area. McAteer, in his first start, looks more nervous than the quicksilver talent that was running rings around Baresi and Maldini. He and Keane and Gary Kelly, also starting for the first time, play some intricate triangles which certainly refute the received image of the Irish team but look more than anything like a temptation to the breaking power of the Norwegians. You can just see it, the foot stuck out, the interception made, the long ball lofted over for Flo – battered by your own bludgeon.

It's one of those games that can look tedious to the neutral, and indeed not even the biggest partisan could claim that it is beautiful, purposeful football, but it has its own drama and as the two teams test one another out it is an absorbing, if occasionally inelegant, contest.

Ireland seem to be running around the pitch like mad things, while the referee seems intent on keeping the game moving, making you wonder if there will be a second-half wilting. That certainly seems to be what the Norwegians are playing for, sitting back for most of the first period, allowing the Irish to smash into the solid wall of their defence, again and again.

Predictably the Norwegians begin the second half at double the pace. Now we have on our hands what we expected all along – a real slugger's match. Bonner loses his temper with his defence, leading to a series of protracted rows, particularly with Phelan. Aldridge heads wide. McGrath saves Ireland again and yet again.

Rekdal finally wrongfoots McGrath, but his snatched shot is straight at Bonner. The Norwegian openings are coming more regularly – it's one of those shifts that you can feel in the power pattern of the game. When the ball loops over Bonner's head, from a set-piece scramble, you can only stand and watch as it hangs, just like the ball hung from Houghton's shot at that very end.

No!

There's me and a man and his wife from Dublin, the three of us standing there looking like *The Scream* in triplicate.

But it hits the bar and we all crumple together, assuring one another it's OK. By the time we can bear to look back at the pitch, the ball is up the other end for a corner to the Republic.

Keane hits a spectacular scissor kick spectacularly high over the bar when you might have expected at least a shot on target. Then a three-man break for the Republic. Sheridan takes the ball at the edge of the penalty area and waits for Thorstvedt to advance before chipping him, and again the ball hangs in the air. Every Norwegian raises hands to face, every Irish arm is raised, until the crescendo dies as the ball comes to rest on top of the goal.

But what's going on in Washington? A draw is likely to be enough for Ireland, but it isn't absolutely certain. There were no scores at half-time, and no radio station is broadcasting coverage of the games. All the same, someone seems to know because the word comes around. Italy are 1–0 up, which puts them first and staying in New York, Ireland second and back to Orlando, Mexico waiting it out to see if they qualify as a wild card. Norway are out unless they score in the next five minutes.

There is one chance; with a minute to go the Norwegians get a free-kick just outside the area. The penalty area looks like the land of the giants. You can see it all too well – Flo rising above McGrath, the downward header, Bonner's despairing snatch at the air, the stunned silence of the Irish fans, the disbelieving joy rising in red and blue pockets all around you, *The Scream*.

In another World Cup perhaps, but not in this one. The ball is lofted in and lands safely in Bonner's hands. The celebrations begin.

Back outside, I see the Norwegians from Desmond's yet again. But we avoid one another's gaze. What do you say? Their team is going home with 4 points and a zero goal difference. Ireland, with exactly the same, is going through on account of scoring one more goal.

Here in World Cup City, and particularly in the Group of Death, some of the people can be happy all of the time and all of the people can be happy some of the time, but not all of the people can be happy all of the time.

It's not until twenty minutes after the game is over that I discover Mexico have equalized, fifteen minutes into the second half in Washington. An American guy, myself and a character with a Yorkshire accent puzzle over this for a minute. But it makes no difference. It's Orlando all right. But even the hottest, steamiest corner of World Cup City seems like heaven right now, compared with the long trip home.

As we get back into Manhattan a man in a suit stops us to ask how it went.

'We're rooting for you,' he shouts after us.

Back at the hotel, as I'm checking out, I notice for the first time the illustration from the *New Yorker* which shows the map of America from the perspective of Manhattan – a great foreshortened country with Manhattan itself looming large in the foreground, Chicago and the Rockies crammed into the middle, Los Angeles the only other discernible landmark in the far distance and, somewhere beyond that, the Pacific.

I check out of the Irish party early; after all, I know what it will be like. I have an early start in the morning for Chicago, and I don't fancy trying to negotiate my way out of Manhattan in the rush-hour while nursing another epic hangover. So I check into a hotel in Queens, which runs a shuttle across to the airport.

Outside the hotel window is a club called Baby Cakes, a large pink building with the title written across the buttocks of a giant, waist-down female facsimile. Neon lights in the shape of nude women flicker in the windows. It looks like some fantasy palace from a movie, and it turns out that that's exactly what it is, a specially built set, ready for shooting tonight.

I take Frau out to the airport and say goodbye again. She's on the last flight out and as they call her in to board the airport begins to shut up.

Now I'm really on my own for the duration in World Cup City.

I share the shuttle back to the hotel with two pilots. There's nothing that can make you more nervous about flying than spending time with a pilot.

'Did you know that on Fifth Avenue there's a Warner Brothers Museum?' says one of them.

'You mean the store?' asks the driver.

'Yeah, that's right,' says the pilot, clearly unaware of the distinction between a shop and a museum, 'and you can buy stuff from all the different eras of Warner Brothers.'

Your pilot today is Mr E Fudd and he has a full-sized model of Bugs Bunny stashed away in his locker.

They spend the rest of the journey back from the hotel fantasizing about the stewardesses on Thai Airlines and girls in California with 'dental-floss bikinis'.

The next day my flight out of New York is delayed as mist settles around JFK and storm warnings come in from Chicago. As we finally take off through a cloud layer with spectacular peaks and troughs that look like the Manhattan skyline, I sit rigid and try to dispel the image that we are being piloted by a Bugs Bunny dummy.

The in-flight movie is *Blue Chips* – an illustration of Tony's point about the American cult of the coach, it features Jeff Bridges as the mastermind of a basketball team, playing Mephisto with the big league corruption.

The next day I will read a newspaper man's explanation of why soccer can never quite be taken to the heart of the American people. They haven't made a movie about it yet.

4

Sudden Death

If New York is a city content in its role as a myth-maker, as first cities often are, Chicago is a town that wishes people would forget its past and let it get on with the present.

The World Cup here is a big thing, bigger than it could be in New York where competition for the city's ever-shortening attention span is all too great. The city lays a weight of hope around Striker's dog collar. Hope that a volume of tourists will be attracted to Chicago for something other than the gangster heritage. Hope that the attendances at the World Cup will be the launch-pad for a successful professional league which will be the salvation of Soldier Field – the grand and largely disused stadium where the competition is taking place.

Of course it's all too much for a mere cartoon pooch to bear. The *Chicago Tribune* hopes that the professional league might attract audiences of fifty to sixty thousand to the Field which indicates that Keith Allen's soccer profile-building adverts have not yet been taken to heart.

In the advert, Allen is walking through an empty stadium, proclaiming in his relaxed and laid-back style, i.e., like a rabid dog on Dexedrine: 'In order to understand the World Cup you have to understand the status of the men who are going to walk out on this field. They're like rock stars. No, they're like gods. No, they're bigger than that, but there isn't anything bigger than that. They're like *God's Rock Stars*!'

Filling a stadium from an international catchment to watch God's Rock Stars is one thing. Getting the sort of crowds that normally roll up to see Messrs Cantona, Giggs, Gullit and Baggio to turn up to see a bunch of college-level no names could be quite another. Now that the USA team have registered on the roll call of the World, the chances are they'll be jetting off, if not to Italy and Spain then certainly to England and possibly to Scandinavia, to replace all those Scandinavians on their way to Italy, Spain and England.

Meanwhile the football fans come to Chicago to watch their team and in the meantime they snap up tours of Al Capone's haunts and tales of the Lady in Red.

And why not? Could you imagine London complaining about the perennial attraction of the Tower of London? Or New York, the Empire State Building? It's all a bit redolent of the Mafia cry of celluloid mythology – we may have been built on crime, but now we're legitimate businessmen. And of course we the observers know in both cases that this is a matter of *plus ça change* . . .

Plus c'est la même Chicago; that's the message of one of the city's greatest chroniclers, Nelson Algren. Algren will chiefly be remembered by mass culture as the author of the book that was turned into the Otto Preminger film *The Man with the Golden Arm*, and for the book whose title Lou Reed stole for his seventies sleaz-erama hit 'Walk on the Wild Side'. But anyone who has read him knows he's the noir-drenched poet of the El train and the arc light. Once you've read Algren, his grim romantic vision will follow you like a pick-pocket through the streets of this 'big-shot town, small-shot town, jet-propelled old-fashioned town . . . whose heartbeat carries further than its shout, whose whispering in the night sounds less hollow than its roistering noontime laugh'.

In *Chicago, City on the Make*, Algren argues that Chicago was built in a wilderness, beginning as a stopping point for horse thieves and attracting the hustlers and the sharps from all around the globe. Chicago was the hustlers' city, it always was and it always will be. On the prairie grass by the banks of Lake Michigan, they built a different type of wilderness – the *Neon Wilderness* that *Algren* chronicles in his book of short stories. The moral of his dark and disturbing vision is stark: it's a thankless town and it belongs in perpetuity to the descendants of the crook and the card sharp.

Reading Nelson Algren on the plane is a tough way to prepare yourself for Chicago.

If you travel for long enough you can become a connoisseur of airports. An airport is a key to the mentality of a city, it is the way the city itself has planned the first impression it creates. London Heathrow broadcasts a separatist island mentality with its A–Z of international destinations down one wall and of British spots down the other. Istanbul and Ilkley, one is exotic, romantic and accessible from here, but the other is British. De Gaulle in Paris is chic and futuristic, the neon window dressing of the very image of the modern city. JFK is New York, and so doesn't care what you think about it.

O'Hare airport is self-consciously hi-tech, its miles of conveyor-belt walkways rolling underneath a sheltering vine of neon. But it's a no-nonsense hi-tech, a mid-Western 'Yeah, we got that fancy stuff out here too, ain't no big thing' image.

I share a taxi downtown with a computer salesman who's in town to close a big deal.

'All I'm going to see of the place is the inside of my hotel room and the contract I'm working on. But you're going to love it. It's a great town.'

This is what everyone tells me. Chicago, a great town. 'Great restaurants' is usually the next line. Chicago is proud of its food; it seems indicative of a certain mentality that its big annual festival, 'The Taste of Chicago', is literally the taste of Chicago, with hundreds of food tents setting up on Grant Park for what the *Chicago Tribune* calls a 'cholesterol-busting treat'. In other towns the festival might focus on dance, theatre or art, with the food being periphery. But Chicago is honest about where its interests lie – here the music is incidental and the cuisine takes centre stage.

The salesman is another reminder of the technological background against which this most primitive of contests is being played out. The television here has had a corporate-image advert about the World Cup database on rotation – the entire history of the game at a finger-tip touch on a computer screen.

He gives the same message that everyone does. 'We've no sooner designed a new bit of hardware than it's out of date.' Amidst all these active matrix screens, World Cup City, with all its quaint notions of national boundaries, is beginning to look a bit like a heritage theme park.

My hotel is in the Loop, what Paul Theroux in his novel *Chicago Loop* called 'this rich-poor, lovely crummy place, the financial district . . . still grubby and real at the edges'. Despite a gentrification process, touched on in Theroux's 1990 novel, the description is still apt. The Loop is a tangle of dowdy offices with wooden chairs and glittering towers, chrome-decked restaurants and downbeat diners.

Grant Park and Soldier Field are to the east, and to the south is no man's land – an area that many long-term residents have still not penetrated.

I walk out of the hotel and head west, out in the direction of Greek Town. The first thing you notice after the sweltering heat of New York is the cool breeze that sweeps across the city from Lake Michigan and can cause a shiver even in the middle of summer. In the winter this seagull of wind transforms into the famous Hawk as described in Lou Rawls's Stateside soul classic 'Dead End Street'. If it can bring a chill like this to mid-summer, you can imagine what it can do in the winter.

I stop first at a sports bar, hoping to find out who will be playing Germany in the game for which I have a ticket. They're following the competition there but not sufficiently closely to have mastered the intricacies for which even a fanatic might need a full-time FIFA guide, or at least access to the database.

Here there's a whole new cosmology to become acquainted with. For the Mets read the Chicago White Sox, for the hapless

Knicks the erstwhile world-conquering Bulls, who swept all before them before the big disease with the little name swept away superstar Magic Johnson, and for the New York Jets, the Chicago Bears.

The White Sox are on the TV here and the jukebox is blaring too. Noise is the engine that drives a bar in Chicago, even if its cogs can grate against an outsider's sensibility. As if the two sources weren't enough, there's a basketball shooting gallery in the corner where off-duty yuppies take pots at a basket, managing about the same strike rate as hapless Knicks front man John Starkes.

This is brash Chicago, not the bustling noise of New York. This is the town of *The Blues Brothers* and Bobby Bland. Paul Schrader's *Blue Collar*, its Beefheart soundtrack echoing the thudding regularity of the production line, was actually set in Detroit, but that sound is the beat of the greater Midwest.

They don't sell peanuts at the bar, but you can have a big basket of heavily salted popcorn on the house – although of course they'll charge you for the pints of Killihan's Red, the rich and uniquely American Irish beer you'll have to drink to wash it down.

Have you been following the World Cup? I ask the barman.

'Sure!' he says. Here it's as strange a question as it might be anywhere else in the world but New York.

You don't know who's playing in the game on Saturday, do you?

But he doesn't follow it that closely. Ten minutes or so with the *Tribune* and we think we've worked it out. We knew it was Germany, but we think, after Holland scraping through past Morocco today and Belgium going down to Owairan's spectacular fifth-minute strike for Saudi Arabia, that Belgium will be coming here to play Germany and Holland going to Orlando to meet Ireland. This not only cheats me out of a replay of the 1974 Final, with Germany meeting Holland, but it condemns Ireland to a much more unpredictable tie. Against the low-scoring Belgians you would bet on the Irish, even with their own goal-shy form, to go through. Holland have been playing uninspired stuff to date, but a team with Bergkamp and Roy is always going to cause breakaway problems.

A few doors down I stop at what looks like a burger joint, opting for not fainting above searching for the perfect restaurant. They tell me the fish of the day is swordfish in a butter and basil sauce and served with wild rice. Hmmm, I see what they mean. Great food.

Across the way there's a group of male office workers plus a lone girl in a T-shirt who are talking about the World Cup.

'You wanna ticket, I can getcha a ticket,' one of them, a spiky-haired individual, is telling the rest. At first I think he's parodying an English accent, but no, it's for real, he's from Essex. As if you cou'n't tewl. His given name is Ian, he comes from Billericay and he's doin' . . . awlright my son.

There follows a discussion on sympathies in the competition that inevitably become a genealogical trace.

'Well, you're Italian, aren't you?' says the girl in the T-shirt to a dark-haired man who does admittedly look like one of the Pacino division. 'No,' he replies, 'I'm Scottish.'

'Scottish?' she asks. 'I'll tell you a Scottish toast – "Here's tae us, whae's like us, damn few and they're a' deed."'

Of all the bars in all the towns in all the world, I have to walk into one where they're exchanging the sort of toast you get inscribed on tea-towels back in Scotland.

Excuse me, I interject, but the one you'd really get in Scotland is 'Slanje'.

The table erupts in laughter.

'Man,' says the girl in the T-shirt, who introduces herself as Jane, 'you are really raining on my brains!'

'Do you think he looks Scottish?' she asks.

'Really,' he says. 'I've been to Scotland and traced my clan.'

Oh, you mean they sold you a tartan plaque.

'That's right.'

Chicago is not the only place that has a few wily hustlers; in the north of Scotland there's plenty who've been bullshitting for a living for generations.

But then there's a lot of Italians in Scotland.

Jane has a theory about this: 'The Italians were the master builders, so they travelled around the world because they were the craftsmen.'

Really, I say, I thought they came to make the ice cream.

'Finally,' comes the chorus around the table, 'she's met her match.'

The men in the gathering are Ian's colleagues, who work in a nearby bank. Jane is a film student, whose secondary occupation is taking the mickey out of the bankers' corporate image.

'The banking thing is just so insidious in this town,' she says. It may not be an exclusively blue collar one, but there's a strong work ethic here, one that Algren also comments on. Art is a frippery in a place like this, a distraction from the business of making money.

'It's just the rhythm of the place,' says the Scot, whose name is John. 'When you're young you work hard and party hard, then you get married, you don't party so much, you focus on your work and your family.'

Jane gives me her own verdict of Chicago.

'It's known as the gateway to the mid-West,' she says, 'and it is, psychologically as well as physically. It's blue collar, conservative, a very racist town. It's the place above all others that denies the myth of America as the melting pot, everything is very separate, the races are separate, rich and poor are separate, everything is quite clearly defined.

'It's a city with a real inferiority complex, because it lives so much in the shadow of the two coasts . . . Mind you, there is one thing to say about it.'

What's that?

'Great food.'

'Hey, Donald,' says Ian, 'how big is your expense account? I'd love to stay for another beer, but I've no cash on me.'

I explain to him that I'm not actually on an expense account, but yeah, I'll buy him a drink.

So we get through another round and debate the great mystery of why it's taken Harvey Keitel so long to be recognized as major league when everyone who knows the name of more than three movie directors has known he's one of the all-time greats for twenty years. We talk about Paul Schrader and how *Blue Collar*, his visceral tale of union corruption with Keitel starring alongside Richard Pryor, is one of the great films that proved inexplicably to be box-office poison.

Then – perhaps it's that time of night – the conversation turns to astrology. I give my opinion that, yes, the notion that your fate is somehow linked with one twelfth of the world's population is ludicrous, but the signs of the zodiac do provide imaginative symbols by which complex things like personality can be viewed.

'Exactly!' says Jane. 'It's not like it's something like Catholicism.'

And then, all of a sudden, the evening sours. I say that, on the contrary, I think it is rather like Catholicism, which is distinguished as a faith by its use of metaphor from the doggedly literal Protestant faith. That's why it is so attractive to artists, whether, like Salvador Dali or Pasolini, they were born to it or whether, like Waugh and Greene, they were drawn to it.

Suddenly a flood of hostility bursts forth from both Jane and Ian. Catholics all have to do exactly what the Pope tells them, they all look really daft with their smears of ash on the first day of Lent.

Another of the assembled crowd, a Catholic, joins in.

'No, I agree with Donald,' he says. 'There's a breadth of interpretation. You don't have to follow to the letter what the official notion is; you can adapt it for yourself within the framework.'

But Ian and Jane aren't having any of it, and their objections become more and more virulent. I wonder, is it just that it's difficult to accord the latitude to a familiar mysticism that you would to a comparatively esoteric one? Or is there a deep vein of prejudice here?

Whichever it is, it's clear that there are two opposing forces at work in the world today. One is federalism, in which national boundaries mean less and less. The other is the equal but opposite force of ethnicity, and the facets that define people's difference – race, religion, national extraction – are all totems to cling to in the face of a mainstream culture tending all the while towards anonymity.

It is in the midst of this flux that World Cup City is forged.

Jane and Ian and I part cordially, and promise we'll try to meet up at the ground, but we all know that something has changed.

I arrive back at my hotel.

Did a Federal Express envelope arrive for me? I ask at reception. I am expecting my other three tickets to be delivered this evening.

'An envelope?'

Yes, it's a sort of paper package that letters get sent in.

'Is the light on your telephone flashing?'

Well, I wouldn't know. I haven't been up to my room yet.

'If the light on your telephone isn't flashing, then nothing has been delivered, sir.'

One thing you begin to notice about corporate America is that when they start calling you sir you're in trouble. This is a code which means, 'I am now about to shut down all listening and logical functions and go into autopilot awkward mode.'

Look, I explain, if I go all the way up to my room and discover that my telephone is flashing, I will then have to come all the way back down here and collect the message. Could you just check, please?

She checks. No message.

I go up to my room. There is a small sweet on my bedcover, and a note telling me that my maid's name is Rosa. The telephone is flashing.

Sparing you the rest of the dialogue (I'm sure you can imagine), it isn't my tickets. It's a fax from Frau.

'You can tell the depth of a love by the silence that descends on departure', it says. I have a quiet night.

The news about Maradona was broken that day. After the classy pull-back and the perfectly placed shot, the mad face screaming into the camera, we are left with a third image of Maradona from this tournament – a legend's last trace on newsprint. It shows the medical officer leading him off the pitch for the 'random' drug test; his face looks full of sadness and resignation. It's over, Diego. The last scene is written with the hand of a medical technician in the urine of Maradona.

The last thing I hear before I go to sleep is the voice of Nicole Simpson. The infamous 911 tape is getting rotation exposure. It's the scared voice of a lone woman – Captain America is outside the window in the dark, and he wants to do her harm.

The next morning, Rosa knocks on my door. I tell her to give me a while and drift back into the luxury of sleep. When I finally surface I bump into her on my way out to a late breakfast. She's a middle-aged woman with crimped hair who still has a girlish way of moving, although she isn't petite.

'Ah,' she says, seeing my hat, 'you come for the football?' She demonstrates a kicking movement worthy of a Wimbledon defender.

'I am from Argentina,' she continues, crossing her fingers; 'it's later today.'

But no Maradona.

'No,' she says, making a clown's sad face, 'no Maradona.'

Chicago has a notably slower pace than New York, which even the run-up to the 4th of July holiday doesn't fully explain. It's also noticeably cooler, with an icy edge to the breeze that blows in from Lake Michigan.

Amidst the hard mirrored edges of downtown, the Loop of the El train is dwarfed by high-rise office buildings, like a silicon body built with a surgeon's knife around a rusty old heart. To the north are the airy malls of Michigan Avenue and the slightly surreal sense of cool blue space created by the lake. It isn't the sea, there's no appreciable waves, although the wind creates a gentle lapping at the shore. But then you can't see the other side. There's just this great quiet immensity of still water, only slightly ruffled by the breeze. The citizens of Chicago cut through the cool air of the lakeside on rollerblades, gliding serenely along the miles of waterside concrete up towards Lincoln Park.

'C'mon you boys in green!' comes a tribute to my Ireland cap. I wave back. It's all smiles in this waterside Utopia.

My only memories of Chicago from childhood were the aftermath of the Weathermen and my Dad falling prey to a rather gentlemanly mugging one night after dark in Lincoln Park. But for some reason I had the image of a fairly dense, concentrated city, something like a lakeside Manhattan.

I had it wrong. The first thing you notice after New York is that you've entered a mid-Western grid based on single strips rather than blocks. Lincoln Avenue in the Near North Side is the old Irish and bohemian area, enough bars, bookshops and restaurants to make an area the size of Greenwich Village, but instead of a concentration like that, it stretches on and on – as far as you can see there's coloured lights against the cool desert night of Chicago, but on either side there's nothing.

In Irish Eyes, a large, blonde barwoman is struggling to keep her severely drunk customers in order. It's 6.25 in the evening. This is a town for serious drinkers.

'You stubborn Irish bull,' she's yelling at one guy in an overstretched Real Men Wear Black T-shirt.

'Never mind us,' she says to me, 'we get a bit rowdy in here. Hey, you want sump'n to munch?'

And she dumps three packets of crisps next to my pint of Killihan's Red. That's Chicago; rowdy, drunken and roughly welcoming.

There's not much interest in the soccer in Irish Eyes. At least not in Argentina v Bulgaria, but they sit me at the far end of the bar with my own TV. At the end by the door they're watching baseball.

Then Charles comes along. Charles is a barman here but he's on his night off and has stopped in to have a drink and watch the game. His mother is Irish, but he was born here.

Like many of the second-generation immigrants in Chicago, he's loosely connected to Irish culture, through places like Irish Eyes, but he knows it's a distant echo. They celebrate St Patrick's night here, but only really as an excuse for a party. They have Irish bands on occasionally, 'but most of them,' says Charles, 'are cod-Irish.'

Together we watch the Maradonaless Argentina confirm Rosa's worst fears. Without him they are simply lacking in inspiration. Sirakov's final-minute strike only hammers home the blow that Stoitchkov's opener struck the team without its flawed heart.

The barmaid has finished her shift and has been replaced by a rumbustious barman with a loud voice and a psycho stare.

'There's been no trouble with hooligans so far,' he says, fixing me with a glare, 'has there? I guess the word is out – this is America, these guys have guns!'

I guess so.

'Where's Bulgaria?' he demands. 'No, wait, don't tell me, I'll guess by the faces. Eastern Europe? Yeah, I see that hungry stare!'

The telephone rings.

'Does anyone want tickets for Ireland against the Netherlands?' he bawls into the room. The crowd has drifted off and there's only about three or four customers left, besides myself and Charles.

I think about it for a moment. In the turmoil, I haven't even thought of where I'm going to be that day.

No, it would be crazy. I'd have to arrive in San Francisco, get a flight straight down to Orlando, then maybe on to Dallas, if they win, for the showdown with Brazil. I think all this aloud.

'Whadya mean, Brazil?' says the Psychostare Barman. 'It could be the US.'

The shakedown means the US are now meeting Brazil in San Francisco on 4 July. But are they going to win? Yeah, dream on.

'That's what America was built on,' says the Psychostare Barman, prodding a finger into the air a couple of inches from my chest. Then just when I think he may be serious, his eyebrow lifts slightly. 'Take that to the bank and cash it!' he finishes with a Psycholaugh.

I work out that the Holland game will be happening the day after I arrive in San Francisco, the same day as the Brazil v US game. It will be ten o'clock in Chicago. Officially Irish Eyes will be closed – the owner is going out of town for the holiday – but Charles and Psychostare will be opening it up specially. In San Francisco I will be staying at a friend's house; I don't know whether he'll have cable, I doubt he'll have the sports channel. At the time of the kick-off it will be 9 o'clock in the morning.

I feel a moment of sudden panic. I may be unable to see the game. I feel in that moment very much alone, in a very big country.

The next day I ask the hotel to put my lap-top in the safe.

'The safe?' the porter asks me, like I'd requested him to jump up and down on top of it for me.

Yes, it's like a cupboard with a lock on it.

'It's a bit big for the safe [it measures about eighteen inches by twelve], but we could lock it up for you,' he says.

I think that's the general principle, I reply, through tensed lips. I have a sensation of observing my own mental state from some distance. That's interesting, I reflect; I feel an overwhelming urge to strangle this man. It is a phenomenon I have observed before, a breed of psychosis engendered by having everything you say repeated in a tone that veers between disdain and disbelief.

I have also noticed supplementary symptoms, like last night I woke up in the middle of the night wondering where the light in the corner of my hotel room was. The light is, presumably, back where it always was, in the hotel in Queens. I have just mixed the hotels up. It's OK, I've had this before. I've never killed anyone. Yet.

It's too late for breakfast, so I order lunch instead.

'Super salad,' says the waitress, and stares at me expectantly, looking like she not only thinks this is a sensible thing to say but also expects an answer.

Oh, really, is it? I think of saying, that's nice.

She repeats herself, widening the gap in the side of her mouth through which she speaks.

'*Soup er salad?*' she says again.

Oh, soup, please.

I read the first line of Theroux's book. 'On West Adams, just inside the Loop, he was almost killed.'

As far as I can work out, this refers to the exact point at which my hotel is situated. This does not seem like a good omen.

But, after two more telephone calls to Roger in LA, the rest of my tickets finally turn up. I take a quick look at them. They haven't been upgraded, as promised, but at least they're here.

Feeling slightly appeased, I go to the tourist information centre for a map.

'A map?' repeats the man behind the counter.

Yes, it's a kind of scaled down facsimile of the city in two dimensions.

He survives, just.

In my current condition, making sense of any public transport network would no doubt prove problematic, so it is perhaps unkind to say that the El map is entirely incomprehensible, but as someone who prides themselves in never having taken the wrong train on the New York system, I couldn't work it out.

'How late are you going to be out?' asks the man at the ticket office, after refusing to sell me a return journey, for reasons I couldn't be bothered to figure out.

I don't know, why?

'Oh, no reason.'

Going to the south of Chicago has the same sort of stigma as going to Brooklyn. It's equally difficult to estimate how much this is to do with reputation and how much with genuine danger. On the way out, at least, there was no threat in the air, just a carriage load of ordinary-looking working people on their way home.

I get out at Halsted and take a walk around what is reputed an Italian area. But the sensation is not so much one of changing countries, as I experienced in New York, as of changing times. With its strip of boarded-up hardware stores and launderettes and museum pieces like 'Let's Groove' records, where you can imagine the seven-inches from Stateside Records delivered hot from the presses, this is like travelling back at least twenty years from the broad boulevards of Downtown.

But there's no more sign of partisan football support here than there is up there. Despite its reputation for being the town where the ethnic groups never merged, wherever I go in Chicago I see T-shirts, hats and posters that celebrate the competition itself, not one particular country. The one exception is an African bookshop in the South Loop which has a window display: 'Stay Black – follow Nigeria & Cameroon.'

I take a left and head down towards the White Sox stadium, which stands on its own amidst a huge radius of hard-edged concrete. A game is about to start and the fans are rolling in with a leisurely pace quite unlike the tense anticipation you feel in the air at a football game.

Taking the train back towards the centre of the town, I stop off for dinner in Chinatown. Unlike the dense warrens of New York, here the pagodas and tassels are built around a broad highway. This is a place to drive out to, not to lose yourself in.

My Singapore Sling is delivered to the table in a china model of a giant panda.

On the way back on the train the atmosphere is different – I am the only white face in the carriage, sitting, trying to pretend to myself that I don't feel conspicuous.

Grant Park by the lakeside really is a different world as I sit at the Marina and watch the sun going down behind the reef of the skyline.

Back at the hotel, two teenagers are on TV being interviewed about their sex lives and putting up with moralistic outpourings from the audience. What you can't work out is why the kids put up with it. Why go on television to have a roomful of people of no fixed expertise mess around in your 'private' life?

I've found myself watching these shows enough to worry me. I've seen the man who slept with both the daughter and the mother, I've seen the two sisters, one of them a heroin addict. I've seen whole panels of manipulative men and freeloading women. The process of watching the presenter's horror-struck face always makes me think of a country probing for some semblance of a moral, like an old junkie trying to hit a vein.

Then we have the highlights of the O.J. Simpson arraignment. Wherever I've been today, the drama has been buzzing away in the background. Hearing the description of the knife that was the alleged murder weapon, I'm struck by how the fastidious detail of the legal procedure begins to sound like fetishism as soon as it is broadcast to an audience.

Unable to stand much more of this diet, I take a taxi down to Buddy Guy's Legends, the Blues club owned by the celebrated guitarist. That's the other part of the Chicago myth – the Blues. It wasn't the birthplace, but this was where the Blues, brought up with the black emigrants from the Mississippi Delta, met electricity.

The atmosphere in Buddy Guy's is convincingly downbeat – there's a row of pool tables in the back, whose clatter provides an offbeat counterpoint to the driving rhythm from the stage. Lamps in the shape of huge Budweiser bottles hang over the tables casting down capes of light tinged blue by smoke. You almost expect Paul Newman in his *Hustler* role to walk in. Almost.

There's two bands on the bill tonight, an all-white support band who knock out a tough set of a music they clearly love, and the headline, Eddie Chah and the Wolf Gang, who remind you without wishing to that it's a long time since the heyday of the Blues, and play old standards like 'Little Red Rooster' with an impressive force but at a pace that makes them sound more like a litany than a sexual growl.

At the more dance-music-orientated clubs, Chicago's tradition of the clash between the downhome and the technological continues. In more recent history Chicago is the place where computerized dance music burst out of its chrysalis; Chicago rocked the house and the whole world jacked their collective body.

When Stuart Cosgrove visited the city in 1986 for the *New Musical Express* he seemed disappointed to learn that the music he cherished as 'black music' was influenced as much by the European syne-drum march of Can and Kraftwerk as it was by the call and response routines of the downhome religion, which can still be seen rocking the networks late at night. It was this that Dele Fadele, the *NME*'s one black writer of the time, meant when he told Cosgrove, 'There's no such thing as "black music",' much to Cosgrove's embarrassment.

Chicago as a city almost seems to represent this clash in its architecture, with the downhome South Side lapping up against the hi-tech towers of Downtown, and in the mesmerizing electronic beats that wash out of my hotel radio day and night, the soundtrack to this schizophrenic city.

Turning on my television on returning to the hotel, I am amazed to find they're showing the movie *Jagged Edge* in which Jeff Bridges is accused of murdering his wife with a hunting knife. In England such a piece of programming would come up only as coincidence and promptly be scotched as 'distasteful'; in the States they probably dusted it down deliberately as a tie-in.

Sweet dreams, America.

The day of the match, Rosa knocks on my door, just as I'm getting ready. Thinking she wants to make up the room, I look out and tell her I'll be ten minutes.

'Oh, it's OK,' she says, and thrusts a handful of picture postcards of Bebeto, John Aldridge and others into my hand.

I find this small gesture particularly touching.

If there's been a cool edge to the wind in my first days in Chicago, the day of the game a big chill descends. There's a mist hanging over Grant Park as I join the procession that is congregating on Soldier Field.

The football fans have nothing like the presence in Chicago that they had in New York. I saw two German fans on my first day, the first of what I assumed would be many, but that was it. Apparently many of them are staying in hotels outside the city and coming in only for the games. Today, on match day, Chicago is transformed abruptly into World Cup City.

And the first thing you notice about this crowd is that it is truly international. There is a noticeable presence of the German colours of black, red and gold, but many of the bearers, when you get closer, turn out to have American accents. Some of those

I speak to have German ancestry, but it isn't generally anything they've thought about until the World Cup came to town. They are supporting Germany, as much because they are the biggest team to be passing through as for the sake of Grandmother Erika and Grandfather Heinrich. Some of them have no national connection at all; they have picked on Germany for the same constellation of personality indicators and sheer coincidences that draws someone to a club side in England.

Most of us in this televisual age would not expect a Leeds United fan to come from Leeds. I can't resist saying that we would be positively surprised if a Manchester United supporter had any more connection with the city than a collection of Happy Mondays records. We are accustomed to seeing the shirts of Milan, Internazionale and Lazio on kids who have simply fastened on to a team through the medium of television, much as many of my generation did, without considering the distance from which these images were beamed in. But for some reason, in an age of multi-nationals, we cling to the idea that a national team should be racially pure and that the qualifications for membership of the supporters' club depend preferably on birth-place and as a last resort on recent genetic memory.

From the perspective of America the participants of the World Cup are teams, and you can choose to root for who you please. After all, this is the land of the free.

But the Soldier Field game, more than the ones in New York, was also something else – it was a gathering of the football fans of Chicago. Amongst the German flags, and the odd Belgian, there were others wearing colours of teams from far away. Like Tony in New York, who had put on his Crystal Palace shirt not so much as a gesture of support for ex-Eagle Eddie as because this was a football match, for football matches you wear your replica shirt, and out here there's precious little chance of that.

So English exiles have dug deep into their closets and dusted down their Chelsea blue, their QPR hoops, and come out to see Germany playing Belgium. Of course they wish England were playing here today. But the World Cup has come to their adopted town, and they're out in their colours to see the game.

And it isn't just the English. Every now and then a Mexican flag will dance past you, borne as high as they can manage by a group of tiny Chicago Mexicans. There's people here from Poland, hustling with the scalpers for tickets for the later rounds, there's a small group of Japanese doing nothing to explode national stereotypes by pointing their camcorders at the spectacle, and at each other. 'Look, there's you filming me, filming you, with a crowd of football fans in the background.' There's almost as many Irish fans here as there were Italians at Giants Stadium.

And of course there's the Germans, the real bonafide Deutschlanders. There's a blond boy in Lederhosen walking across the bridge shouting 'Hello! Hello!' and waving, and an old guy in a World War I helmet, and all around there are impromptu brass band processions of overweight men in replica shirts. I should say at this point that I don't share the clichéd view of Germany as a nation. The old Berlin was one of my favourite cities, full of clever, sophisticated people with a sharp, ironic sense of humour. I even call my wife Frau, although neither of us is German, in a homage to that land of Dietrich, Brecht, Syberberg and Wenders.

But it is difficult in this crowd, which looks like it's been imported from some spiritual Bavaria, to dismiss the significations of these images – that you expect the boy in the Lederhosen to break out any second into a chorus of 'Tomorrow Belongs to Me'. There is also the simple fact that the Oompah band is just not as seductive to the outsider as the samba drums of Brazil.

Soldier Field was built to commemorate the dead of World War II, but as a military monument it has the pseudo-classical grandeur that Hitler's architect Albert Speer was so fond of, with its rows of pillars and its imperial boxes built high above the pitch.

In fact this grandeur is one of the reasons why the spectacular piece of power architecture has become a slightly decaying mausoleum. The boxes are too far away from the field of play to attract the corporate market, who want to be close to the action, not viewing from the rulers' perspective of height and distance. The Chicago Bears, whose home ground this is, play here only a handful of times a year. A few capacity World Cup games has staved off economic collapse, for now.

By kick-off the wind is icy and a thick layer of cloud has settled over the stadium. I take my seat a few seats away from a small Belgian division decked out in red wigs. In front is the most vocal section of the German support.

As the teams are announced the Belgians try to put up a brave show, roaring at every name, except, for some reason, the defender Emmers.

Then comes an announcement which puts such considerations into perspective.

'There will now be a moment's silence for the Colombian defender Andrés Escobar, who died early this morning in tragic circumstances.'

The television this morning had been dominated by the O.J. Simpson case. What did they mean, tragic circumstances?

The hush falls. But in the land of the shrinking attention span, when they say a moment they mean a moment. There is no time to consider how long a minute lasts in perfect quiet. The teams just break away and the hubbub starts again.

When the game starts, I find it difficult to imagine why the Belgian defence should have been so difficult to breach hitherto. The Germans seem to walk through it for the first goal, Matthäus crossing for the totally unmarked Völler to nod in. But then, bizarrely, the Belgians are level within minutes: a speculative shot from Grun, looping over Illgner's head and into the net to have the Belgians attempting to project their tonsils towards the far side of Soldier Field again.

Germany, realizing how easy it had been to score the first, simply go out and score another, Völler beating two and laying off to Klinsmann whose task in finishing is no more difficult than Völler's had been five minutes earlier. The game is eleven minutes old. Still, the *Chicago Tribune* tomorrow will whinge about soccer as a low-scoring, non-eventful sport.

The Belgians are subdued again, knowing that if the equalizer came from the realms of the unlikely a second one is asking their team to score two for the first time in the competition. As if to emphasize the fact, a slow drizzle begins. The man selling plastic capes is doing a roaring trade; the unfortunate who's trying to peddle ice-filled Cokes to a shivering crowd slightly less so.

Germany threaten to score several times before Völler makes it three, and the Belgians are looking resigned. The American family on my left, meanwhile, are having a whale of a time. They're all carrying German flags, but only the little girl seems to distinguish between events at either end.

The dad is bellowing advice and encouragement to both teams. 'Shoot it!' he counsels whenever the ball reaches the danger area. 'There it is!' he points out as either defence opens out, and 'You betcha!' as either goalkeeper is forced into a save.

Like their compatriots in New York, they seem to be fascinated by the length of the goal-kicks.

'Sometimes the goalie kicks it all the way into the other goal,' the dad tells the daughter. 'Imagine that.'

It wouldn't count, I point out, having come over all pedantic.

The dad gives me a look that is part hurt, part resentful. The daughter looks sceptical. The mother, though, is interested. 'Really?'

Yes, a goal-kick is indirect; the only time there was a goal from one was once when the opposing goalkeeper touched it on the way in.

The dad gives the daughter an 'I told you so' look and turns his attention to the Oompah band behind us.

'Yeah!' he bellows. 'Let's get the drums goin', Deutschland.'

Then a Mexican wave starts which he greets with massive enthusiasm.

I have to confess I've always thought the Mexican wave a trifle daft. What changed my mind was a reference in the *Chicago Tribune* again, which described this harmless piece of fun as being 'in defiance of dignity and local habit'. Well, sod you, parochial son of a bitch. If you want our money to boost the income of your bars, restaurants and hotels, and to stave off the bulldozers from your stadium, you'll just have to put up with a Mexican wave or six, even if it's not what you do around here.

I stand up and make a fool of myself with the rest of them, defiantly.

At the half-time break I meet a German in a Celtic shirt, who won't let go of my hand when he hears I'm from Glasgow. But otherwise it is difficult to do anything other than spectate on the German party. Unlike the Irish or the Brazilians they are not keen to encourage you to join in. This is their moment, the enjoyment of it is their birthright. Not yours.

Still nobody I speak to knows what Escobar's tragic circumstances are.

Then in the second half we witness once again the great German collapse, as Belgium begin to recover some control over their play, and Germany begin to look anything but confident, despite their two-goal lead.

By the time Weber is dumped to the ground as he was raising his leg to shoot on a lone Illgner, the sympathy of the neutral crowd has swung in Belgium's favour. None of the Americans around me can understand a decision that's evidently so bad. The referee is twenty or thirty yards away from the play and partially sighted, but he is still too arrogant to even think of consulting his linesman. I wish I could say it's a long time since I've seen a decision as ridiculous, but it isn't. No wonder there's a call for a second referee with a video monitor in the stand. Talk about undermining the referee's authority is nonsensical when they constantly put their own competence so much in doubt.

Within seconds Völler is on the floor, rolling around feigning injury. The whole stadium is filled with the sound of booing and you realize just how neutral this crowd is. Now everybody, except the die-hard nationals, wants Belgium to pull off a miracle comeback. Oh, and the little girl next to me.

'I just want Belgium to score so we'll get extra time,' Mom explains to her. The little girl just grips her flag a little tighter. She isn't convinced.

They threaten enough times, but by the time Albert shoots

home from close range, not even the red-wigged ones believe Belgium can do it. As the final whistle comes, three of them wrap themselves in their flag and try to hide from the cold.

Mentally they are clicking their red heels together and saying, 'There's no place like home.' Tomorrow they will have vanished from World Cup City.

Outside the stadium, the Germans are dancing, the Mexicans singing. Finally I find out the fate of Escobar.

He was shot??!!!

'Yeah,' the Mexican tells me, 'but it wasn't to do with football. It was the gangs, the corruption.'

One of the theories about conspiracies is that we like them because they are comforting. The idea that there is one secret that will explain everything if only we can figure it out is more acceptable than the alternative – that life really is a confusion of single incidents, none of which is connected to any meaningful pattern.

In the case of Andrés Escobar it is preferable to think of the player being tangled up with some complicated betting plot, one so complicated it seems to defy all the rules of gambling, than to consider the alternative – that this passion we kindle can burn so hot it can lead to murder.

But think of the venom you can spit at a hopeless forward. Just think about it.

The next day, I check out of the hotel. On the way down the hallway, I run into Rosa again.

'Today is the big day for Argentina,' she says, holding two hands up with fingers crossed. 'I go home soon to watch it.'

She is almost levitating with excitement. I wish her luck and wave goodbye.

At the airport I read the *Chicago Tribune* for the last time. They have an article on the success of the Saudi Arabia team, focusing on the financial investment that has transformed them into a force to be taken seriously in world soccer. Perhaps, it postulates, one day we will see the headline: 'Saudis buy Italy's Baggio for $20 million and six oil wells.'

It seems interesting to me that the US press simply don't understand how national sports work. This isn't an isolated incident, either. The New York press had referred to supporters complaining about the amount of money the Italian team had paid for Baggio, not realizing that international teams don't pay for players. Also I see more than one reference to the American stars who will be leaving the country after the tournament, implying that they will no longer be able to play for the US team.

Their idea is that your nationality is defined entirely by where you live.

But then, in the case of the *Tribune*, ignorance is a quality they display with nauseous regularity. In another part of the paper they run a list of 'Things we won't miss about the World Cup' which includes: 'Soccer fans moaning about how their dog's breath sport doesn't get enough attention.'

It seems a shame that a city that has welcomed the competition so warmly should be let down so badly by the narrow provincialism of its newspaper.

Things I won't miss about Chicago – guess what's number one?

5

Samba Partying in Suffragette City

While I'm in the air, Dumitrescu and Hagi tear apart Argentina and break Rosa's heart. Hearts are broken daily nowadays in World Cup City.

I am met at the airport in San Francisco by Ken Prestininzi.

Ken is a playwright, a friend of Frau's – they once spent six weeks as guests of the bean million-heiress Drue Heinz in her writer's retreat castle in Scotland. Much of Frau's leisure time was devoted to joyously driving the social-climbing administrator, Dr McLeer, as close as possible to a mental breakdown; Ken was her partner in this service to humanity.

I'd met Ken only once and was surprised when he offered me the spare room in his apartment for my stay in San Francisco. But having spent three weeks starting conversations with complete strangers, he seems like an old friend, despite the difficulty we have in recognizing one another.

As we drive back to the city, with the San Francisco Bay out to our right, Ken laughs uproariously at my first impressions of Chicago.

Well, I was only there for a few days, I say, it's always difficult to judge. I'm very conscious that when Americans write about England, Bog Brush Buford being a good example here, they tend to get it wrong.

'Well, I don't know,' says Ken. 'I lived there for ten years and I think you've got it about right. It is a place with a tremendous chip on its shoulder. There is this thing called the "Mid-West" and Chicago is very conscious of itself as being the focal point of the Mid-West. It has a very strong work ethic and a dedicatedly non-pretentious attitude which can get seriously irritating.' He laughs again, probably from bitter experience.

'San Francisco is very different.'

This is immediately apparent as we park the car and my things, and take a walk around the famous Haight. Ken lives on the Lower Haight, a more downbeat area than the celebrated section a mile or so down the road where Haight crosses Ashbury. Lower Haight is the centre of a lot of the black population, and there's often a distinct edge to the atmosphere, particularly at the corner of Buchanan which is a big hangout late at night. You can feel a slight bristle as you walk through, and sometimes you'll get a slightly ironic greeting. But, as with most places, the threat turns out to be superficial. At least as far as I'm concerned.

Another friend tells me that a lot of people she knows have been mugged down here. But as Ken says, here as in New York 'You're more likely to get mugged if you look like you deserve it.'

We walk past a bar called 'the Mad Dog in the Fog'.

'That's a big Irish hangout,' says Ken. 'Maybe we should check it out later.'

But for now we walk on. The thing that surprises you, when you've only heard about the gentrification of the Haight, is that it still has, like Portobello Road in London or the Village in New York, any of its bohemian atmosphere. But it does.

'I think they've worked very hard to maintain that. You'll find there's a Gap store on the Haight Ashbury crossing, basically because that is just such a big company there's no way of keeping them out, but in general there's a lot of effort put in to make sure that the shops are in keeping with what is regarded as the spirit of the Haight.'

There's a distinctly European feel to the city, from its predominantly white architecture and its cool sun to the visible café culture.

'Yes,' says Ken, 'you see what I mean about the difference from Chicago? When my parents came here they were genuinely shocked that the bars and the cafés could be packed during the day. My Dad would say, "But where are these people's *jobs*, where do they *work*?" It's just not like that out here.'

He's keen to know what my image of San Francisco was prior to arrival.

Comfortable and weird around the edges, I say.

He laughs again. 'Hey,' he says, 'you're really good at this!'

It isn't difficult, in fact my view of the city comes wholesale from Hitchcock's *Vertigo*, perhaps his strangest and most poetic film, and one of those movies where the city is the lead character. James Stewart is the height-sick central character, who is tricked into an obsession not with a woman but with a ghost of the old bohemian days of San Francisco. The city, in Hitchcock's vision, is full of ghosts. It is San Francisco itself, the memory contained in its broad empty streets, the strange beauty of its buildings, which conspires to haunt Stewart, a man attempting to lose his own past only to find himself ensnared in the past of another. The plot, as Chris Marker points out in the tribute to the film contained in his brilliant film-essay *Sunless*, is too labyrinthine to convey to anyone who has not seen the film – even when you've seen it four or five times your own grip on it can falter because, like memory and obsession, it is deceptive. The film creates its own echoes, its own ghosts. Everyone within it is trying to shake off the past – the only one who succeeds does so at the expense of committing a murder. Walking round the city, it is impossible to shake off the feeling of the film.

San Francisco has created a few more ghosts since then. The Haight is still associated with the Summer of Love, but San Francisco also had its part to play in the Summer of Hate that was 1969, when the nihilism and psychosis of the seventies burst out of the multi-coloured chrysalis of the sixties.

The Haight was the place where Charles Manson recruited his Family, preying on the innocence and gullibility of the American youth who were drawn to the site of the psychedelic revolution and looking for a leader now that it was too late to catch the

Magic Bus. Once he had his brood of bewitched females, he took them out to the desert and the murder of Sharon Tate was conceived.

On the outskirts of San Francisco is Altamont where the violence that underpinned the Rolling Stones' mojo finally burst through to the surface as Hell's Angels took pool cues and baseball bats to hippies with peace signs, and a knife to a young black boy.

The decade of Seconol, The Stooges and The Sex Pistols was born.

But for now my concern is with the immediate future and how I'm going to get to see Ireland play Holland for a place in the Quarter-Final of the World Cup. Returning to Ken's apartment, overlooking the Bay Bridge, we make a call to the Mad Dog in the Fog. They are opening tomorrow morning at eight. It's fixed.

We head over to Chinatown for dinner. There's a thrill to filling in the blanks of places you have heard about but have never seen. Chinatown is a symbol of a broader middle-Asian influence in San Francisco, deriving from the historical links that physical proximity brings but replenished by the growth of Silicon Valley, one of the major US centres of the computer industry.

Wandering up into the hills above where Chinatown meets the Italian sector, you can find yourself, just for an instant, in a mini-Japan, with two or three houses built in oriental style surrounded by the distinctive stunted firs of a Japanese garden – then a few paces on you swoop down a hill and the mood changes again.

There's a subtlety to the design of everything in San Francisco. The neon is all cool blue and muted red, floating serenely in the night like an echo from an era of late-night drifting jazz and Edward Hopper pools of haunted fluorescence. Like Paris or Prague, it's a city that seems to maintain its atmosphere by some magical trick of time – a city composed of many parts which nevertheless has a sense of being a single entity, a sense that London, for example, has lost.

Between Chinatown and the Italian section is City Lights

Bookshop. The Beat Generation was really born in New York, where three would-be writers, Jack Kerouac, William Burroughs and Allen Ginsberg, shared an apartment off Times Square. But the Beat was first broadcast to the world from here, when Kerouac's 'mad to live, mad to love, mad to be saved' novel *On The Road* and Ginsberg's 'Howl' to the 'angel-headed hipsters' were first published by Lawrence Ferlinghetti.

Next door, the bar where some legendary drinking sessions took place also holds its memories within the walls. You can see why the Catholic Kerouac would have liked it. With its bar lights, the colour of stained glass windows, hanging in the gloom, its dark wood and its gallery, it has the hallowed atmosphere of a church – together with an impressive array of spirits of the more down-to-earth type. It still seems like a place where people get blind drunk and manage to talk about poetry regardless.

For an hour or so I even forget about World Cup City.

For Adrian and for Sylvie it's twelve noon in Orlando, but for me it's a cold and misty nine in the morning in San Francisco as I drag myself, with great reluctance, out of bed and hurry around the corner to the Mad Dog in the Fog, just in time for the kick-off.

Watching anything at this time in the morning is a strange experience; the images your brain takes in seem to join seamlessly on to your dreams. But it's clear before my coffee has been delivered over the bar that this is no dream. This is a nightmare.

There is an early opening for Staunton, but when the chance falls to a player who has not done a thing right for the whole tournament, you just know that someone is going to step up and get in the way. Once the pattern of play has settled, two things are apparent. The first is that the lackadaisical Holland who scrambled their way past Saudi Arabia have found their motivation and their pace, with Van Vossen making Gary Kelly prove his growing reputation as a speedy full-back, and Overmars making Terry Phelan look like he is running through thicker air.

I have scarcely sat down when Phelan nods the ball feebly back in the general direction of Bonner, and Overmars is on to it. Babb gives chase, leaving Bergkamp unmarked in the middle and a silly goal is given away.

Some prat at the bar with an English accent and a partial harelip, wearing leather trousers in a forlorn stab at sex appeal, is holding forth. Hearing the commentator eulogizing the danger of the Dutch team, he starts on a predictable spiel about how Ireland are OK playing their defensive football against inferior teams, but against an outfit with class like the Dutch . . . etc., etc. All of which is total nonsense from start to finish.

Firstly, in case no one had noticed, the Irish haven't been playing particularly defensive football in this World Cup; even against Norway it was the opposition who sat back and made it look, however illogically, that they were playing for a draw. Secondly, if they're only effective against inferior teams, how come they beat Italy? And if Holland are such a superior team, how come the Republic beat them in the warm up?

Really the Republic's problems are clear enough. Phelan, who has disappointed enough at Manchester City to be out of the team and on the transfer list, isn't really up to it, despite the impeccable game he played against the Italians, and the midfield is composed of the walking wounded.

Then there's the lack of a real front man, which leaves the two best chances coming to the head of . . . Ray Houghton. Once again, you don't really hold your breath. Well you do, but not with any real conviction.

Even so, the battling spirit could still have won through had Ireland not shot themselves in the other foot too. Jonk's shot just before half-time is no more than a hopeful punt, but Packie Bonner is caught quite by surprise and flaps at it like a schoolboy who's been too busy watching the girls play hockey to notice the shot coming. And you know it's over. Adrian's words from the Top 32 Club come back to me.

'I just have a feeling he's going to let us down.'

Somewhere in a stadium in overcast Orlando, he's wishing he hadn't been proved right.

The prat at the bar goes on about how Romania are the best team he's seen, because 'they have the best counter-defence'.

'What's a counter-defence?' asks Michael, an Irish guy from Cork who's sitting behind me.

I don't think he knows, I reply. Romania will be playing Sweden in the Quarter-Final, the next game I have a ticket for. I'm looking forward to seeing the team that now has everyone talking. But awesome though their performance against Argentina might have been, it isn't just irritation at the prat in the bar that makes me suspicious of Romania. I remember those early games too well.

The matches were largely unseen in England, but none of the US pundits (self-appointed or otherwise) seems to remember an unexceptional Swiss team tearing them apart, or the faltering performance against the US. All the same, I hope they sweep away my reservations with a display of power and fluidity.

There is one thing we like better than being right in World Cup City, and that is being entertained.

Meanwhile, for some reason, they're showing the goals from the 1966 World Cup Final. A massive cheer goes up, and I realize what in a state of complete wakefulness I might have realized an hour ago. The Mad Dog in the Fog is a reference to Noël Coward. This isn't an Irish bar. It's an English bar.

I take a look around me. There's an Aston Villa shirt behind the bar, Watney's Red Barrel (which I believed to have ceased to exist years ago) on tap, and a Rangers scarf above the Celtic one on the far wall.

Michael, his friend Sean and myself are the only Celts in here.

'Ireland have never scored more than one goal in their World Cup history,' the commentator is telling us.

'We're here to make history,' says Michael.

All right! I shout and we slap hands.

But we both know it's a gesture.

With an hour or so gone, they show a replay of the first goal. A few who have looked away from the screen for a minute or so look back and see the ball going into the net the Irish are attacking and cheer what they think is a Dutch own goal. But realization dawns soon enough.

Paul McGrath does get the ball in the net, but it's in the last minute and it's disallowed anyway.

Some minutes later, I have to point this out to the prat and his friend who are still celebrating long enough after to make it annoying.

'There was nothing wrong with that!' he opines, despite the fact that the replay shows McGrath nearly taking a Dutch player's ear off with his studs. Even McGrath gives a little smile to himself when he sees the decision.

It's eleven o'clock in the morning. I'm awake now, and Ireland are out of the World Cup.

'I just came in here because I live around the corner,' Michael tells me. 'The real Irish centre is down on Geary. But I'm glad I'm not there; it'll be all tears, I'll tell you.'

Ken gives me a lift down to Geary to watch the US v Brazil game, but if tears there were they've been mopped up in time for the second kick-off, and amongst the Irish contingent there's more of a mood of quiet resignation and a lingering sense of disbelief. Maybe we'll all wake up soon, and the match won't have happened.

A large part of the crowd in Kitty O'Shea's, though, is American. Not entirely surprisingly, given the name. Katherine O'Shea, nicknamed Kitty, was the mistress of Charles Parnell, the great campaigner for a United Ireland, but it was his affair with her, a married woman, that brought about his downfall.

On returning home, I will be surprised to discover that this game is seen as a signal of Brazil's inferiority not only to the 1970 team (an impossible comparison in the first place) but also to the current Romania. If anyone suspects that my conviction that the Brazil of Romario and Bebeto would crush the Romania of Hagi and Dumitrescu is informed by hindsight, they may address requests for verification to the Prat in the Leather Trousers, the Mad Dog in the Fog, Haight St, SF CAL. Because from my seat in Kitty O'Shea's, their all-out assault on a defensively minded American team looks a great deal more convincing than Romania's attempts against the same opposition.

If anyone was wondering where the luck of the Irish was today, there was one simple answer. The Americans had it, because despite the US packing the entire team behind the ball, the Brazilians manage to produce enough chances for a rout. The American supporters I talk to are just here for a party, they don't dare even dream that their team could breach the underestimated defensive powers of the Brazilians. What this is all about is how long the US can last out.

Mauro Silva heads wide from five yards and the crowd whoops. Romario heads against the post and there's a cry of 'Whooooow!' I realize what all this reminds me of. It's a rodeo! Brazil is the bucking bull which we know is going to throw the cowboy, but it's fun watching just how long he can hold on for.

For an instant the US begin to play it around a bit, inspired by an audacious back-heel as Brazil begin to show their frustration, but as the first half comes to an end Brazil come back again and again. After a continuous wave of attacks, which the American defence can only parry, Meola gets his hands on the ball at last and the relief is tangible.

Then Leonardo finally loses his temper after being held off by Ramos, and delivers an elbow to the ear. The referee delivers a red card.

Now there's a thought beginning to dawn in the bar that maybe this could be America's day. After all, this is the fourth of July.

Romario hits the post once more, just for good measure, before half-time and applause breaks out around the bar.

The second half continues just as the first half finished. Romario squeezes the ball over Meola and it's heading into the net – there are squawks and screams – but then from nowhere Dooley appears to scoop it clear and the crowd cheers like the cavalry is coming.

A drunk bursts in through the door.

'No score?' he asks. 'Shit!' and slams it shut again.

'Thanks for stopping by, pal!' the barman shouts after him. 'A fine example of the American male!' he eulogizes.

Then Romario rounds Meola and (screams) places his shot (squawks) . . . into the side netting.

Once again around the half-way mark the Brazilians begin to look exasperated. It seems like they're thinking slower than usual and the passing has lost its exhilarating pace.

Then Romario turns provider, running down the right flank. He centres for Bebeto who takes it perfectly, and slowly the ball rolls into the net, and this time the screams are followed by hush.

The final whistle blows and there's an 'Ahhhh', followed by a round of applause, and then a lull.

'Hey!' says the barman. 'I've got the Giants game!' and life and the fourth of July go on.

A little further down the road, I stop in another bar, whose title makes its sentiments quite clear. It's called Ireland's 32, a reference to the number of counties a united Ireland would have. Inside it's even clearer. Posters around the wall carry slogans like: 'Stop the strip searches in Armagh' and 'Oppose State terrorism in Ireland'. Behind the bar are books on the IRA, Bobby Sands and the SAS in Ireland.

Here, amidst the ashes of disbelief, the Irish party is beginning again in an attempt to prove that the 'win, lose or draw' promise holds true. Van Morrison is booming on the jukebox and two girls in Ireland shirts are swinging one another around on the dance floor, singing along and punching the air with beer bottles.

I'm sitting at the bar, watching a sour-faced barmaid try to deal with a clientele that's already getting out of order at two o'clock in the afternoon.

Standing next to me is John, who's berating her for not giving him a free drink.

'I've been drinking here all morning,' he says. And by the looks of him I'd take him at his word.

Are they giving you a hard time? I ask her.

'No,' she replies, without breaking a brow made of concrete, 'I'm loving every minute of it.'

She must be one of the kind that believes in bullying the customers into leaving bigger tips.

'It's hard, isn't it?' says John, in my direction.

I look over.

'Living in America.'

He tells me he's from Waterford, he's been out here for two years. 'Trying to make me fortune,' he laughs.

What business you in?

'Lifting furniture.'

So we discuss the game for a bit, and then before we both get too depressed we have another drink. I put The Pogues 'Fairytale of New York' on the jukebox. This always reminds me of driving through Glencoe with Frau one Christmas time. As we looked out of the car at the haunted, windswept majesty of the pass, Frau said: 'I wonder if you can get a hot dog anywhere?' I collapsed with laughter. But round the next corner was a lay-by, and we pulled in. Parked in the corner was what looked like a disused bus, but inside they were selling caramel wafers, macaroon bars, tablet . . . and hot dogs. This song was on the radio.

'C'mon,' says John, catching my faraway look, 'it's no time to get maudlin.'

So we have another drink.

We're half-way through this one when John taps me on the arm. A girl standing behind us is bending over to pick up something from the floor. John makes the pained face of frustrated lust at me.

'When I get drunk,' he says, 'I'm dying for my hole.'

Now John seems like a nice enough guy, and he's been buying his round and all that, but he's already confided in me that he's been on a three-day bender, during which he's not had a bath or a shave. But even if he hadn't told me, I could have guessed the cause, and certainly the symptoms I'd noticed for myself. So I just nod and smile, thinking he's as much chance of scoring as Tommy Coyne does of a transfer to A.C. Milan.

Then I come back from the Gents and there he is with two girls perched on the bar stools next to him.

Suzanne and Joanne are friends from Phoenix. Joanne works

for an accountancy firm here in San Francisco, so when Suzanne came to music college here, she moved in to share her apartment.

I tell them I've always wanted to go to Phoenix.

They want to know why.

I tell them it's something to do with the way Jodie Foster says 'Phoenix is Weird City' in Martin Scorsese's *Alice Doesn't Live Here Anymore*.

They look at me like they think I'm strange.

'So what do you do?' they ask John.

'I'm training to be a doctor,' he tells them, without blinking.

When Joanne turns to talk to Suzanne for a moment, John leans behind my back and says, 'Which one do you want?' thereby echoing Johnny Boy in *Mean Streets*.

'I'm married,' I tell him. 'I'm just kidding around.'

'Jeez,' says John, 'don't tell them that.'

So I don't. Instead I just hold my left hand up a lot, and start playing with my ring as though absent-mindedly. John tells me he's after Suzanne, but before long he's huddling up close to Joanne, who seems more interested.

'It's a hard city to meet people in,' Suzanne says to me.

Really? It seems quite sociable to me.

'Oh, it is,' she says, 'but everyone's gay.'

She goes on to tell me that Joanne, whose grandparents were Irish, has a longstanding ambition to marry an Irishman and go back to Ireland with him. I figure that John's idea would be more like marrying a rich American woman and settling out here for his retirement.

They ask me to join them to watch the fireworks for the fourth down at the bay. Joanne wants Suzanne to come, so that she won't be left alone with John, and John wants me to come along so that he won't be outnumbered.

John is telling them how much he made, shifting furniture with a bunch of Paddies last week, the proceeds of which he's presumably been drinking for the past few days.

'But don't you have to do your hospital training during the summer?' asks Joanne.

180

'Oh, you can do that,' he replies, remembering the line he's spun them and trying to keep a straight face, 'but you won't make any money at it.' Then he stuffs a piece of bread in his mouth in a doomed attempt to stop laughing. The breadcrumbs spray all over the table.

John assures them that he'll be taking a cab back over to Pacifica, the infamously foggy district where he lives, after the fireworks. But there's a distinct gleam in his eye.

We take a bus over to the girls' apartment. A Chinese punk gets on with two thin antennae of hair extending a foot above his head. In New York this would not seem like a surprise, but somehow in quaint San Francisco it seems like a genuinely surreal sight.

'Is this a bed?' asks John, investigating the sofa.

'Yes, but don't get any ideas,' says Joanne. A bit late for that, I feel.

I am caught between a feeling that I can't stand to see any more, and a voyeuristic curiosity. But I am also curious to see a fourth of July celebration at close quarters. My only memory of the last one I saw was looking out of a window in New York and seeing a limousine pulling up in front of the apartment building. The window came down and a skeletal hand, like something attached to a Disney villain, came out and dropped an unidentified device into a dustbin that was standing on the sidewalk.

As the car drew away, the dustbin exploded. This seemed to me like the epitome of controlled abandon, a ghoulish way of joining in the fireworks and fun that seemed somehow to symbolize an idealistic celebration in an age of cynicism.

The gathering down by the waterfront is largely Asian. It's easy to conclude that the concept of America still means more to people who haven't lived with it all their lives. And indeed the Caucasians in the audience adopt a self-consciously removed stance about it all.

Martin Luther King's 'I have a dream' speech is played as part of the soundtrack to the fireworks, to give a broad perspective of the America we are here to celebrate.

'Doesn't it make you feel patriotic!' says one girl to her crowd, her voice dripping in irony, in case you should mistake her meaning.

'What do you think of the fireworks?' Suzanne asks.

I always think fireworks are impressive at first, but they lack a sense of drama. You see one explosion and that's great, then another one in a different colour, but that's about the extent of the variation. I usually get bored long before they finish. And you?

'Oh,' she says, 'it just seems like a typical cheesy American thing.'

Joanne and John, who by now are calling one another Siobhan and Sean and planning their wedding, seem more impressed. By the time we head on up the hill, Suzanne, perhaps not wanting to put a damper on things, is enthusing too.

We go into a bar, the Royal Oak on Polk Street – another of San Francisco's haunted taverns, dripping in yellow, green and red art-deco fittings. But here the ghost is in residence. At a table behind us is sitting an old woman. Her face is sharply defined and pale with a subtle hue of blue. She's dressed all in black and is wearing a close-fitting black skull-cap which also covers her ears and the back of her neck, like a helmet.

Sitting in front of her on the table is a small Martini glass filled with a blood-red cocktail.

She's amazing, I say.

'Oh, she's always in here,' Joanne tells me.

After a medicinal Jack Daniel's, my first long day in San Francisco begins to take its toll on me, and I leave Joanne to continue fantasizing about what kind of cake she will have at her wedding, and John whispering 'Could I just maybe stay on your sofa bed?'

Suzanne says if I come to the restaurant where she works as a singing waitress, she'll sing an aria for me.

As I leave, I notice the woman in black has gone.

Happy birthday, America.

The next day I am back round at the Mad Dog in the Fog which, despite my first experience of it, has been adopted as HQ.

Normally the idea of an English bar abroad would fill me with contempt, but I've been out here for long enough to appreciate a place that has a darned fine bacon and sausage sarnie on the menu just as much as the exiles who hang out here. Besides which, it's right around the corner, it's showing all the games and each game brings in a new crowd. You can sit here and watch the world revolve around you.

Italy versus Nigeria has brought out a sprinkling of Italians, and a horde of honorary Nigerians. Many of them are from other African countries, showing a loyalty to the continent. This surprises me: my friend in London, Kofi, at least up to a couple of weeks before the competition, was dead set against Nigeria after they triumphed above his native Ghana in the African Nations Cup.

The guy I'm sitting next to tells me he's from Kenya.

'I have three teams. One was Cameroon, but I still have Nigeria and Brazil.'

He wants to know who I'm supporting. But this one is too close to call. Nigeria have the African charm, but here they lack the sparkle of ambition, and I have this old-fashioned feeling that Italy have something to contribute to this World Cup.

When Amunike sticks out a foot from a scrambled corner and hooks the ball over Italy's second-choice keeper Marchegiani, the whole place goes wild. For the first time I notice a couple of English blokes behind me, all decked out in Nigeria T-shirts and hats. Their wives, who are with them, look on indulgently.

But just as it looks like Italy's uncharismatic grafting for an equalizer has come to nothing, just as the commentator is giving Roberto Baggio's scoring total for the competition as 'zip', it happens. Mussi breaks away down the right, Baggio takes up the perfect position and aims his shot perfectly in the corner.

It's a well-taken goal all right, but it looks more than a little lucky on the replay. The Nigerian defender seems to move out of the ball's way, perhaps thinking it's going wide, perhaps afraid of a deflection that will wrong-foot his keeper. But Baggio has come to life, right at what was almost the death.

Then towards the end of the first period of extra time, his perfect pass for Benarrivo catches Eguavoen thinking too slowly and it's a penalty. I can feel the silence in the Café Sorrento, in St Peter's Church in Farringdon, all the way from San Francisco. And when Baggio's penalty skims past Rufai's fingertips I can hear them breathing again with a roar.

'Well, there's still Brazil,' says my Kenyan pal, with a grin. Indeed there is.

By the Mexico/Bulgaria game, I'm suffering from football fatigue, and fighting to stay awake. Stoichkov's opening goal is brilliant as he beats his man and sends the ball smashing into the top corner before Campos can move. But the rest of the game is notable only for a surreal display by the referee that brings the Mexicans an equalizer from a questionable penalty.

Campos finally gets the chance you feel he has been waiting for, to take centre-stage for a penalty shoot-out. And he does manage one acrobatic save, but unfortunately his team-mates are incapable of scoring from any one of their first three kicks, and the Man with the Peyote Pyjamas and his faltering team head back south of the border, leaving their legion of fans to turn also to Brazil.

Bebeto and Romario feel the eyes of more than one nation, more than one continent, turning to them.

With three rest days in the competition, I have some time to go out and have fun in San Francisco. So on the Wednesday I meet a friend for an early dinner.

Kathy is a New Yorker, who lived in England for a while but has returned to the States and settled here. She understands my enthusiasm for San Francisco. It has an undeniably seductive magic, but she is beginning to feel it a little limited in comparison with bigger cities like London and New York.

'Apart from anything else, Don,' she says, 'I'm so fed up with being a lesbian.'

Kathy has always had her lesbian phases, but she is the first to say that she's keener on men than women.

'But I have no choice here!' she says. 'I had one boyfriend, who was a Zen monk, when I first got here. That was kind of interesting because he was in with all the politicians. But that was it. It's just the scene here. I keep getting pursued by all these twenty-year-old dykes. So it's either that or remain celibate!'

What is interesting, she says, is that lesbian culture is beginning to occupy the position that male gay culture used to. The women are increasingly successful, self-confident and sexually voracious. The fact that lesbians are under considerably less risk of Aids than either male gays or heterosexuals is a major contributory factor.

'They have these things called play parties,' Kathy says, 'which are basically orgies. But it's "play" because the sex doesn't mean anything, so you can go with your girlfriend, have sex with all these other women, and then go home like nothing has happened.

'Apparently they can get quite heavy, too, like there's a lot of serious S&M involved. They keep inviting me to them, but I'm a bit nervous about it.'

The male gay scene, meanwhile, which used to dominate the gay section of Castro, just below the Haight, has changed places with the lesbian scene. Devastated by Aids, the men have become more monogamous, more caring.

The focus of the new scene among the young dykes (their term) is a band called Tribe 8.

'They're totally wild,' Kathy says. 'The singer, Lynne, is a friend of mine. She has this tendency to take her clothes off all the time. The last time I saw them play, she was up there on the stage, wearing nothing but this pair of leather trousers. And you can tell she's packing, right?'

She stops for an instant. 'Do you know what that means?'

She's wearing a gun?

'No, a dildo.'

Oh, OK.

'Then she takes the trousers off and this huge grey dildo flops out, and one of the young dykes gets on stage, and starts sucking it. It's wild, I tell you.'

The conversation turns to friends of ours who live in the city, the artist Mark Pauline and Andrea Juno, who edits the magazine *RE-Search*. Pauline mounts shows of violent machine sculptures made out of military surplus and material looted from heavy engineering firms; a process he calls 'involuntary sponsorship of the arts'. Andrea's magazine is an A4 book format which takes one theme as its subject. 'Pranks' was one, including the quite brilliant suggestion of freezing a bag of pig's blood, removing the wrapping and throwing it through a jeweller's window. When the police come to investigate, all they find is a blood stain on the floor. 'Tattoos and Body Piercing' was another, an issue which may have been partly responsible for the explosion of piercing from cult to mainstream.

Mark and Andrea were once an item, the emblematic San Francisco Underground couple. But, rather famously in the locale, they are no more.

'Oh, you didn't hear about that?' Kathy asks. 'Well, basically it was a bad break up. Like Mark tarred and feathered her car.'

He what?

'Well, you know he has all that machinery at his disposal, he tipped a vat-load of tar over her car, then coated it with feathers.'

Another celebrated San Francisco resident is Fakir Musafar, the performance artist whose particular métier involves hanging himself up with fish hooks.

'Oh, he's a really nice guy,' she says. 'He just wants to float body piercing on the stock market, that's his ambition now.'

Comfortable in the centre and weird around the edges indeed.

The next day Kathy rings up.

'Tribe 8 are playing tomorrow night,' she says. 'Do you want to come?'

Well, is it safe?

'Oh yeah, I think so. They don't beat men up any more.'

So that's all right, then.

I take a walk down the Haight and find myself struck by an irresistible urge to hear The Beach Boys' *Pet Sounds*, so I stop off at Reckless Records.

I'm in luck, they have a second-hand copy of it on cassette, so I put it on my Walkman and take a hike up Buena Vista, the hill that rises up behind the Haight. The guide book has promised me that the Golden Gate Bridge, which I've yet to see, is visible from any high point in the city. But every time I have got into a position to see it the famous San Francisco fog has rolled in and obscured my view.

If you don't like the Beach Boys, then all I have to say is that you don't understand pop music. *Pet Sounds* is about as close as the medium has ever come to sounding not raw, energetic or sexual, or any of the other qualities we associate with great pop music, but simply beautiful.

Needless to say, as I reach the top, the fog comes in right on cue and the view the hill is named for is shrouded in white – an occurrence that has its own drama.

Just at that point the tape spools on to Sloop John B and any unsuspecting San Franciscan out for a walk hears an out-of-tune voice coming towards them out of the fog, finding the collision of words, tune and moment just too much to resist.

'Drinking all night/Got into a fight/Well I feel so broke up/I wanna go home.'

Then, with one perfection building on another, comes God Only Knows (what I'd do without you).

In the fog, no one can see a tear in your eye.

I come down, quite literally out of the clouds, with my spirits refreshed.

The night of the Tribe 8 concert is a Friday and the Haight is so crowded it takes me ten minutes longer to walk its length. There are Guardian-Angel-like patrols in berets maintaining a very visible presence.

'There've been some shootings recently,' I'm told, 'and so we've got numbers out tonight, just to make sure it stays calm.'

The restaurant we eat in, Cha Cha Cha's, is Cuban/Spanish and full of voodoo schtick. But voodoo is quite a serious part of the culture here, just as Zen Buddhism is.

'You have to search around a bit to find it,' says Kathy, 'but it's here all right.'

Part of the new tribalism which sees the primitive and the pagan gaining a distinct ascendance.

It's a long time since I've been to see a band live, although I have picked up that there seems to be a punk-like undercurrent to music recently that seems to be more than just crude revivalism. For reasons that are hard to pin-point, rock music seems to have recovered its relevance. As a friend of mine says, whereas until a year or so ago the dance-music medium seemed to be the locus of the most interesting developments, now rock has gained an unexpected centrality.

Standing in the bar of this Upper Haight club, I am suddenly gripped by the feeling that I'm in the middle of the monster scene in *Star Wars*. And I mean that in the nicest possible way. There's a comic diversity here that you used to get in the early days of punk. Kathy, who remembers early gigs by Patti Smith and Richard Hell and the Voidoids, has the same feeling.

Looking in the bar mirror there's a woman in a leopard-skin jacket next to me, a hairy old hippy in the background, a leather Cruella to my left and a skinhead girl, who's clearly speeding off her box, on the right. Meanwhile up on the stage, the first band, another all-girl outfit, have a gawky charm to their musical adeptness. There's a sophistication to the composition that belies the naïvety of its execution, much like the early postcard bands like Orange Juice and Aztec Camera.

The guitarist finishes the set by kissing the bassist, to great applause.

Tribe 8 take the stage in a cavalcade of guitar that sounds like heavy metal ought to sound, like energy directed, however haphazardly (The Stooges), rather than wasted (Iron Maiden). It takes me about thirty seconds to recognize what this reminds me of.

It's *Radio Ethiopia*! I shout in Kathy's ear.

A few moments later we're joined by a Joan Jett lookalike, the girlfriend of Lynne, the lead singer.

'Don't tell her I told you so,' she says, 'but she plays that record before she goes on stage, every time.'

Evidence of good taste, Patti Smith's chunk of bleeding, visionary metallica was unjustly maligned when it came out in 1977, but it stands up almost as well as the verbal pyrotechnics of *Horses*. The way the guitar lopes in behind her voice as she asks in a restrained scream, 'Go ask the angels if they're calling on me', it sounds like the epitome of slow pulsing sexuality – a thrill that Tribe 8 know all about.

But if sophisticated metal is their milieu, then there's a side to Tribe 8 that likes to play at hardcore. That for me is when they're less successful, although it has its rabble-rousing appeal to their audience.

'Are there any fraternity boys in the audience?' Lynne asks.

'Yeah!' shouts one deluded Pavlovian dog.

'And you admit it?' Lynne comes back. 'Well, this one's for you!'

The dog is pleased for a moment, but even he realizes something's up.

'Cos I know you guys like to gang rape girls, so this is about a game that we play that's a bit like gang rape, it's called "Gang Castrate".'

Then, when the body-slamming rant is over, 'Yeah, I have nothing against penises,' she says. 'I have one at home in a drawer.'

By this time she's naked from the waist up, à la Iggy Pop, except for one vital difference, of course.

'Stop looking at my tits!' she yells at another man in the audience.

Well, honey . . . I mean there is an answer to this, if problem it be: either you make your gigs women only or you keep your shirt on.

'Who's that girl over there?' says Joan Jett to Kathy, indicating the leather Cruella. 'She is beautiful. Boy, couldn't you just die.'

Then another girl arrives, who looks like a fifties cartoon strip in her tartan trousers and blonde bubble hair cut short at the back and sides.

'We're just rounding up the dates for a mild play party,' she says to Kathy.

What's a mild play party? I ask, after she's gone.

'No S&M,' Kathy tells me.

It was fun crashing a party in Suffragette City, but it's with a certain amount of relief that I return the next day to a more familiar place.

I have breakfast the next morning in a café which advertises on its menu the 'World Cup is Almost Over Omelette'. Yes, but almost is a long way.

I cross the road to the Mad Dog to watch Italy play Spain in the first Quarter-Final.

Once again the now-familiar sensation of waking up as the first half progresses. Then Dino Baggio's perfectly curled shot gives Italy the lead in the first half, for the first time in this tournament.

Daniele Massaro starts the move. 'Nobody had heard of him before this World Cup,' raves the commentator. I think one or two people did notice when he scored a hat-trick in the European Cup Final, but never mind. Sitting on their one-goal lead, Italy look as dull as Milan's machine, but for once they get their comeuppance from a freak goal by Caminero, which deflects off a defender and loops over the keeper. Suddenly I realize that the Mad Dog crowd, which seemed to be predominantly Italian, is full of Spanish fans.

Now Italy are on the ropes, rarely getting out of their own half. But, despite the mounting drama and the continuous action, the commentator finds time not only to repeat the sponsor's catchphrase every few minutes, but also to plug tonight's feature film.

Salinas breaks through, almost casually dummying Pagliuca, who nevertheless manages to catch the ball with his foot and scoop it away. Another shot is tipped over the bar, Costacurta clears off the line. Can Italy even make it as far as extra time?

And then a great run by Signori, who lofts the ball over the back line to Baggio in the penalty area. A shuffle around Zubizarreta. The touch isn't perfect and the defender has a chance to get back, but the shot, from the tightest of angles, is just too quick. He's done it again.

Thousands of good Catholics convert to Baggio's preferred Buddhism instantly. Zen and the Art of the Last Gasp.

While we have been transported away to the drama of World Cup City, the morning mist has burnt away outside and the street life of the Lower Haight is coming to life in the sunshine. A circle is sitting around listening to old Roy Orbison.

'There's a candy coloured clown they call the sandman,' sings the Big O in a line that will forever call up the image of Dennis Hopper in *Blue Velvet*.

'How you doin', my fren'?' smiles a toothless old guy, nursing a can of beer.

Another old black guy with a naval captain's hat and a bottle in his pocket is making an intent study of the front fender of a car. A dice player rolls, just as I walk past.

'Seven!'

I've been told that the place to watch the Brazil game is down the road in a club called Bahia. And I'm obviously not the only one who's got the word. By the time I get down there, fifteen minutes before the kick-off, there's a queue right down the street.

D'you think we'll make the kick-off? I ask the two guys behind me.

'Jeez, I hope so,' says one of them, a Latin-lover type with slicked-back black hair who introduces himself as Mario.

'Last time we were in here we got into a fight,' his friend confides, a big bear-like man called Andy with a face that's lined in the shape of a smile.

When was that?

'Oh, nineteen-seventy,' Mario replies. 'We were watching the Final, but there was this Italian guy who wasn't too happy about what was going on.'

'Hey, you're Irish,' says Andy, observing my hat. I'm not about to argue. 'Our martial arts teacher was Irish.'

Their teacher, Bill Paul, it turns out, was a legendary San

Francisco figure. A gay martial arts guru, he brought diverse sections of the community together, sometimes quite literally.

'His Christmas parties were always a lot of fun,' says Andy. Until Aids intervened.

'Even now he's remembered, though,' Andy continues. 'Just last week I had this guy being macho with me – "Oh yeah, you do martial arts," he says. "Who did you study with?" I told him Bill Paul, he said "Buy you a beer?"'

By now we're nearing the front of the line. Mario is looking nervous.

We'll make it, I say, there's still five minutes till kick-off.

'No, I'm thinking about the game. I couldn't sleep last night, my wife was saying, "What's wrong?" I said "I'm worried about Brazil."'

They'll win, I say.

'That's what she said. I wish I could be so sure. I'll tell you what, I'll buy you a beer if they do. In fact I'll buy you a beer anyway!'

No, I'll get them, I say, figuring these are good people to be on the right side of.

'To the luck of the Irish,' is the toast. 'Let's hope it's with Brazil today!'

So what do you guys do?

'Oh, we're lawyers.'

With a huge mural showing a tangle of tropical greenery at one end, and creeping plants all around the place, Bahia is the nearest I've ever come to watching a football match in a jungle. There's a giant screen and the place is packed to the rafters, heaving and pulsing with drums.

Just in front of us is a table with four or five orange Dutch shirts around it, but other than that the place is decked in the yellow, blue and green of Brazil. A favourite T-shirt has 'Brazil – Champions of Romantic Football' written in English and Portuguese.

There's a bull-fight atmosphere, with cheers being accorded to Brazil's flair in dealing defensively with Holland's early forays, but it's an edgy first half. Mario goes to buy some more beers, and the beat begins again.

When it comes, the first goal is deceptive brilliance, Bebeto running down the left and sending in an inch-perfect cross. But Romario meets it with a strike that is elegance incarnate, catching the ball perfectly on the volley to send it shooting into the corner.

Bahia explodes. Mario's beer goes everywhere. Andy and I are soaked, but we don't care. High fives are struck and a mood of celebration begins. Then within minutes Bebeto himself is through the centre of the defence. Normally there's a nervousness that accompanies the anticipation of the lone run on the goal-keeper, but Bebeto just looks intent. Just the slightest swivel of the hips is enough to take him round.

In England they are debating an application of the new rules. Romario, who is running back at the time the ball is played, is clearly not interfering with play by the new interpretation. There is no linesman's flag, let alone a whistle, but for some reason, the Dutch defence stops.

Andres Cantor is not concerned with any of that, though. Instead he's leading a chant that is taken up around the bar.

'*One two three four five six*,' he shouts in Spanish, '*Brazil is going to win the fourth championship!*'

The last syllable has only just been pronounced when Bergkamp catches the Brazilian defence asleep and gets a goal back. What was turning into a celebration party reverts to tension. We're trying to peer round a giant climbing plant. At one point we see the ball heading for the Brazilian net, but then Taffarel appears from nowhere and catches it.

Then the Dutch get a free-kick. Koeman lines it up. We don't even dare think about it. But it crashes against the wall and deflects for a corner. But from the corner Overmars heads the ball high into the Brazilian net. And after all that, we're back where we started.

Two Dutch girls are standing on their chairs roaring like their tonsils are dispensable. From the far side a Brazilian girl motions for them to sit down. Whether it's a piece of advice for their own safety or just because they're annoying her isn't quite clear.

'I can't stand this,' says Mario.

But now Brazil have a free-kick. Branco is lining it up . . .

A Brazilian forward pirouettes in front of the keeper's vision, the ball threads through the gap between him and the Dutch defender, a conjunction of balletic movement, destiny and sheer chance, and the ball settles contentedly into the corner of the Dutch net.

Goooooooaaaaaaaalllllllll!!!!

Cantor is outdoing himself, and this is a man for whom the apoplectic is commonplace. Everyone is going crazy. Mario is grabbing my wrist and shouting into my face, 'I've been watching them at practice for weeks, they do that all the time!' The three of us are dancing an improvised conjunction of a samba and a three-hand reel.

And then it's over. The whole place spills out on to the street where a corner has been cordoned off specially for the occasion. A band appears from somewhere, don't ask me where, these things just happen in World Cup City. There's cars with Brazilian flags everywhere, a cacophony of car horns. This being San Francisco, there's a Brazilian queen, wearing only a pair of skin-tight black bathing trunks, dancing with a Brazilian flag on the back of a black convertible.

There's an impromptu football game on the go. Each player takes the ball, juggles it and passes it on, all to the rhythm of the samba band. As the game goes on, the flourishes become more extravagant. It's like breakdancing. A crowd gathers and cheers at the most skilful moves.

The sun is shining, I have a ticket in my bag for the Semi-Final and I'm going to see the magical Brazilians in the flesh at last. How are things in World Cup City?

Perfect. Just perfect.

The university town of Stanford, where the games are taking place, is about an hour's drive from San Francisco. My plan is to hire a car, drive down there, and after the game keep on going to Los Angeles and Brazil, who will meet the winners of the game I'm going to see, Romania and Sweden.

Just as I'm buying supplies for the journey, the first World Cup shock of the day unfolds in front of my eyes. The television is on. Every other time I've been in this shop it's been O.J. Simpson. Now it's the World Cup – an American event at last.

'One–nil to Germany,' the storekeeper tells me. Then we're both looking up at the screen when Stoichkov curls his free-kick over the heads of everyone and into the net. We both let out an involuntary noise that's somewhere between a cheer and a laugh.

I'm still there watching moments later when the ball skids off Letchkov's bald pate to put Bulgaria up. It seems in that moment that Germany have finally seduced the disaster they've been courting.

Then comes the second World Cup shock of the day. The first one caused a ripple around the world, this one causes a cataclysm that affects one person only. But since that one person is me, Germany's exit diminishes to the realms of the insignificant.

I haven't got a ticket.

Well, that's not strictly accurate. I decide to check that I have my Quarter-Final and my Semi-Final ticket with me before leaving. Semi-Final – check. Quarter-Final – *Aarrrrrghhh!!!!!* What I have is a ticket to the Brazil/USA game. A week ago this was worth somewhere up to $500. Now it is a strip of meaningless cardboard.

I get straight on the phone. Amazingly, considering it's a Sunday, Michael is in the office.

'OK, look,' he says, 'you'll get a ticket outside, there's going to be thousands on sale for this one. We'll reimburse you for the ticket you got.'

Suddenly from a leisurely drive down to Stanford in the sunshine this becomes a hell-for-leather escapade. On the way down I twiddle through the stations, hoping I might get some news of the Germany game, but no. Still no radio stations are providing commentary.

I did hear that the Spanish station broadcast the Brazil game, because I was talking to a German, Rolf, who was driving over to see the game with his Brazilian girlfriend, and they'd missed the kick-off. 'I only know two words of Spanish,' Rolf had told me. One of them was 'arriba' which apparently means over the top. The other, of course, was *goooooooaaaaaaaaal*.

But I can't even find that today, so I just stay in the dark.

Arriving at Stanford, I hit a traffic queue straight away. Pulling into a shopping centre to buy a bottle of water, I see a FIFA official being ferried to the ground in a limousine with dark-tinted windows.

'How far to the ground?' I ask the driver, who I figure must have made the trip before.

'About half a mile,' he says.

I decide I may as well stay parked here and walk the rest of the way. But a few hundred yards on, the traffic queue has now cleared and there's nothing up ahead but a long, empty road with lush green verges, lined with suburban houses. The odd garden sprinkler provides the only sound.

I look back, wondering if it's worth going back for the car, when I see two figures jogging towards me at a steady pace. As they pass, I fall into step.

How far to the ground? I ask.

'I think it's about two miles,' one of them says.

Oh, what the hell, I could do with the exercise. So we run for a bit. My fellow joggers are middle-aged. One, who has a benign, lined look is Peruvian and the other, small and dark, is half-Polish and half-Mexican; both of them live in San Francisco. Neither of them has a ticket either.

At the next junction a Chinese American in a World Cup baseball cap is turning the corner in his pick-up truck.

'You wanna lift?' he asks.

You betcha. We climb in the back and the junction disappears behind us. We're racing towards the stadium with the speed cooling our brows after running in the heat.

'Hey, Ireland!' shouts the passenger of a white van, draped in the *Ordem e Progresso* flag of the Brazilians.

Hey, Brazil! I salute back, clapping my hands in the air. You will win! And they smile and wave. Then a car full of Italians drives past on the other side, tooting their horn and shouting 'Baggio! Baggio!'

A little later, I hear there is a vogue amongst Italian fans to wear little Buddhas on their heads.

None of our teams is playing, we're just going to a football match, together, in the sunshine, to see what these Romanian and Swedish cats have to offer.

As we get nearer the stadium, any worries we have about securing tickets fall away. They're being waved at us from all angles, fistfuls of them. Scalpers who thought they were going to make a killing from all these foreign football junkies have found themselves with a stack of tickets for a game between two countries who have brought maybe two or three thousand travelling supporters between them.

'Eighty dollars,' says a giant black guy to my new-found friends.

I tell them there's someone back there selling for sixty. 'OK, sixty,' he says, 'and you' – turning to me – 'take a walk, you've fucked up my business once already.'

'Isn't it great watching these guys squirm?' says my Peruvian pal.

I buy a Category 1 ticket for half-price, but they're now set on getting the perfect seat, at the lowest possible tariff. And with the way the market is going, they look like they'll get them. And there is something great about watching the football lovers grind the money grubbers into the dirt.

Inside the stadium one thing is clear. For all the talk of the magnificence of the US grounds, not all of them are up to scratch. Much is made of the toilet facilities at grounds in Scotland and England, but I've never had to queue for fifteen minutes outside a Portaloo until now. They had these things at Giants Stadium outside the ground, but here they've had to instal them inside, to make up for the paucity of the regular facilities. Inside the door a small notice informs you that this unit is designed for five people for one working week.

The steps up to the ground are far too narrow and too few to cope with a crowd this size, a problem that is aggravated by the fact that some cholesterol junky fat American bastard insists on nudging me up with his stomach.

I point out that he's already taking up more than his fair share of room.

'What about you, skinny!' he comes back. Joan Rivers he ain't.

Being too thin is like being too intelligent, I tell him. I expect him to work this one out about five minutes before the full-time whistle.

Inside I feel particularly glad that I am not sitting next to gut-buster or any of his ilk. My 'seat' (face value $125) turns out to be a marked number on a plastic bench. Perhaps Burger Butt will get the last laugh after all, since he is sure to find the conditions more comfortable than I will.

Sitting next to me is an American who caught the football bug while on holiday in Spain in 1982. Like all of the American fans I speak to, he's eager to talk about everything.

'What do you think of the American TV coverage?' he asks me. I try to say something non-committal, in case he gets touchy.

'I think it's terrible,' he says. 'They're so into what they call "color commentary", because American sports are based around short bursts of action, so they're telling you all these anecdotes all the time. They don't realize that with soccer the build-up is what's important, how the power of the match is swinging. I've ended up watching a lot of the matches on the Spanish channel instead, because at least they tell you who's on the ball.'

San Francisco is normally cool, and Stanford Stadium in particular has a reputation for catching whatever breeze is coming up from the bay. This may have contributed to the fact that two of the best games of the tournament so far (Brazil v Russia and Brazil v Cameroon) plus the highest scoring (Russia v Cameroon) have taken place here. But today the sun is beating down on us. With no shade at all in the ground, you feel a bit like a prisoner of war in a Japanese camp, pegged out in the blistering heat.

And indeed for much of normal time, the match could have been conceived as part of the torture. We are gathered here together in these inhuman conditions really to watch one man – Gheorghe Hagi. And the Maradona of the Carpathians has proved that there is one aspect of the poison dwarf's game that he has mastered to perfection. It is . . . falling over. Dumitrescu holds the ball up, plays it back to Hagi and Hagi falls over. The keeper Prunea plays the ball straight out to Hagi and Hagi falls over. Yup, even from this distance, John, I can see that he's doing it quite without assistance from anyone. Whoops! look here comes the ball, wallop! He's over again. The nearest we come to excitement in the first half is when he picks up the ball in the penalty area, controls it and . . . falls over. Will the referee be fooled? Nope, so we all go back to sleep again.

Most of the neutral support, myself included, had turned up here hoping for a sweeping and stylish Romanian victory. But as the game wears on, and believe me it does, we find ourselves drawn increasingly towards Sweden, who at least seem to be putting some effort into the odd attack.

The only explanation I can think of for this display of negativity from Romania is that, having been taken apart by a Switzerland team who turned out to be quite ordinary, they are cautious of committing themselves too much against another set of dour Europeans.

Whatever the reason, their tactic for the first half seems to be for Petrescu, the full-back, to push forward, Hagi, who's playing so deep he could be a midget centre-half, to fall over and for the rest of the team to wander around looking aimless, like a bunch of fourth-formers out on a nature trail. Hmmm, yes, warm today, isn't that an interesting blade of grass down there? I wonder what all these people are doing watching us.

Many of the football fans I've spoken to so far seem disturbed by the blithe way in which Americans get up to go for a hot-dog mid-way through the half. In this game I envy their detachment. I sit there and watch Petrescu run all the way up the line as his colleagues stand around and think, Duh, I wonder what Dan's running for. And then I watch him run all the way back down again.

The second half begins, and Petrescu is running in a different direction, but other than that nothing has changed. 'Have I missed anything?' says an American guy behind us, coming back in with a hot-dog. Well Hagi fell over a few times. 'Oh, OK.'

When I say Hagi did nothing in this match, I mean he did nothing. I knew at Giants Stadium that I wasn't watching Roberto Baggio at the top of his game, and yet all I heard said afterwards was 'Baggio – he's class, isn't he?' Because, even in a quiet game, you could tell that he was; there was a turn here, a flick on there. Even if McGrath had his measure, you always thought there was the possibility he could produce something magical that would turn the game. With Hagi you hoped that he might give us something to justify his billing, but every time, all he does is fall over.

And then at last I am rewarded for my persistence. For a free-kick from outside the area, Brolin joins in the Romanian wall, the ball is slipped wide of the last man in the line and Brolin breaks on to it, smashing a shot high into the net. After nearly eighty minutes of total predictability it was a triumph of the totally unexpected, a move executed with joyous panache.

Even now, Romania's movements scarcely rise above the languorous. All the same, they do manage to get a free-kick on the edge of the Swedish area.

They need an Italian job now, I tell my neighbour.

Hagi's free-kick is blocked, but the rebound falls loose in the penalty area and Raducioiu is on to it like O.J.'s lawyers will be on to a flaw in the prosecution's case. His finish is venomous.

Now, suddenly, we have a game. Not a beautiful game full of flowing movements and sweeping passes, but a blood, guts and thunder total scrap.

Romania are finally looking if not like contenders at least a little better than mediocre. Another free-kick, in an almost identical position. Hagi takes it short, Dumitrescu is surrounded by four Swedish defenders, but in their haste to get a tackle in they let the ball run free to Raducioiu again, and again his shot is beautifully placed, this time down low and hard into the corner. Romania 2–1 up and beginning to wake up to a place in the Semi-Finals.

In their best move of the game, Dumitrescu plays a neat one two with Raducioiu, but Schwarz, making a decent attempt at making it look like a collision, takes him out. Second bookable offence, and Sweden are down to ten.

Now the Swedes are coming forward in a great blond cavalcade, like they have the *Ride of the Valkyries* behind them. Cometh the long ball, cometh the goalkeeper, cometh the head of Kennet Andersson. 2–2.

The Americans around me want to know what the rules are for these penalty shoot-outs they've heard about.

No, the goalkeeper isn't allowed to move, but usually that doesn't make a difference. Yes, it has actually happened that the whistle has been blown, the ball has gone in the net, and the kick has had to be retaken, all because of a keeper moving.

An American with his face painted in the Swedish colours takes exception to this.

'*No!*' he says. 'If he *makes* the save he calls it, if he *doesn't* there's no *call*.'

Now he's made a mistake, and because I'm hot and irritable too no fucking American is going to tell me about the rules of our game, no matter what Colin fucking MacInnes says.

So I give him a list of grounds and names.

'That was *years* ago,' he says, unshaken in his belief in the American prerogative to be right all the time even with something they know nothing about. Of course every other American I have met has, if anything, understated their knowledge, but in this instant his annoying behaviour becomes a national characteristic.

Excuse me, pal, but I said it had happened, not that it had happened recently.

'I'm not going to *argue* with you,' he comes back.

Well you could have fooled me.

By the time he's finished not arguing with me the penalty shoot-out has already been called.

Let's face it, penalty shoot-outs are punishment beyond the call of duty when it's your team. But when you're a neutral they're great. And don't give me any of that crap about being a lottery.

Maybe if the players were blindfolded, or if there was a law that the mascot and the manager had to take one of the first five, but otherwise, what's the problem? Taking a good penalty is all about skill, judgement and nerve, and I have no problem with a game being decided on those qualities. Better that than tired limbs leading to an own goal, a defender's fluff or a goalkeeping gaffe in sudden death, or finishing a game with all the players in their own penalty areas, booting it backwards and forwards all night because they're too scared to lose.

Penalty shoot-outs, no problem. I'm not going to argue with you.

So it's the long walk from the centre circle for Prunea and Mild. Mild takes a short run and blazes it over the top. I try to work out if I'm pleased. On the one hand maybe Hagi's just having a bad day and maybe if he recovers Romania might make for a better Semi-Final. On the other hand anything that pisses off the fuckwit with the face paint is OK by me.

From here on in we're treated to a display of why the penalty shoot-out is not a lottery. Raducioiu plants his in the corner. Andersson strikes his high into the roof. Hagi stares out Ravelli as he tries to psych him out, then wrongfoots him brilliantly. Brolin gets revenge by treating Pruneau with equal disdain. Lupescu scores his too, as does Ingesson. It's all down to Petrescu now, the one Romanian who's played his heart out today. If he scores, Romania are through. He places it to the right, close to Ravelli and about eighteen inches off the ground. Ravelli scarcely has to bend to scoop it away. Petrescu crumples to the ground.

Now we go into sudden death, with Sweden kicking first. Nilsson scores his and you can feel the pressure is bearing down again on Romania. Dumitrescu steps up and scores to keep their head above water. Then Larsson ducks them down once more.

Belodedici, a defender, is the next Romanian to face Ravelli. He strikes the ball to Ravelli's left, realizing too late that the keeper has anticipated him. Mid-way through the air, Ravelli adjusts his dive, raises his arm a couple of inches, and palms the ball away.

Romania are sunk.

You can feel sorry for Petrescu, but not for Romania. Apart from ten minutes or so in extra time, they played like this was on their mind, and they lost.

I console myself by thinking that the team of the bastard with the face paint are going on to meet the mighty Brazil, and I'm going to be there when Bebeto and Romario run them ragged.

I drive off towards the coast road. I have $60 in cash, two credit cards and a ticket to the Semi-Final. Like everyone else in the world I have my heart set on one of those magical loops of time that football can make. I think of being ten years old and the particular texture of grainy screen that the TV reception from Mexico created.

Brazil v Italy. The past is getting closer.

6

The Fear of Finishing

You don't really see America unless you drive through it. Although, like everywhere else, time is at a premium in World Cup City. I met a man whose tribute to Jack Kerouac and his epic journeys with Neal Cassady was to look out of the window on a clear day, for the duration of a coast to coast flight, and keep his eyes focused on the ground.

'If Kerouac could drive from coast to coast all those times,' he said, 'the least I could do is watch it all the way across.' His conclusion was 'There must be a lot of lonely people out there – all that space!' The major cities of the United States are so far apart as to make you feel there is virtually no connection between them; they are worlds unto themselves, particularly New York, which is really a small island off the coast of America. The real United States, if you can call anything real whose common reference point is television, resides in the great rural tracts where the majority of people live.

Rural America is simply too vast to be penetrated between football games, but you can see a bit of the road – although to refer to the coast route between San Francisco and Los Angeles as a bit of road is like calling the last act of *Götterdämmerung* a good tune.

First you drive through miles of conifer glades, past roads with names like Dry Gulch and Memory Lane. Outside a Hell's Angels' watering hole, a line of Harley Davidsons shine like a constellation of gleaming metal as the light falls in slower, diagonal beams through the trees.

Something else had happened while I was in San Francisco. I had spoken to my mother, who was seriously ill and lying in a hospice bed. It seems now prophetic that I had first been gripped by the desire to drive this section of my journey while watching the Peter Weir film *Fearless*.

In the movie, Jeff Bridges survives an air crash, against all the odds. The airline offers to fly him back first class from San Francisco to Los Angeles, but he declines, taking what is to them the peculiar decision to drive. Only one scene is shown of his journey. He stops, in the middle of a desert highway, with a line of windmills behind him, and listens to the earth as the sun sets. I suppose I had a premonition that this would be a good place to come and do what Jeff Bridges was doing – think about death.

This is also the road that James Stewart drives Kim Novak down for a second time at the end of *Vertigo*, and by forcing her to recover the past he indirectly causes her to fall to her death, also for the second time. But this time for real.

I reach the point where the woods open out to the sea, and clamber down the rocks. There's something about the inelegance that such an action forces you into which recalls childhood immediately.

Football matches, like movies, are a way of contacting the past – a stitch through time which allows memories to leak. Sometimes they make the past better – when your team triumphs in a game that echoes an important disappointment of the past – and sometimes they make it worse – when the reverse happens.

With Italy playing Bulgaria and Brazil against Sweden in the Semi-Finals, it seems unthinkable that the Final will be anything other than a repeat of the 1970 game between Brazil and Italy. All of us who are old enough are returning to a corner of our memories.

For me it was my first real World Cup, when I was old enough to study the moves in the hope of trying them out myself in a schoolboy game; the first time when we imagined in the televisual fantasies that ran parallel to our games that we were Jarzhinho or Pelé, rather than, for my school-mates, Astle or Hirst or, for me, Dennis Law or Jimmy Johnstone, or, for all of us, the inevitable George Best.

I remember watching the 1970 Final with my grandparents. My grandmother was behind Italy. She had been there a lot on holiday. But there was something else. I pushed her.

'Well,' she admitted, 'I wouldn't like to see a black team winning it.'

She was the only person I knew who didn't want Brazil to win. To me it was inconceivable that anyone would not want the best footballers in the world to take the trophy. And there was no doubt in my mind that these leonine figures, striding through the static of our black and white television, were the best players in the world.

In this World Cup, after Ireland's exit, I had not looked for another team. But I realize now, sitting watching the sea, how much I have been caught up again by this country Brazil, because of the warmth of their celebrations but also because of the exhilaration of watching those triangles cut with devastating speed across the turf, while the drums accentuate the course of adrenalin.

If it's Brazil against Italy, I think to myself (in that conscious way where you know the thought is ridiculous but you give it an inner voice anyway because it pleases you, and because nobody else is listening), I'll have a part of my childhood back. And I know, in that moment, whether or not they admit it to themselves, millions of others are thinking this same thought, all across the world.

The words of Michael, the Italian boy in St Peter's Church, come back to me. 'You can measure your life out against World Cups.' We like to believe there is an intricate pattern here, like the signs of the zodiac, and that in our own small way we are a part of that pattern.

In the evening the mist begins to come down, giving a bleached quality to the light as I drive on further down the coast. The past of this region is embedded more visibly in its landscape than elsewhere in America; the Mission buildings, like the one where the final scenes of *Vertigo* are shot, are memorials to the often brutal Spanish missions which converted the native Americans to Catholicism. Even the Mexican restaurants, like the one where I stop in Santa Cruz for a dish of spicy prawns, which clears my head, are in some small way a reminder that Mexico once extended this far.

Stretches of barren sandy coastline are punctuated by industrial plants that rise up out of the mist, eerie in the silence of their own pools of light.

Finally, fatigue overtakes me around Monterey, where I follow a pick-up truck, driven by two black women. The kid in the back waves at me. The bumper sticker reads 'Operation Desert Storm – Support the Troops' against the background of stars and stripes.

I'm still wondering where I might stay when I see a sign for Cannery Row, the name of a book by John Steinbeck I read when I was young. That sounds as good a place as any.

The guide book tells me that the area is named after the Steinbeck book, but the local I ask gives me a different story. He argues, quite plausibly, that it was called Cannery Row because of the pilchard canneries that still line the sea front. One thing is certain: Steinbeck lived here when the canneries were thriving businesses and he used the place as the backdrop for his love story between a shy marine biologist and a whore with a heart of gold.

Now the canneries are rusty, corrugated iron shacks left standing only to give a sense of the past for the tourists who stay in the luxury hotel, overlooking the beauty of Monterey Bay.

Even here there's an Irish bar, where one or two local characters hang out. After a long day of football and driving, and a pint or so of Guinness, I fall for the illusion that the new Cannery Row may be as interesting a place as the old, lacking only a latter-day Steinbeck with the time and the inclination to fictionalize it.

I have a drink with two Dutch fans, who have sought out the Irish bar deliberately. Not to gloat in a victory that is already too far in the past, but because they got a taste for the Irish craic in Orlando. Having struck up an accord while both their teams were playing there in the second round, the Dutch and the Irish had a party after the game.

'There was one point,' one of them says, 'when we were singing "Holland" and they were singing "Ireland" and then someone started singing "If you all hate the Germans clap your hands", and the whole room joined in.'

After Bulgaria's sensational victory, they don't mind that Holland are going home now. They know this wasn't a classic Dutch team, and they pushed Brazil further than either of them had expected.

'But tell me,' one of them asks, 'why is it that the Irish hate the English so much? I mean we hate the Germans because of the Second World War, but why the Irish and the English?'

I try to condense five hundred years of complex history into five minutes.

'So you mean the Irish are not British?' says the other, confused.

'No,' his friend corrects him, 'and we must never call them that.'

I find myself quite moved by this, that through football a Dutch fan has learnt a little more about how an Irish fan sees the world, even if it's only the reason for his hostilities. We exchange cards and names, and of course we will never see one another again. But then stranger things have happened. World Cup City can prove to be a smaller place than you might imagine too.

South of Monterey is Big Sur, a stretch of mountainous coastline where the road is etched into the rock, taking you high above the most dizzying vistas where ravines plummet down to the sea, inches from the wheels of your car. You look down to see the surf foaming at the rocks, hundreds of feet below.

This is where Jack Kerouac became disillusioned by his own inability to transcribe experience direct into words. Big Sur was just too big a subject. In his book of the same name he spends pages spelling out the sounds of the ocean in the hope of representing the feeling of being here, but knowing that he was failing.

Its beauty is almost tiring; each time you think you've passed through it, you turn another corner and find that the sheer height of the swooping rock clutches at your stomach, and you have to make a conscious effort to breathe. Vertigo indeed. It goes on like that for hours. Even when you pull in and stop, the shadow of the coastline follows you as you fall asleep.

At the end of Big Sur the coastline reverts to its sweeping dunes, and you reach the Hearst Castle, on which Xanadu in *Citizen Kane* was based. It's a national monument now, but I arrive too late to see round. So I pull into the entrance way and watch the sun set over the sea. Even with the tourist coaches pulling out around me, there's a sense of windswept isolation about this place.

San Luis Obispo, where I stay on my second night on the road, is notable chiefly for being the site of the first motel. A convenient stopping point either for the Coast Road or the more anonymous highway between Los Angeles and San Francisco, it's a place meant for short stop-overs. Its classic art-deco cinema – a museum of pink neon that climaxes with an ornate spiral, rising high above the lighted cashier's window, which projects out on to the sidewalk – gives the place a feeling of small-town timelessness.

But the conversations you overhear at dinner – 'My room-mate, he's going out with a lesbian.' 'Oh, cool.' – are enough to let you know that this is not rural America.

Outside my motel room a hummingbird is hovering at a flower bed as the light turns gold and translucent.

Inside, *Beavis and Butthead* are on MTV.

Kathy told me that her students are bemused by her affection for these anti-heroes of our time. Beavis and Butthead are not their idea of serious entertainment. I told her I think that their memory of adolescence is too fresh, they are intent on escaping into the adult world. For those of us who have lived there for long enough to get bored with it, Beavis and Butthead, with their gleeful anti-authoritarianism and their dumb irresponsibility, bring back some of our own past. Because although they are partly a satire of the generation of the incredible shrinking attention span, they are also Everykid. Like it or not, there is a Beavis and Butthead in all of us.

In the commercial break, MTV informs us that it is going 'on line'. If MTV itself provided a revolution in popular culture, through giving an outlet in every home for the visual side of pop music, the next revolution will be happening on the Information Super Highway. Are you ready for virtual Woodstock? In cyberspace imaginary guitars are real and nobody needs a Portaloo.

For my first night in Los Angeles, I decide to stay out at the Beach. I've been warned off Venice, which, after dark, has been taken over entirely by gangland. So instead I head further south to Hermosa Beach, the slightly grungier sister of Manhattan Beach.

Paul, an artist I had contacted in London through mutual friends, is staying out here too. He's watching the football as a fanatic, but also as an artist, gathering material to put together a show – visualizing World Cup City.

He's out when I ring – he's gone up to the ground to put his name down on the stand-by list for press tickets for tomorrow's game. So I go out for a walk on the beach.

The walkway by the beach is a long procession of bikinis gliding by on rollerblades, and slightly older women, jogging with baby buggies – two-wheeled contraptions with heavy suspension that allow you to run with your offspring. Out on the boardwalk, the men are dangling fishing lines into the glittering water, seemingly not put off by the industrial plants that nestle on the horizon in both directions. Life here really is a beach. They're even building a mini stadium around a patch of sand right outside my motel, where Brazil are to play the United States at beach soccer. It's not an entirely flippant affair either; Junior will be playing for Brazil and a couple from the current US team, including Cobi Jones, have announced that they will be playing too.

When I get back to the motel, the telephone rings. Paul's in a bar close to the motel. He gives me directions.

'Oh, and by the way,' he adds, 'George Best is here.'

Oh yeah, I say, assuming he's joking. Well tell him mine's a bottle of Sam Adams.

But when I get there George Best is indeed there. Not only that, but he's sitting within inches of me.

Having been a journalist for ten years, I had thought that I was immune to the power of celebrity. But there is something about someone who played such a pivotal role in your childhood. I sit there, attempting with some difficulty to talk to Paul, but the only thing I can think of is the pair of George Best football boots I was given for my Christmas present when I was seven years old.

It's as if I have become once again that seven-year-old, having a flash of the future, seeing myself in twenty-seven years' time, sitting in a bar in Los Angeles, next to George Best. I want to do something really stupid like ask to shake his hand. Fortunately, after hearing football talk starting up, he pays his bill and leaves, before I can embarrass myself. Talking football is something he does for money.

'Just think,' says Paul, 'we're exactly the type of people he comes out here to get away from.'

Did you try to talk to him? I ask.

'Yeah, I asked if he was out here for the football, but it was clear he didn't want to chat. Mind you, I spoke to some girls yesterday who said they'd seen him last night in one of the bars, and they said he was totally off his head, so he probably just came in here with a stinking hangover to have the cure.'

And instead he finds two people from the land way beyond here, where he will always be a superstar, his locks swinging as he turned, a symbol of the days of innocence.

We are joined by Paul's American friend George. We try to explain to him what it meant to us, to be in the same room as the man who's just left. But it can't be done, you had to be there. Similarly, we may be curious about the O.J. Simpson case, but it can never mean as much to us, as we weren't brought up watching the Juice run.

And yet Best, although he was the bad boy to O.J.'s Mr Clean, is more of a point of comparison in the Simpson case than he may at first appear. Because O.J., like Best, is a symbol of his age. This is becoming clear in the so-called 'race issue' emerging in the proceedings.

'What nobody is talking about,' the newspapers say, 'is that O.J. is not just a man on trial, he is a black man on trial.' In fact, this is total nonsense; a lot of people are talking about it, particularly the black and the politically correct brigade. What the media mean is that *they* have discovered a new angle.

Much of the arguments around the 'race issue' are muddled at best. The black lobby object to O.J. becoming the 'symbolical black man', in other words the black who, through his celebrity, becomes an honorary white. This is the argument represented in Spike Lee's *Do the Right Thing*, where the racist brother explains to Lee's character: 'Magic Johnson, Prince, they're not like niggers, they're black, but they're different.' But the black lobby's argument against his objectification is then contradicted once they begin to complain about the fact that when he became a celebrity, he turned his back on black womanhood in favour of the status symbol of a blonde wife. You can't object to someone becoming a symbol of something and then complain that he is not a good enough role model.

The other strand of the argument is that black heroes have been making a habit of falling from grace recently. Mike Tyson, Michael Jackson and now O.J. Simpson. This is a perfectly valid observation, but you can't make it a causal factor unless you're going to hatch some involved right-wing conspiracy theory. Sure enough, this is exactly what begins to follow.

But bearing the weight of all those hopes and dreams is difficult. O.J. Simpson just broke more drastically, and more violently, than Best did, perhaps because whatever weights he had to bear, Best was never expected to be perfect.

Controversy follows Best even here. There is a rumour that the bar he has shares in, down the road from where we are in

Hermosa Beach, may lose its licence. Best is not implicated himself, but there has been talk of barstaff dealing drugs. But even out here there isn't a bar he can take his troubles to without finding a couple of football fans staring, awe-struck, in his direction. This is World Cup City, George; there is no way out.

Paul's friend George has a muscular build and an Attila the Hun haircut. He's one of many ordinary Americans who bought up a strip of World Cup tickets in the hope of making a profit on reselling them. Instead he's ended up making a bad loss. The tickets were expensive in the first place and, as with Romania v Sweden, you could easily find that your investment had just gone through the floor.

George drove all the way from Los Angeles to Stanford for that match – a good six-hour haul even if you keep your foot down and don't stop. And how much did you get for your ticket, George?

'One bottle of Budweiser!'

What?

'Oh, I just got really fed up with trying to sell it, and there was this Swedish guy who really wanted a ticket, so I thought, what the hell, it's his team! You gotta like that!'

'You gotta like that' is George's catchphrase and it sums up his attitude to life, but underneath his exterior of cheerful resignation it's clear that there's some tension building up between the World Cup and its hosts.

When I recount the hostility displayed by the *Chicago Tribune*, George says he can understand a bit of that. After all, what is this competition doing here, demanding such an inordinate amount of attention? But on the other hand, hey, look, there's a bunch of Swedish fans just walked in. Hey! You gotta like that!

Paul and I want to talk football to someone else who speaks the same language, recognizes the same humour, but we hold back as much as possible for George's sake. George, for his part, is watching the baseball game behind our heads. He tries every now and then to explain what's going on, 'But hey!' he says with a touch of petulance at one point, 'you don't care anyway.' We protest otherwise but ultimately we don't. At any other time we might have been curious, but this is the final run in of the World Cup; of course we don't care about anything else. The Atlantic may not be as wide as it used to be, but it's still a long way.

George finally leaves us to it, and Paul and I go on to get something to eat and talk some serious football.

'Good luck tomorrow,' we say to the Swedes.

'You'll need it,' adds Paul.

And once George has gone, the other side of the irritation comes out, and for twenty minutes or so football is forgotten in favour of a British tourist tirade on the subject of American hotels, airport staff, etc., etc.

And you know you're in trouble when they start calling you sir.

'Exactly!'

The next day at ten in the morning Paul and I meet on a misty boulevard and drive up to Pasadena. The first route we take is the 405, the scene of O.J.'s last run.

On the way through downtown LA we pass the Soccer Convention building, a giant exhibition centre which is running a collection of memorabilia and technological trickery throughout the duration of the World Cup. Paul got free entry with his press accreditation.

'There's not actually much in there, for the size of it,' he says. 'It's stuff like Beckenbauer's boots and that sort of thing.'

But there is a virtual reality game where kids get taped up to appear as goalkeepers in a three-minute clip. Johan Cruyff fires a shot and they dive to save, or not. It isn't live, it's Memorex.

Pasadena, unusually for Los Angeles, has an atmosphere of the past about it. Its opulent, slightly Gothic buildings reek of faded elegance, echoes of the Golden Age of Hollywood. Los Angeles, as everyone knows, is not a single city, but a collection of towns, linked together by freeways. In Los Angeles the World Cup is just something going on out there. But in Pasadena it has taken over. As it proceeds, World Cup City gets smaller – for the moment it still encompasses Giants Stadium in New York, but in a couple of hours' time the whole of World Cup City will be defined by the ruined palaces and palm trees of Pasadena.

Unlike other centres for the competition, here a large proportion of the fans are staying within a couple of miles' radius of the stadium. It's set up to be a hell of a party.

As Paul and I arrive in town the sun is just rising to its full height, giving a clear, hard edge to the buildings. There's still over four hours to the kick-off, but there's a proliferation of tickets being sold on the streets. Characters are standing out on the main drag of Colorado Boulevard holding handfuls of the things, the World Cup holograms glinting rainbow colours in the sun.

I had expected as we got to this point that the number of tickets available would have reduced; instead it seems to be the other way round. Presumably some genuine fans bought up seats for the earlier rounds; for these later games it seems that the majority went to small-time speculators. Another triumph for FIFA.

We have enough time to check out the various bars for a good spot to watch the first Semi-Final, Italy v Bulgaria. There's scarcely a bar or a restaurant that isn't showing the game. The Brazilian and the Swedish fans are doing just what we are – watching the first game here before heading out the mile or so to the Rose Bowl. But there's also a large Italian contingent, some of them no doubt Pasadena residents, and others who have come out here to watch the game from World Cup City, even if it is on TV, and to be on the spot for the party later.

After a quick tour around, we find what looks to be a good prospect – a restaurant with a large bar and a giant screen, not too crowded. It seems perfect until we are struck by a perfect example of the American illogicality we spent last night moaning about.

Having the fat reserves of the average superwaif and with a metabolism that runs faster than Bebeto, I realize that I'll need some sustenance if I'm going to make it to the end of the game. Now you wouldn't have thought this would be a problem; we are in a restaurant, right?

'Sorry, all the tables are booked.'

Well, could I just have something to eat at the bar?

She gives me the menu. Someone else comes to take the order.

'You'll have to sit down before I can serve you.'

But all the tables are booked.

Well, you can sit out in the other room, there's tables there.'

Is there another screen?

'No.'

Kind of defeats the point.

'Well, maybe if you can find yourself somewhere to sit, I can serve you.'

But how can I find myself somewhere to sit if all the tables are booked?

'I don't know, sir.'

Aaaaaaaaarrrrrghhhhhhhh!!!!!!!

I'm just explaining this to Paul, who'd been off to find the Gents, when a guy in an Italian shirt with an American accent says,

'No, she told you the right thing, I understood her.'

I am still ranting about not giving a toss about his having a sense of logic that's as imbecilic as the waitress when Paul drags me out of the door.

'Probably not a good idea,' he says.

OK, good point.

Finally we find an overcrowded bar where, after some pleading, they promise to do their best to find me a sandwich. So I'm there trying to keep my feet, between fainting with hunger and the general heaving and jockeying for position you get when you have too many human beings in one place. This makes standing on the Geldard End for a Roses derby look like a seat in the directors' box.

A huge Brazilian behind me insists on trying to occupy the same space as I do. Every time I shift an inch, he moves into the space. *Lebensraum, lebensraum!* With his mirror shades and his beard, he looks like a giant Fidel Castro. To complete the resemblance he pulls out a cigar.

I glare at him. Paul covers his eyes. I can't help it, hunger makes me aggressive.

'And stupid.'

Yes, that too.

The Brazilian glares back.

While this has been going on, Bulgaria and Italy have been testing one another out, and then it happens. Baggio's goals so far have been fortuitous in timing, but they have come from distinct opportunities, whether the snatched shot against Nigeria or the long pass that put him through on the keeper against Spain. But this one comes out of nothing; from a throw-in, he spins off one man, beats another and then curls it inside the post.

The audience at Giants Stadium goes mad, the Italian contingent in the bar goes mad, even the rest of us applaud, then we shake our heads and think. Roberto Baggio. At last. A ripple runs around the crowd. My sandwich arrives. The Brazilian smiles, shakes my hand and asks me if I want a beer. Even in the blazing sunshine outside, it feels as if a cloud has lifted. And for fifteen minutes we're bathing in the heat of the Italian brilliance.

Albertini hits the post, then the ball comes back to him from Baggio and he tries a chip over the goalkeeper which begins to fall just close enough to Mihaylov to finger tip it over the bar. Then from the corner Albertini again plays a ball over the defence, Baggio is through on goal and his shot again bisects the space between keeper and post. Throughout the world, kisses are bestowed on graven images of a pony-tailed man who has just had his deity confirmed.

Even Sacchi is smiling.

It seems like a comfortable ride home for Italy. Experts at sitting on a one-goal lead, they're now sitting pretty with two. Then, just as the half draws to a close, Sirakov makes a run, straight through the centre of the Italian defence. Costacurta elbows him but it's Pagliuca, spreading himself to close down the angle, who raises a foot to trip him up.

This time, though, there's enough of a tangle of limbs for an element of doubt to protect him from the red card.

Stoichkov takes a run on the spot-kick, shuffles, sends Pagliuca the wrong way and rolls the ball into the net. That sound in the bar is the sound of Italian blood, pulsing a little faster around the system now.

In the second half Costacurta makes two or three timely interventions, including one where ball strikes hand, or was it the other way around? But no penalty is called.

'It's a FIFA fix,' bellows a bull-necked American. Wherever there are initials in this country there is a conspiracy theory waiting to happen. 'They want a Brazil/Italy Final.'

The minutes of extra time drag on. There are scares, but no serious ones. Once it seems that the referee blows up. They think it's all over. But there's another thirty seconds for the Italians to endure. It is now.

After the claustrophobia of the bar, even the stifling heat of the California sun comes as a relief. All along Colorado Boulevard the bars are spilling out a parade of yellow and green shirts. Even I am wearing a Brazil T-shirt, which I bought at the last game. In the semi-drunken euphoria of the Brazil/Holland game, I said to Mario and Andy in San Francisco I would come to this game wearing a Brazil shirt and an Irish hat, and here I am, falling into step with the Brazilian army.

Of course, a football fan hates neutrality like nature abhors a vacuum. You have to find a bias, and usually they're easy enough to come by, even when sitting watching a game on television. Supporting a team by proxy can never give you the ecstatic highs and lows of watching your own team do battle, but it allows you to participate, rather than just watch, and that's the difference between us and the commentators.

Nationality has been swept away. I've never even been to Brazil, I have little idea about its politics, although I'm learning about its music all the time. Brazil to me is the most dynamic football team in the competition, with a pair of killer forwards, but there's also an infectious *joie de vivre* that matches the Irish. It's a party you would have to be a killjoy not to want to join. The

World Cup? They're going to dance away with it. My conviction grows stronger by the second.

But then of course I'm not Brazilian. In San Francisco, I will discover later, Mario is saying to Andy: 'We need Donald here.' In the pre-game nervousness, he wanted to hear me assure him, 'Brazil will win.'

Sweeping down the hill to the Rose Bowl I am struck by the starkest contrast between watching on television and being here. Just the sensation of the crowd and the colours around you. American television has grappled with the idea of the fans as part of the event, interviewing them outside as part of the build-up, showing scenes from bars. But I realize that what I have missed in the games I've watched on television here is something that is quite routine in the coverage you see in England or Scotland – the close-up shots of supporters. That particular look of distracted absorption that you see on the faces reminds you instantly of what it feels like to be there.

We round a corner and see the football-shaped helium balloons of the Rose Bowl floating above the conifers.

'Hey, you gotta good seat, buddy,' the steward grins at me as he points from the entrance down towards the goal. I walk down and down and down. Finally I find my seat – if I was any closer I'd be playing in goal.

Of course we know it's not exactly the best place to watch a game from, except if you want to study a goalkeeper's perspective. But it's close to the action, and that is what is seen as the most desirable place around here.

As the teams walk out, I'm not complaining. There's something strange about seeing them so close. Usually features are things you distinguish only on television, like you're used to distinguishing one player from another by a manner of movement – the way Gary McAllister seems to dance through defenders as though the ground is moving and he's just picking up his feet, or the way Paul Merson charges around like Pigpen in *Peanuts*, so that you almost expect a cloud of dust and flies around him.

But there they are, walking right past me. Bebeto's smooth

features, Brolin's baby face, Romario's heavy-set looks. I still find it strange that most players are younger than me now, in the same way that it's strange that a street or a park you knew in childhood is smaller than you remember it. When I look at a football match, I look at it always from the perspective of an adolescent. I will get a Brazil/Italy Final, I have never been so certain of anything in football, but I really do get a part of my childhood back every time I watch a football match. That's what being a fan is all about.

For the first half, Brazil are coming right at me. And I really mean right at me, there's only Ravelli and a nylon net between me and the rampaging Brazilian blue. Unlike other games, where they've limbered up to pace in the first half, this time they've come out and gone straight for the jugular. The interplay is already dazzlingly fast, but as I'm applauding one sweeping movement, the bank of fans to my right are on their feet berating the final ball. Even for Brazilians, abuse is part of the experience of watching the game. We demand success but, Arsenal fans apart, we demand that it is delivered with panache.

To my eyes Brazil are displaying plenty of flair – the problem is not in carving out, or even sculpting the chances, but in taking them. Ravelli boots the ball out, but it just comes back through the Swedish defence as though it were no more than a cumbersome impediment, emphasizing just how difficult it is to mark this speed. Bebeto takes the ball from an advanced midfield position, turns in a single move. He's got a Swedish defender on him, and two or three players running for possible passes, but what does he do? The slightest hesitation and he just beats him solo, with his runners scurrying through and the Swedes lagging at their heels looking punch-drunk.

Bebeto puts Zinho through. This is it! But no, he shoots wide. He does the same for Romario. This time! Yes! Romario teases Ravelli with the ball and then with a quick two-foot shuffle, snatches it away from him and rolls it towards the empty . . . No! Patrik Andersson appears from nowhere to hoof it off the line.

It seems like there's something wrong. There's no shortage of hard-headed determination. But the killer instinct has gone missing. At the time I felt their inability to punish the United States as much as they might was just down to luck, but perhaps there was something else at work – the striker's fear of the open goal.

Everyone has seen it with their own team; the striker who displays a dazzling ineptitude for a period of months, then hits a vein of form – and instead of tripping over himself, or rocketing the ball over the bar, he smashes it into the roof of the net, or curls it inside the post.

The striker is like the cartoon figure who's walked off the edge of the cliff. As long as he doesn't look down, he can do the impossible, he can walk on air. As soon as he stops and looks below, there's a gulp, an 'Uh-oh' and the sound of whistling air.

The further we get into the second half, the more Sweden seem to be coming back into it. They could be four or five down by now. But they're not, and that means something. Perhaps they can reassemble their own belief. Just one break might be all it needs.

Brazilian hearts stop as Dahlin makes a break through on a long ball from Brolin, but Aldair nicks it away from him. Sweden are beginning to put passing movements together as though they are inspired jointly by Brazilian brilliance and by their inability to find the net.

Then Thern swings wildly at Dunga, and the red card comes out. You feel like this could be the last omen stacked against Brazil, because virtually every team who has gone down to ten men in this competition has gone on to win.

Then again these teams weren't playing Brazil.

All the same, the continuous, pulsing noise of the Brazilian fans is beginning to ebb away. They still chant the name of their team, but the expectation as they reach the penalty area is tangibly less.

Bebeto is displaying a capacity for work that I had never previously suspected him capable of; digging out chances from the rock face of the Swedish defence, playing like a Cantona, as danger-man and creator simultaneously. Jorginho is playing like a model of the attacking full-back, overlapping with Raí again and again and whipping crosses in.

Finally, just as we're settling for another half an hour of this exhausting, brilliant football, it's one of these crosses that does it, picking out Romario on the far post, nipping in between two exhausted defenders. The ball flashes down and bounces high and the net ripples. Next to me Herbert, a Guatemalan living in LA, hesitates for a moment, as if he can't believe it has finally happened. And then we both jump up and dance the samba jig.

Bebeto tries to match Romario's feat once again with a curling shot, but Ravelli pulls off a final save.

As the whistle goes, Herbert raises his hands to the California sky and pours the last of his bottle of mineral water over his head. The last remnants of his face paint, already caking off with sweat, pour down his grinning features in yellow and green trickles.

And so, with the game out of the way, the party can begin in earnest. They've set up a stage on Colorado Boulevard, and there's a samba band playing. Were they booked at half an hour's notice? Or do they double in Scandinavian folk music? Or perhaps it was a FIFA fix after all.

But as the yellow tide dances its way back from the Rose Bowl, it's the Italians, who have been congregating here ever since the final whistle went in their game, who are running the party. One of them clambers up a lamppost and takes down the German flag that's flying there. The crowd cheers. Then as the Italian tricolour replaces it, the cry goes up. 'Italia! Italia!'

By now the Brazilian crowd has arrived, and they move to the other end of the street where an *Ordem e Progresso* flag is raised from the opposite lamppost. 'Ole, ole, ole, ole / Brazil, Brazil,' comes the chorus.

The chant backwards and forwards continues for half an hour or so. In the middle the fans are bouncing up and down, catching one another's arms in an impromptu reel. There is an aspect of facing off, of strutting your stuff the night before the battle, but there is none of the violent undercurrent that you feel, even now, at an English football ground. There is just the feeling, communicated through the dancing and the shouting and the singing, that this is the centre for tonight, not just of World Cup City, but of the world itself, and, for the moment at least, there is room for both parties in the same space.

There may even be room for a third party, because, from the other end of the boulevard, a pair of horns is visible, making its way through the crowd, just above head height. As it comes closer, we see the yellow and blue of the Swedish colours and a third chant harmonizes with the polyphony.

'Svenya, Svenya.'

They aren't coming from the direction of the ground, so they've obviously been back to a hotel somewhere to recuperate from what was, after all, a disappointing performance. For a team that had come so far, they never really had the faith to seem as if they might make it any further. But the Swedish fans had held their heads in their hands for a while and then come out to play.

There's a slight lull in the noise level for a moment as they approach, then a Brazilian shouts: 'Hey! Sweden wants to party too!' and a great cheer goes up for their spirit. All around there's Swedish fans hugging Brazilians. And the dance goes on.

Now I'm as cynical a son of a bitch as ever strolled this boulevard, but in that instant you could have fed me any utopian cliché you care to mention.

The car park my car is in closes shortly, but the night is only just getting going, so I decide to move it and come back. For as far as the eye can see, the street is bumper to bumper. Every car has a flag and every horn is blaring. The place is alive with colour and noise, creating one great joyful throbbing cacophony.

A promotional poster in New York, with copy in the style of the *National Enquirer*, had posed the question 'How long will it be before Martians win the World Cup?' Well, if they have ears up there, they must be wondering what all this noise is about.

A black sports car with a group of Italians in it passes a bunch of Brazilians in a green one. 'Baggio, Baggio,' shout the Italians. 'Bebeto! Romario!' shout the Brazilians as the Italians make the thumbs-down and clutch their crotches. Then the traffic begins to move and they shake hands, the passengers sitting in the back, holding on until the last possible moment and then waving.

A woman with a small child on her back sees me watching. 'That's nice, huh?' she says. She is Mexican and watched the game on TV, but she's come all the way across town to join in. As we speak, we're joined by her husband and some friends who all want to shake my hand. Where am I from? Was I there today?

And then they dive into the throng, the child on the woman's back still waving at me.

When I get back to the car, Paul is standing by it. We'd arranged to meet earlier in the bar we had been in previously. But we'd managed to miss one another in the crowds.

So we park the car on the street and walk back. Above us a helicopter moves across the night sky, shining a spotlight down on the congregation, bringing forth another cheer. What would a performance be without the follow spot? And looking down, the 'copter pilot sees an array of colours as flags are waved just for him.

In a club called Menage, they're playing back-to-back samba, and the place is leaping, flags waving. As each chorus comes around, punctuating the rhythm with a chant that sounds like the natural ebullience of the music bursting out into words, the whole place joins in.

'Jesus!' says Paul. 'What is it about these people? It isn't just getting to the World Cup Final that makes a party like this.'

Well, no, but it's something to do with it. We look around and every face looks like the glory of the moment is shining back from the surface of the skin. And we raise our bottles in salute and begin, both of us at once, to put Northern Soul steps to a Brazilian beat.

A while later I go to seek out the Gents, which is buried in a corridor below the club. From here the music is a distant echo and the place is full of smiling, panting people, wiping the sweat of the day and half the night from their brows, and catching their breath to carry on.

225

A fat guy from Dallas comes in and shouts, 'Any Brazilian guys want to smoke some grass?'

How about Scottish guys? I ask.

'Scottish guys, sure!' he shouts.

So his mate, a small skinny character in a baseball cap, rolls a number and we all pack into a cubicle. There's one Brazilian, a Peruvian, the two Dallas cowboys and me.

'I wish I was Brazilian!' says one of the cowboys. 'You guys have the best women and the best soccer!'

'Hey, what's your name?' he asks the Brazilian who's doing his best to devour the entire joint.

'Gastao,' he says.

'What?'

'*Gastao!*'

Just in case we don't get it this time, he turns around to show it written on the back of his shirt, above a number five. The cubicle erupts with laughter.

'Oh, Gastao?' says Paul when I recount the tale. 'I saw him staggering around earlier. He looked out of it already. He's a fuckin' wild man!'

Given that the music and the colour, already intense, are building to an incredible plateau, and I only had two drags on the joint, somewhere out there is a wild man who is totally off his samba trolley.

Finally, as fatigue overtakes us, we drive back down to Hermosa Beach, where the quiet is lined by the lapping of the sea.

Then after that heart-warming evening, we have an argument about Eric Cantona.

Paul is a Man United fan.

7

Dancing in the Streets

The day after the Brazilian party, I wake up to shouts outside the window from kids on the beach, the sound of the sea in the distance and Van Morrison belting out from an open window down the alley.

Yesterday afternoon he was playing *Gloria*, now he's worked his way through to the *St Dominic's Preview* LP, one of the finest ever recorded.

'Jackie Wilson says, I'm in hee-eaven.'

I get on the phone to the ticket agency straight away. Michael is sounding downbeat, and no doubt regretting his rash promise to refund me the money on the Brazil/USA ticket I was sent instead of Romania/Sweden. He knows that the black-market value was lower than I had paid him, so I come out of the deal better off and he loses out.

'Look, you did order that ticket. I've got it written down here.'

And I've got my original credit card receipt which says I didn't.

'Well, OK, look, do you want anything for the Final?'

You bet I do.

'Well, I've got a ticket here, it's right behind the goal, I'll give you that for four hundred dollars.'

I should have tried to bargain, of course, but all I could see was Brazil and Italy walking out on to that pitch and I was a ten-year-old boy again, being told that one day I would be there, inside the television when all this was going on. I had never really thought until last week that I might be able to get to the Final, never really believed it until this moment.

Of course I could wait, and maybe the price would go down further. But what if it sells out?

I tell him I'll bring the money in tomorrow and pick up the most expensive but the most genuinely precious strip of cardboard that I'll have ever seen.

Outside, the sun is shining, the roads are quiet and courteous fellow drivers beckon me across crossings. I smile, wave and glide on towards Venice, and, yes, I am indeed in heaven.

You think of New York as being the ultimate city, but in the back of your mind you know that the real model of the modern city is Los Angeles. Its malls and drive-ins are the blueprint for much of what has happened across the world in the last fifteen years.

The suburb is by definition a self-conscious Utopia, an oasis in the urban desert. As a city of suburbs, Los Angeles is a megatopia and takes its role as man-made Eden very seriously. Look at the reaction that attended first the South LA riots and secondly the earthquake. They were received in the city of Angels almost as divine judgements; the earthquake itself was more than just a natural disaster – it seemed to attain a symbolic status as an indication that all was not well in the Californian dream, like the earth had been shaken by the secret fear of its millions of 'haves' and by the righteous indignation of its 'have nots'.

As the race issue explodes in the O.J. Simpson case, the LA media is full of references to this being the 'city of the Rodney King beating', a self-fulfilling prophesy visited on a city that takes its hidden guilt seriously.

First we heard the discussions, then came the newspaper articles, then the mention on the news and then, lo and behold, it was leaked that the policeman who found the blood-soaked glove at O.J.'s estate was a suspected racist. The conspiracy that had been dreamt of, particularly by the black population who were statistically more likely to cling to the notion of the Juice's innocence, had taken form.

On a radio talk show, as I'm heading up towards Venice, a caller disputes the notion that the cop is a racist, just because he used the word 'nigger', when while in the armed forces he found himself at the frontiers of the race war. 'You might use that term in exasperation,' he says, 'but it doesn't mean you are disposed towards organized racism.'

The talk-show host is all liberal outrage. 'Well, my friend,' he says, 'how would it be if you came with me to Watts and we'll ask some of the people there if they think that you're a racist for using that term?'

But whatever else he is, the caller isn't stupid. He snaps right back: 'Well, how would it be if I just went there, on my own. What do you think would happen?'

The host relies on bludgeoning him with the 'You're not answering my question' line, but the truth is that the caller has touched on a very sensitive area. There is no easy answer.

One of the reasons Charles Manson had such an unsettling effect on the Californian dream is that in an age of middle-class peace and love delusions he came screaming out of institutional America saying: 'There's a race war happening.' Where he came from there was. It was an uncomfortable notion then, and it still is now. But the fact is that there is a huge section of Los Angeles living in poverty, and the vast majority of them are black.

I click in a cassette that just happens to be Steely Dan, the sound of the paranoic edge of the seventies, wrapped in a smooth funk arrangement, which tells me that only a fool would believe in a world of salads and sun because 'Everybody on the street has murder in their eyes.'

For the second time today I experience the alchemy of music and mood, although this time it's a darker fusion.

*   *   *

Midweek, Venice Beach is quiet, but far from deserted. The famous outdoor gym on the boardwalk is bereft of the steroid-popping hulks, although a little further down a guy is selling testosterone-boosting psycho tablets to a group of bare-chested bloods.

There are dummies that mime life and an old man who mimes dummification, while a little further along the boardwalk a fat man with a beard and shades jams with a female bassist, a shady-looking drummer and a horn player on a loose Blues number. If the Blues at the Buddy Guy club had lost all feeling from repetition, this is proof that the music can still live and breathe. As they torture the notes, the rattle of the frets brings the hairs to life on the back of your neck.

At a record store I find a copy of one of David Byrne's compilations of Brazilian music and relive the feeling of last night's carnival.

Driving in to take a run along Sunset Strip and on to Hollywood, I realize I'm going to run right past the number given on the ticket agency's card. This Sunset Boulevard address gives them an aura of respectability, nestled in amongst a line of restaurants where women who know they have money and think they have taste sit and sip mineral water at outdoor tables as the sun begins to sink into the car fumes.

But when I reach the number I'm looking for, it turns out to be a bathroom fitting shop. A couple of doors along is a beauty parlour, which no doubt styles the all-hair-and-tan brigade. But there's people in there, so I step in and ask if they've ever heard of World Ticket Service. They haven't, but the girl behind the counter offers, helpfully, to give their number a ring and takes the card in her scarlet talons.

'I see what it is,' she says. 'Come this way.'

She leads me out the back into a parking lot, and round to the back of the bathroom suppliers. There, sitting in a small, cramped room, are Michael and Roger, who welcome me like an old friend.

'Come in, mate!' says Michael. 'D'you want a beer?'

Something happens when you've seen a football match with someone.

After a day of driving around in hot and dusty LA I fancy a beer too. Roger gets some out of the fridge.

'Jeez,' he says, 'd'you know, we've been in this office since five o'clock this morning. We've been dealing with Europe so much, you see. I'm knackered.'

Still, I say, you must be happy, with Italy meeting Brazil in the Final. Roger doesn't seem so sure.

'That's the thing about this game,' he says. 'You're not thinking about what's good for football, you're thinking about what's good for business.'

With Brazil and Italy in the Final, he explains, the price of the tickets goes up. It's only then that I realize that Michael and Roger aren't dealing in tickets, they're brokering them – rounding up the interest in England, then buying the tickets from other black-market sources out here. Of course they set the prices to the buyers in advance, then hold out until the prices come down as low as possible.

If we had landed up with a Sweden/Bulgaria Final, they would have cleaned up, buying up tickets for fifty dollars apiece and handing them over to punters who had pre-booked at five or six hundred.

It's not a game without risks, though. For one thing there's the travel agents, who have a habit of taking a hundred or so, only to return them at the last minute when they can't sell their expensive packages on the back of them. But there are other hazards.

After I had seen them at the Ireland/Italy game, Michael and Roger had been forced to make an unscheduled trip to San Francisco, after being landed with two hundred tickets for the Brazil/Russia game.

'We got to the airport,' Michael says, 'and all the flights was full. So we were told we'd have to fly out here to Los Angeles on the last flight out, and then get a connecting flight up to San Francisco. And would you believe it, because we hadn't booked in advance they charged us twice the going rate!'

He looks injured, even at the memory. I venture to suggest that upping the price because of the demand is a principle he should maybe appreciate.

'Urgent traveller, they called it,' he continues. 'We didn't get a cup of tea, or nothing to eat. We had one drink, which we had to pay for. Disgusting it was.'

'Then,' Roger picks up the story, 'we got to Los Angeles and there was no connecting flight after all. There we are, stuck at the airport with all these tickets!'

Thinking that having made it this far they were as well going through with it, they hired a limousine at $1,000 for the round trip.

'So,' Michael carries on, 'we're selling the tickets and doing OK when this character comes up to me. He asks how much the tickets are and I tell him two for 'undred, cos we're just trying to off-load them by this time. He goes into this pouch he's wearing, like he's going for his money and pulls out a pair of handcuffs.'

The pair of them were arrested.

'He claimed I'd been asking two hundred for hundred dollar tickets.'

Perish the thought.

They were locked up, and told that their chauffeur had deserted them. But it turns out the guy had regretted leaving these two affable Arthur Daley types and had returned and staked his limo as bail for them.

When the competition is over, they will have to stay out here – their passports have been confiscated – and face a charge of scalping that could carry a prison sentence.

The whole system of ticket distribution for this competition is crazy, and I'm as critical of a system that's so wide open to abuse as anyone. But having sat at a game with them I wouldn't wish a year in an LA jail on Michael and Roger. So I take my leave and wish them luck, and I mean it.

I have a drive around Hollywood which seems, since I was last here, to have lost even the sleazy Tom Waits-type downbeat charm it used to have. Now the whole place just looks like an anonymous estate.

So I cruise back down the length of Sunset, through Beverly Hills and out to Santa Monica, which is supposedly a great hangout. Along the main precinct there's a line of massive bars selling frozen drinks with names like 'Pink Panties' and 'Purple Orgasm', the latter sounding quite alarming. These are the hangouts for mall-spawned kids like the strangely poetic creatures that inhabit Douglas Coupland's highly successful first two books *Generation X* and *Shampoo Planet*. There is a certain surreal fascination to this world that Coupland captures brilliantly. But I choose a more conventional sports bar instead.

Here I get told the O.J. jokes for the first time.

'Knock, knock.'

Who's there?

'O.J.'

O.J. who?

'OK, you can be on the jury.'

And:

'What's the last thing O.J. said to Nicole?'

Don't know.

'Your waiter will be with you shortly.'

The other victim in the murder case counted waiting amongst his professions.

Back at the motel, the television has a story of two holidaymakers who return home to find their house has been trashed. The graffiti on the walls reads: 'Charlie Manson is my father.'

Los Angeles may not have a centre, but World Cup City has. Or at least it has now, and it is Pasadena. So I check out of this Hermosa Beach suburb and move to the hub of the action.

Everyone who visits LA states the obvious about it being so easy to drive around, but all that depends on finding the entrance to the freeway. Today I take the same route that I did two days ago, or at least I think I do, but instead of finding myself swept on to the four-lane highway, I zig-zag underneath it and wind up in the middle of a wasteland, with the smooth progression of traffic I want to join lining my horizon instead.

Fortunately I drive past a petrol station at one of these desert crossroads, where the pump attendant, another Mario, puts me right.

'Pasadena?' he says. 'You going to the game?'

For the first time I get the chance to say 'Yes' with all the anticipation that word contains. I'll be there. Mario is Mexican but he's been following Brazil since Mexico made their disappointing exit. He shakes my hand and waves me out. Together we are a part of the great multi-national that is Brazilian football.

On to the freeway at last, I flip through a few stations on the radio in the vain hope of finding something listenable. Finally the digit counter comes to rest on the punk rock station, and I realize why the rest of it sounds so bland. With an MOR station on the radio, the cars on the freeway seem to sway serenely from lane to lane. With the nervous adrenalin of some hyped-up grunge merchants blaring out, it looks more like it is, a great weaving network of psychosis.

LA has always had its underside – the melodies of The Doors wound around some of the darkest visions of the sixties, while the bands that revolved around the SST label in the eighties, many of which were captured on the soundtrack to Alex Cox's *Repo Man*, anticipated the manic metallic brood that have come home to roost in the nineties.

LA is a no bland city; it just clings to MOR culture because beyond those suffocating harmonies it's a genuinely scary place.

I sleep out the heat of the afternoon, then set out for a walk as the light begins to fall. My only regret is that the Final will be played in blistering noon-time heat, instead of the sudden desert cool of the Pasadena evening. I can just see it, the helium balloons beginning to silhouette against the sunset, the realization that the pitch has started to glow as anticipation rises and the floodlights warm up, then the explosion of flash lights around the ground as the teams walk out. It won't be like that, shame.

In this light, the Gothic splendour of the Pasadena architecture is shown to perfect advantage. One building in particular, the Green Street Building, has a sinister, haunting quality. With its decorative windows and hanging arches it has obviously been created with a quite deliberate intention of summoning up an echo of some forgotten Golden Age of Venice or Rome. Now, like the house in Billy Wilder's *Sunset Boulevard*, it recalls the time in which those faraway places of the past were re-dreamt in the imagination of a Hollywood of pioneers, of D.W. Griffith and Erich von Stroheim.

A man in the street stops and talks to me for fifteen minutes about the history of the building. You can do that here in a way that would be unimaginable in London or New York, simply stop someone in the street and ask. He seems pleased that people are coming from around the world to Pasadena, and want to know about it.

'It dates from the eighteen nineties,' he says, 'when the society people from New York would move out to California for the winter time. That was one of the Grand Hotels, now it's an apartment building.'

Rarely has a building given me so vivid a sense of the past. Something you don't expect in California, where yesterday is already history.

In the centre of Old Pasadena the carnival is starting, taking off from where the night of the Semi-Finals left off. Families are parading whole broods of little Romarios and Bebetos through the streets, flags are flying from car windows and the whole of Colorado Boulevard is like a honking, bellowing, flag-billowing, bumper-to-bumper jam.

It may be paranoia, but I begin to get a sense that some of the Brazilians are not quite as happy as others at the whole world crashing their party. As I queue up for some food, one says to another in English: 'Do you speak Portuguese?' then, apparently inclining his head in my direction, says something of which the only word I catch is 'Gringo'.

I'm wearing a bootleg approximation of the magical Bebeto number 7 shirt, which compensated for not being strictly authentic by its cost of $10, as against the $50-plus price tag of the real thing. But I get the impression that, at least as far as he is concerned, this reluctance to make a major investment marks me as being exactly what I am, an outsider.

It is, of course, understandable. It's all very well loving their football, but why should just anyone be able to claim a part of this success? We hate it when England claims a stake in Scottish triumph, the Irish likewise. What right do we have to a piece of their pride?

A little further down the road there's a rangy, bearded man juggling a football and trying to sell a coaching manual, a ring-bound desk-top number. Profits, claim a sign, go to the Youth Soccer Association, but he acts a little cagey when I ask exactly what that is. He tells me he played in the North American Soccer League, but someone else standing next to me says 'Hey! So did I. What team?' After an interchange, the newcomer, who introduces himself as Rob, turns to me.

'There never was such a team,' he says. Rob was once the team-mate of the Portuguese master Eusebio. Fakes beware, this street is suddenly thronged with experts.

The next day is the third and fourth place play-off, for which Roger and Michael gave me a ticket free, gratis and for nothing. They did try to sell it to me first, mind you, but it had to be worth a try. Many of their American counterparts don't have their sense of realism about it, because as I walk along to the ground, already cutting it fine for the kick-off, I'm offered tickets at $100 a time.

I hook up with an American Brazilian who's on his way down. He offers one of them ten bucks.

'You crazy?' says the scalper, going wide-eyed.

'No, you're crazy!' we chorus together.

I stop off at the supermarket to buy a bottle of mineral water. Then I'm half-way down the road before I realize that the security won't let me in with the one I've got, which is a glass bottle, the only type they have cold. So I turn back and buy a warm, plastic one. By this time, I'm late for the kick-off. Even so, scalpers are thronged outside the ground, still asking prices that are higher than face value for a game that all the fans know rates just above giveaway stakes. You can see the forlorn hopes of making a killing fading in their eyes. By now it's a matter of making their money back.

I am stopped by the security guards, who in their cod military uniforms and purple berets don't believe in keeping a low profile.

'You have to take the lid off this bottle,' they say.

Look, this is a glorified friendly, who's going to throw a fucking plastic bottle of mineral water at anybody?

'I'm not going to argue with you.'

This is his cue for six of his colleagues to gather around me. OK, guys, since you insist.

So I open the bottle, which naturally enough, having been shaken about a bit in my bag on the way down the hill, splurges and spurts all over the place. Seven cod military uniforms get liberally doused.

You might have thought in this heat they'd find this refreshing. But apparently not.

'Get him outta here!' shouts the first one. 'Stick a bomb up his ass!'

His colleagues advance towards me with intent. But it's hard to stick a punch on someone who's collapsing in fits of giggles. You try it some time.

So the boss of the gate, a giant black man, saunters over.

He seems to think it's quite funny too and just waves me in, advising me to 'keep walking'.

'It's a good job you're not in my neighbourhood, punk!' the first guard, who now looks like a victim of inadequate Portaloo provision, shouts after me.

When I get back to England, I will discover that Eric Cantona was expelled from the ground on the day of the Semi-Final for punching one of these jobsworths in the mush. For the first time since his goal against Stuttgart at Elland Road, I will drink a toast to the eccentric Frenchman.

Yeah, I wouldn't go near your fuckin' neighbourhood.

*   *   *

237

Sweden, who have made comments in the press about not wanting to play this game after the rigours of the Semi-Final, look on the day like they're fired up to send their small but vocal group of supporters home a bit happier. Basically they tear a lackadaisical Bulgaria to pieces with Eriksson and Brolin far outshining Stoichkov. It is only a glorified friendly, but perhaps there is more ability in Sweden than was apparent when the stakes were higher. Like Ireland, now that they have established a position based on tough competitiveness, they may in the next four years begin to flower.

There's a feeling from this World Cup that the one-dimensional football of the long ball game has been defeated. We are entering an age of the multi-faceted attack, and Sweden show sufficient hidden depth to survive.

At the final whistle, the Swedish team throw their shirts to the supporters – well, it saves carrying home dirty laundry, doesn't it?

For this game, I have a Category 1 ticket, one of the most expensive ones; it's behind the goal but closer to the pitch than I'd really like. Tomorrow, for the Final, I have a Category 3, which is a cheaper band. I decide to find the seat and see what my view is going to be like.

It turns out to be just perfect, three quarters of the way up, right behind the goal, and with the whole pitch spread out beneath me. I stand there in this almost empty stadium and think, so this is it, this is where I'll be, tomorrow, when Brazil walk out to play Italy. The World Cup Final. Having scoffed at the travel brochures that used the full title when Final would do, it has now become my new litany. The biggest game of football in the world.

The next day, the Italian presence is certainly more visible than it was way back at the Irish game in Giants Stadium, but it's the Brazilian colours that dominate on the way down the leafy hill to the Rose Bowl. But these two are not the only contenders. A Brazilian woman walks down the road hand in hand with a man in an Ireland T-shirt, a group of Mexicans fly their flag,

Swedes, Belgians, they're all here. None of us can quite believe it. This is it, the last match, soon it will all be over.

Jeff, in Azzurri shirt and mirrored wraparounds, is talking in a loud voice with a group of Brazilians.

So, I ask him when we get chatting, are your parents from Italy?

'Oh no,' he says, 'I'm Jewish.'

He's been following Italy since '82, and has stuck with them as an adopted nation, although he has been behind the US in this competition.

'But I totally respect Brazil, man; that team is awesome. When I saw what they did to Sweden, boy, at least it made me feel better about what they did to the US. Because that game, it could have been six, man.'

We shake hands as we get to the gate. Have a good one, Jeff.

In the scramble at the gate an American Brazilian manages to get in without a ticket. While the searches are going on, he just walks right through.

'Lend us your ticket just for a second,' he pleads, planning to pass it somehow to another friend outside. Just how he plans to do this through a twenty foot no man's land between the double fencing is academic, because I'm not parting with anything I spent four hundred bucks for, not even for a second. Just as I'm walking away, a security guard approaches him.

'Hey you,' he shouts, 'where's your ticket?'

He knows someone has slipped past him, but he's not sure who. The Brazilians scramble and within seconds they're lost in the crowd.

Inside it's largely Brazilian around me, but I'm sitting next to a guy from Nepal, and behind me is an entire extended family of Chinese.

An Italian flag is waved by the entrance and at first a cry goes up of 'Brazilia', then the owners of the flag come into view – two Italian babes with glossy hair swinging down to the level of their micro shorts.

The Brazilians beckon and indicate two vacant seats in their midst, but the babes just smile and sashay past, revelling in the whistles.

Daryl Hall pops up again, shaking his locks and singing 'Gloryland', and I've obviously been out here too long, because this schmaltz is beginning to get to me.

Carlos from Colombia is running up and down the central aisle, waving a wad of notes around shouting 'Hey, Italy! Two hundred dollars! Two hundred dollars says Brazil wins!' One group behind me make out they're interested in taking him up on it, but when they realize he's serious they back out. Carlos takes this as a personal triumph and jumps up and down the aisle again, holding his hands aloft in celebration.

When he takes his seat again, he turns back and calls, 'Hey, Italy!' They look down. 'Baggio who?' he asks to the great amusement of the Brazilian fans around him.

Just at this point I feel a sharp jab in my kidneys. Turning around it turns out to be Mrs Tong, the Chinese brood mother behind me.

'You sit down!' she yelps with all the common courtesy of a prisoner of war commandant.

All right, keep your hair on. Everybody's standing up, I point out to her; we'll sit down at kick-off. Thirty seconds later, as the teams take up formation, we do just that.

As the atmosphere starts to rise, Mrs Tong is still jabbering on. 'What you mean everybody standing up? Not everybody stand up . . . etc., etc.'

Look, I try, we're going to watch the game now.

But this doesn't placate her.

Oh look, shut up, would you, I snap in terminal irritation, the game's starting.

That's it! Inter-racial warfare. Mr Tong kicks me in the back, all the little Tongs – about fifteen of them – are doing martial arts poses around me. Number 1 son is exposing his tonsils while yelling at me: 'She's a *woman*!!!!!'

Well, thanks for clearing up that little ambiguity, but so what, exactly?

'Whadya mean, *so what!*'

Look, does anyone have an American to Cantonese dictionary?

'Do you want to go outside?' Mr Tong asks me.

For one of the few times in my life, I am totally speechless. The World Cup Final is about to start, I have paid $400 to be here and this moron thinks I'd rather be out rough-housing with him by the Portaloos.

I am still standing dumbfounded when the security guards, all of a sudden not such bad guys, turn up and suggest that sons 2 to 15 return to their places.

'All she did was ask him to sit down,' says Number 1 son. 'He just turns round and says "Fuck you!"'

With the aid of a tiny Mexican who has been trying to hold them at bay singlehandedly, the guards finally persuade the Tongs that I have no desire whatsoever to have sexual intercourse with Mrs Tong.

By this time the game has started. My first ever World Cup Final, and when the ball was first kicked I was arguing with a bunch of Chinese psychopaths. Well that never happens at Elland Road or Celtic Park.

Italy seem to be settling better in the opening few minutes, although it's Romario who has the first real chance, a free header from a cross of typical radar accuracy from Jorginho.

Then Brazil begin to take hold, Romario and Bebeto's lightning interchanges sending Bebeto through, but his shot from a tight angle is deflected by Pagliuca for a corner. Then at the other end Massaro makes a break but with Santos bearing down on him his shot goes straight at Taffarel.

For a few minutes it feels as if this might settle down to the Final we have all hoped for. But the further it gets into the first half, the clearer it is that the nervous edginess has taken hold. This is one of those games that never seems to resolve the tension of the first few minutes, the teams taking quick snaps at one another, but never seeming to have the time or the assurance to really build a move.

The other thing that becomes evident is that Sacchi has got his tactics down perfectly. Where Sweden's defensive approach looked forlorn from the start, Italy are aiming to hold the ball up in midfield. So where Sweden sat back, with their midfielders playing deep and allowing the Brazilians to run at them, Italy have their midfield pushed forward, leaving Romario and Bebeto to run alone up front. For all their much-trumpeted lack of midfield flair, Brazil have been playing the simple passing game with devastating speed in this competition. By holding them up, Italy have put a sock in the samba rhythm.

It's an impressive game-plan; not a pretty one, but an impressive one. However, it might not have worked so well but for a couple of other factors. First, after twenty minutes Jorginho has to come off injured. Bemusingly the crowd cheers, presumably because Cafu, the São Paulo player who replaces him is a favourite, but although he has the same attacking impulses he lacks Jorginho's close control, and more importantly his crossing ability. In the second half, as Brazil begin to press more, he will allow the ball to run away from him, or loft in a no better than average cross. Jorginho was inclined to be more deadly.

Then secondly there is . . . the fear of finishing. It's twenty-four years since 1970 and Brazil have never been this close since. The nervous finishing that caused them to hesitate so badly in what should have been a destruction of Sweden is now a genuine affliction.

This is never more evident than in the crucial point of the first half. Branco takes a free-kick and sends a screaming, dipping shot towards the bottom corner. Brazil have committed men forward for the set piece and Mazinho is on to the rebound. With four unmarked players closing in and without a challenger near him, he just has to steady himself and centre, but instead he snatches at the ball and falls over.

It's one of those pivotal points in a game. If it had gone in, Brazil would have settled, Italy would have been forced into a more attacking formation, and the space that the game needed would have opened up. Instead you knew it would have a superstitious effect, and Brazil become doubly nervous.

And of course there's another factor at work, or rather not. What's that, Carlos?

'Baggio who?'

Precisely. Roberto Baggio was doubtful for this game, with a hamstring injury from the Semi, and the obvious fact is that he isn't fit. With his mojo misfiring, Italy are a team lacking the balance and refinement that you expect from them.

Of course all of this is lost on Mr Tong, who's having a good time anyway. Every time the ball gets over the half-way line, he yells 'Shoot it!' When the movement comes to nothing, he says sagely, 'Shoulda shot it.' Move over, Arrigo Sacchi.

In the second half Stigo from Brazil comes and squeezes on to the end of our row. Either his own seat is further back or he's miraculously sneaked in without a ticket. Number 1 son Tong tries to give him a lecture for standing up as Mauro Silva breaks into the box only to dive rather ineffectually in the hope of a penalty.

Irritation being the better part of valour I tell Number 1 son to leave him alone. Stigo's team are in the World Cup Final and if he doesn't like people standing up he should have gone to the ballet instead. Miraculously Number 1 son does as he is bidden and no one hears a peep out of him for the rest of the game.

Meanwhile Brazil are beginning to apply some of the pressure that has been the hallmark of their second-half game, albeit without the killer's confidence. Stigo grabs my arm. 'It's going to happen soon,' he says, 'just five more minutes.'

Within seconds Taffarel nearly drops the ball right at Baggio's feet. But then Romario nearly breaks through, only for Baresi to cut in again.

'We'll make it,' says Stigo. Tension rises as both sets of supporters sense that one goal will take it. Brazil continue to press, but just as they seemed unmarkable against Sweden, so the Italian defence seems unbreachable today, five of them standing across the field now, beckoning Romario and Bebeto at them.

We know it's extra time, the teams know it's extra time, there's just five minutes to be played out before the whistle goes.

Even Stigo is now beginning to wonder whether one Italian break will take away the trophy, after so long. But at the beginning of extra time it's Brazil who are still coming forward, and then at last they catch Italy coming out for the offside trap, the ball is played out to Cafu on the right, his cross just bends away from Pagliuca, but the keeper reaches out after it. Bebeto at the far post tries to touch it back for Romario rushing in, but the ball loops off his left foot. It's a fifty-fifty ball between Romario and Pagliuca, Bebeto stands on one leg and waits. But Pagliuca snatches the ball from Romario's toe.

You also notice that the new refereeing guidelines have come to a logical impasse. If the guidance is to give short shrift to players who dive and feign injury, and yet to clamp down on the tackle from behind, how do you tell which is which? This ref has seemed, throughout the game, to err on keeping the game moving, and there have been some blatant dives which he has ignored. But towards the end, the Italian defenders seem to have discovered just how much they can get away with here, and are taking it to bemusing extremes. The ref isn't blowing up for anything, even clattering from behind.

But now the exchanges have some force. Brazil's substitute, Viola, begins to run at the Italian defence. Romario just misses. Baggio comes within inches.

'Baggio who?'

But still it's mainly the Brazilians who take the initiative, beginning to leave gaping holes as they do so, and the Italians are hitting back on the break. Baggio slips through again, but again he shoots straight at Taffarel.

'Baggio who?'

And we get to penalties.

Stigo can hardly look. This is the way Italy really might take it.

Baresi steps up, but as he tries to place it over the diving Taffarel, his foot skids underneath the ball and it sails over the empty net.

The Brazilians are going mad.

Santos kicks. And . . . Pagliuca saves it!

The Italians bay their revenge raising flags in clenched fists.

Albertini places his shot right in the corner, low and hard.

Romario steps up and Brazil's hero sends Pagliuca the wrong way, but his shot hits the post and for a heart-stopping instant it seems like it might bounce back across the face of the goal. But it's struck with enough force, it hits the post at a sufficiently sharp angle to hang for a second and deflect into the back of the net. A sixteenth of an inch from fifteen yards keeps the dream alive.

Evani scores for Italy.

Branco scores for Brazil.

Each set of supporters in turn, haunted, expectant and delivered.

Now Massaro places his kick. And Taffarel saves. This time the Brazilians hold their fists in the air, and the Italians gulp.

As Dunga steps up, chests are crossed, hands are held in prayer position. And as the net ripples, Brazilian arms shoot up into the air and Italian hands cover faces.

Baggio steps up. He has to score this one to leave Bebeto to take the kick that could give Brazil the World Cup.

And as the ball sails over the crossbar, and the Italian fans stare in disbelief, the last word is left to Carlos.

'Baggio who?'

On the way back into Pasadena, there's a slightly leaden-footed feel to the celebrations this time. After all, it is the first Final to remain scoreless. There is the feeling that we have been cheated of the *coup de grâce* of a Final that we might have hoped for. And after the sheer euphoria of the Semi-Final celebrations, it takes a while to get the party going.

But if it wasn't a classic Final, it made an absorbing clash of tactics which easily beat the cynical spectacle that was Argentina v Germany in 1990. Brazil were the romantic winners, even if they were more fearful than dashing in carrying away the prize.

An American, swathed in a Brazilian flag, sees my shirt and crosses the road. We slap palms, as a Scot and a Californian celebrate a South American victory on a street in Pasadena.

I have a Mexican meal on Colorado Boulevard, and raise a margarita to deserving winners. Already the disappointment of the game fades in the afterglow of the simple fact that I was there.

As I'm eating alone, a young native of Pasadena asks if he can share my table in the crowded restaurant. He's been at the game too, rooting for Italy, although again he has no Italian blood.

'Do you think they'll shoot Baggio?' he asks me.

No, I don't think so, but the Buddhist monasteries can cancel all those plans for building extra wings.

By the time I come out, the dancing is well under way, and once the beat picks up it takes on its own momentum.

There're more people here than there were for the Semi-Final, it's even difficult to make your way along the street, such is the pressure of bodies. The coalition of South Americans that has thrown its weight behind Brazil begins to break up, as the Mexicans, who have been shouting for their continent's Champions, return to the cry of 'Mehico, Mehico!' leading the Mexican flag in a twisting, snaking path through the revelry.

Inside Menage the atmosphere isn't quite the same as it was after the Sweden game, and this time in the Gents I come across a trace of conflict, to offset the drug-assisted scene of unity I saw the last time. A few Brazilians are surrounding one Colombian, questioning his right to take a part in this victory.

'Hey!' he's saying. 'We're all the same blood, we're Latin.'

They don't seem impressed.

Well I'm Celtic, I say to his interrogators, and I'm glad you won it.

'That's it,' says the Colombian, 'it's football we're here for.'

'Fuck you!' says one of the Brazilians. 'What happened to Escobar?'

Going back inside, I have a mooch around, half expecting to run into Paul, who I know is going to hang around before taking his flight out of World Cup City at 4 a.m. tomorrow morning, but there's no sign of him. Instead I hear a voice drifting over.

'We beat Manchester United, the scum of England.'

The speaker is a young Indian girl.

Did I hear you right? I ask.

'Why?' she asks. 'Are you a Man U fan?'

No, I say, I'm a Leeds fan.

She warms up instantly and invites me to take a seat. She's been talking to a boy with a Sweden shirt on.

'This is Anders, as in Limpar,' she says. 'My name's Alka, as in Seltzer.'

Alka, an Aston Villa fan, is out here staying with an American friend of hers, John.

'We met in France,' she says, 'on a train, on our way to the Olympics in Barcelona. He'd always wanted to come to a football game, so I said if he was coming to England I'd take him to Villa.'

In the end, John arrived during the close season. But then a few months ago he rang her up and said: 'I've got tickets for the World Cup, come out and stay with me.'

'There's nothing romantic going on, mind you,' she says. 'I made it quite clear to him from the start that I had a boyfriend.

'Although he does get into my bed every morning.'

Anders and I express a certain amount of surprise at this, but Alka doesn't seem to be overly bothered, so we figure it's her business.

'That's John over there,' she says, pointing to a figure who's cutting a swathe through the crowd. On his shoulders there's a Brazilian girl who appears to be dressed only in a flag. Later someone else takes over and John comes to join us, although he casts a jealous eye back in the direction of her new carrier every now and then.

Alka implores me to tip John and his friends off about Bog Brush's *Among The Thugs*.

'They all take it really seriously,' she says. 'Would you tell them what a lot of rubbish it is?'

Well, put it this way; if you offer to buy someone drinks in return for stories about football violence, you'd be a fool to believe what they say.

'And what about that scene where a hooligan sucks a policeman's eye out!' Alka says. 'For a start it's a physical impossibility!'

Shortly afterwards we are joined by Betty, a Chinese American who works for the same accountancy firm as John. She orders a round of drinks.

'You guys are drinking with me!' she tells us. 'We'll have a round of kamikazes,' she tells the waitress.

'D'you want a drink to go with that?' John asks me.

Isn't that a drink?

'No, that's a shot, have a margarita.'

If you insist. The kamikazes arrive and are knocked straight back. The margaritas follow, and the entire entourage, comprising two Swedes, two Mexicans, one Chinese American, two other Americans of undetermined background, an English Indian and a Scot, hit the dance floor to the mad hedonistic rush of Brazilian samba, while around the perimeter a series of television screens run the penalties, again and again. Outside, Colorado Boulevard is turning dark, but in the shadow you can still pick out the flash of a smile amidst the throng as the whole street throbs to the same rhythm.

In this last night in World Cup City every bar you've been in flashes before your eyes. In New York, Chicago, San Francisco, London, everywhere across the world they'll have a dance of their own. But I'm here in Pasadena and outside the streets themselves are dancing.

Goodnight, and goodbye, World Cup City.

The next day I begin the drive back to San Francisco – it costs an extra two hundred dollars to drop the car off in LA, nearly a hundred dollars more than the petrol and the flight back from San Francisco again. Back in the real world, everybody's broke.

Two days later, I pull into town and, with an hour or so to spare, I think, the Golden Gate Bridge; perhaps I'll get the chance to see it, after all. But it appears and disappears on the city's signposts like one of its phantoms, and I get caught in the rush-hour traffic.

Finally, after two hours of thinking it must be around the next corner, I give up, and head back to Ken's.

From there I ring Mario, and arrange to meet him and Andy at Bahia, the bar in which we'd all watched the Brazil v Holland game.

The doorman is wearing a Brazil – World Champions 1994 T-shirt. I take a seat in the empty bar. They're showing the Brazil v Cameroon game on the TV screen. As with all football matches you instantly remember where you were when you watched it. Boo Radley's, New York, with Roland and Mike. It seems so long ago, so far away. The game is already a museum piece – a recorded live transmission that is three weeks old and by now a contradiction in terms.

The same thing seems to occur to Andy and Mario as they walk in.

'Strange to think this was what we were getting so worked up about,' says Mario. 'That stupid screen.'

We all look around expecting to find an echo of the emotions amongst the creeping plants and the jungle murals. But there's nothing. Until we start talking.

So what were you doing when the penalties were being taken?

'I couldn't watch,' says Mario. 'I was hiding there, behind the mirror.'

We looked at the mirrored wall he points to and suddenly the atmosphere reassembles around it. I can see Mario, standing behind there, unable to look.

'But I couldn't prevent myself either,' he says. 'There was a stepladder behind there and I kept peering over the top. I was saying "Where's Donald? We need Donald now."'

But in the end it was OK. Now the bar is empty. The only evidence of the triumph is the doorman's T-shirt.

'So,' says Andy, 'is there anything you wanted to see while you were in San Francisco and didn't get around to?'

Well, actually there is one thing.

'Sure, we'll take you to Golden Gate Bridge,' he says. 'What kind of San Franciscans would we be if we allowed you to leave without seeing it?'

So I get to add another one of the modern wonders of the world to my personal memory bank. First we take a trip to the other main tourist attraction, down the cracked carriageway of the world's most crooked street, and then there we are, heading over the dizzying span.

'See the tower that's coming up?' Andy says, opening the sun roof. 'Wait till we get to it, then look up through the roof.'

He giggles.

As we pass underneath, I look up and see the tower receding above me into the mist.

'It's great, isn't it?' Andy giggles again. 'I love doing that – I do it sometimes when I'm driving.'

We reach the other side to where the suicide is faked in *Vertigo*, and look down. It's only when you look down that you really get a sense of scale.

'This is where the Italian team jumped off yesterday,' jokes Mario.

Then we're back, driving through the city.

'This bar here is owned by a Brazilian,' says Mario. 'He had a giant flag up outside. There's still one in the window.'

But as we drive past, the window is bare.

'Oh, he took it all down,' Mario comments.

Yup, it's all over, so soon.

'Now we have to go back to reality,' says Andy, dolefully.

World Cup City is already gone. The next day, I fly out of plain old San Francisco back to Los Angeles, and later – much later – find myself standing in the arrivals area of Heathrow airport, waiting for Frau to come and take me home.

FEVER PITCH
Nick Hornby

Winner of the
WILLIAM HILL SPORTS BOOK
OF THE YEAR AWARD

Shortlisted for the
NCR AWARD

'The best football book ever written'
GQ

'Good books about football could be counted on the teeth of
Nobby Stiles' upper jaw ... *Fever Pitch* is a small classic'
MICHAEL PALIN

'Hornby should write for England'
OBSERVER

'*Fever Pitch* is the anatomy of an obsession, a knowing, bitter-
sweet, and very funny autobiography in which the writer's life
is measured not in years but in seasons. I've read no better
account of what being a fan really means'
PETE DAVIES

'Funny, brilliant, relentless'
INDEPENDENT ON SUNDAY

'The best author of my generation'
JULIE BURCHILL

New format edition   £5.99 paperback   0 575 05910 9

Two photographic books published in association
with *When Saturday Comes*:

SHOT!

A Photographic Record of Football in the Seventies

From Barry Endean to Franz Beckenbauer, and ticker tape welcomes
to pitch invasions, SHOT! brings to life one of the most vivid decades in
football history with a collection of evocative images, many of which are
published for the first time.

'An unforgettable tour through the memory bin of that often brilliantly
freakish decade' *ESQUIRE*

'A compilation of great photos' *MAIL ON SUNDAY*

'This beautiful, grainy book has it all: sideburns, orange balls, Cruyff,
toilet rolls...' *THE FACE*

'It's a pleasure to look back over these snaps and remember what made
one fall in love with the game in the first place' *THE IRISH TIMES*

'It now means I spend far too long in that little room at the end of the hall'
STEVE COPPELL, *DAILY TELEGRAPH*

Gollancz/Witherby   £12.99 paperback   0 85493 237 2

THIS IS SOCCER

Images of World Cup USA '94

THIS IS SOCCER brings together a unique and largely unpublished
selection of photos that tell the story of how football not only survived its
four-week journey across America but produced the best tournament since
1970. It includes a foreword by the *Observer*'s Patrick Barclay.

Gollancz/Witherby   £9.99 paperback   0 575 05892 7

Published in association with
When Saturday Comes